PRIMATE FIELD STUDIES

D0219980

Series Editors:

> Robert W. Sussman, Washington University
> Natalie Vasey, Portland State University

Series Editorial Board:

> Simon Bearder, Oxford-Brookes University
> Marina Cords, Columbia University
> Agustin Fuentes, Notre Dame University
> Paul Garber, University of Illinois
> Annie Gautier-Hion, Station Biologique de Paimpont
> Joanna Lambert, University of Wisconsin
> Robert D. Martin, Field Museum
> Deborah Overdorff, University of Texas
> Jane Phillips-Conroy, Washington University
> Karen Strier, University of Wisconsin

Series Titles:

> *The Spectral Tarsier*
> Sharon L. Gursky, Texas A&M University
>
> *Strategies of Sex and Survival in Hamadryas*
> *Baboons: Through a Female Lens*
> Larissa Swedell, Queens College, The City University
> of New York
>
> *The Behavioral Ecology of Callimicos*
> *and Tamarins in Northwestern Bolivia*
> Leila M. Porter, Northern Illinois University
>
> *The Socioecology of Adult Female Patas*
> *Monkeys and Vervets*
> Jill D. Pruetz, Iowa State University
>
> *Apes of the Impenetrable Forest: The Behavioral*
> *Ecology of Sympatric Chimpanzees and Gorillas*
> Craig Stanford, University of Southern California

Forthcoming Titles:

> *A Natural History of the Brown Mouse Lemur*
> Sylvia Atsalis, Brookfield Zoo
>
> *The Gibbons of Khao Yai*
> Thad Q. Bartlett, The University of Texas at San Antonio

PRIMATE FIELD STUDIES

Many of us who conduct field studies on wild primates have witnessed a decline in the venues available to publish monographic treatments of our work. As researchers we have few choices other than to publish short technical articles on discrete aspects of our work in professional journals. Also in vogue are popular expositions, often written by nonscientists. To counter this trend, we have begun this series. **Primate Field Studies** is a venue both for publishing the full complement of findings of long-term studies, and for making our work accessible to a wider readership. Interested readers need not wait for atomized parts of long-term studies to be published in widely scattered journals; students need not navigate the technical literature to bring together a body of scholarship better served by being offered as a cohesive whole. We are interested in developing monographs based on single or multi-species studies. If you wish to develop a monograph, we encourage you to contact one of the series editors.

About the Editors:

Robert W. Sussman (Ph.D. Duke University) is currently professor of anthropology and Environmental Science at Washington University, St. Louis, Missouri and past editor-in-chief of *American Anthropologist*, the flagship journal of the American Anthropological Association. His research focuses on the ecology, behavior, evolution, and conservation of nonhuman and human primates, and he has worked in Costa Rica, Guyana, Panama, Madagascar, and Mauritius. He is the author of numerous scientific publications, including *Biological Basis of Human Behavior*, Prentice Hall (1999); *Primate Ecology and Social Structure* (two volumes), Pearson Custom Publishing (2003); and *The Origin and Nature of Sociality*, Aldine de Gruyter (2004).

Natalie Vasey (Ph.D. Washington University) is currently assistant professor of anthropology at Portland State University in Portland, Oregon. Her work explores the behavioral ecology, life history adaptations, and evolution of primates, with a focus on the endangered and recently extinct primates of Madagascar. She has presented her research at international venues and published in leading scientific journals. She is dedicated to educating students and the public-at-large about the lifestyles and conservation status of our closest relatives in the animal kingdom.

The Behavioral Ecology of Callimicos and Tamarins in Northwestern Bolivia

Leila M. Porter
Northern Illinois University

PEARSON
Prentice
Hall

Upper Saddle River, New Jersey 07458

Library of Congress Cataloging-in-Publication Data

Porter, Leila M.

The behavioral ecology of callimicos and tamarins in northwestern Bolivia / Leila M. Porter.
    p.   cm — (Primate field studies)
Includes bibliographical references (p.   ) and index.
    ISBN 0-13-191470-7
    1. Callimico—Behavior—Bolivia. 2. Tamarins—Behavior—Bolivia. 3. Callimico—
Ecology—Bolivia. 4. Tamarins—Ecology—Bolivia. I. Title.

QL737.P925P67 2007
599.8'5—dc22   2006023636

Publisher: Nancy Roberts
Supplements Editor: LeeAnn Doherty
Editorial Assistant: Lee Peterson
Full Service Production Liaison: Joanne Hakim
Marketing Director: Brandy Dawson
Senior Marketing Manager: Marissa Feliberty
Manufacturing Buyer: Benjamin Smith
Cover Art Director: Jayne Conte
Cover Design: Kiwi Design
Cover Photos: *Main image front cover* courtesy of Edilio Nacimento, Vincent C. Sodaro/Brookfield Zoo, Leila M. Porter; *top band images 1-4* courtesy of Robert W. Sussman/Washington University of St. Louis
Manager, Cover Visual Research & Permissions: Karen Sanatar
Director, Image Resource Center: Melinda Patelli
Manager, Rights and Permissions: Zina Arabia
Manager, Visual Research: Beth Brenzel
Photo Coordinator: Annette Linder
Full-Service Project Management: Bharath Parthasarathy/TexTech International
Composition: TexTech International
Printer/Binder: RR Donnelley & Sons Company

Credits and acknowledgments borrowed from other sources and reproduced, with permission, in this textbook appear on appropriate page within text.

Pearson Education LTD., London
Pearson Education Singapore, Pte. Ltd
Pearson Education, Canada, Ltd
Pearson Education—Japan
Pearson Education Australia PTY, Limited

Pearson Education North Asia Ltd
Pearson Educación de Mexico, S.A. de C.V.
Pearson Education Malaysia, Pte. Ltd
Pearson Education, Upper Saddle River,
    New Jersey

10 9 8 7 6 5 4 3 2 1
ISBN 0-13-191470-7

For Garoto, whose help made this study possible

Contents

List of Figures   xi
List of Tables   xv
Acknowledgments   xvii

1   The Elusive Callimicos   1

Callimico Taxonomy   2
Distribution, Behavior, and Ecology of the Callitrichids   6

2   The General Research Plan: A Comparative Study of Callimicos, Saddle-back Tamarins, and Red-bellied Tamarins   13

Study Species   15
Study Area   18
Trail System   22
Study Groups   23

3   Fungi and the Dietary Niche of Callimicos   29

Methodology   32
    Behavioral Observations   32
    Diet Overlap   33
    Monitoring Plants, Fungi, and Arthropods   34
Results   35
    Overall Diet   35
    Fungi   35

Nectar 38
Fruits 42
Exudates 44
Arthropods 47
Vertebrates 51
Vertical Stratification: Height Class Use 53
Diet Overlap 55
Feeding Competition 55
Discussion 56

4 Habitat Use and Activity Budgets 61

Habitat Specialization 61
Activity Budgets 63
Methodology 64
Analyses 66
Results 67
Home Range Size and Density 67
Sleeping Sites 68
Activity Period 68
General Activity Budget 70
Changes in Callimico Activity by Season 72
Locomotion 72
Callimico Substrate Use 72
Height Class Use 73
Microhabitat Use 73
Seasonal Changes in Microhabitat Use 75
Discussion 76

5 Polyspecific Associations 83

Potential Costs and Benefits of Polyspecific Associations 83
Methodology 86
Analyses 87
Results 89
Patterns of Associations Between Callimicos and Tamarins 89
Effects of Polyspecific Associations on the Behavior of Callimicos 93
Discussion 97

**6 Social Organization and Reproductive Strategies
of Callimicos 103**

Overview of the Social Organization of Callitrichids 103

Methodology   107
Results   107

  Breeding Females   107
  Breeding Males   107
  Predation and Dispersal   108
  Birth Season   108
  Interbirth Interval   108
  Infant Development   110
  Communal Care   110
  Mortality   112

Discussion   112

  Male Reproductive Strategies   112
  Female Reproductive Strategies   113
  Infant Care   114
  Benefits of Allocare to Caregivers   118
  Why Don't Callimicos Twin?   120

7 Conservation   **121**

Conservation Status of Callimicos   121
Speciation   122
Population Density   124
Geographic Range   127
Habitat Requirements   128
Reproduction   130
Interspecific Competition   131
Role of Callimicos in their Ecosystem   132
People and Forests in the Department of the Pando   133
Future Conservation in the Department of the Pando   138

8 Summary   **141**

Diet   141
Habitat Use   142
Reproductive Strategies   143
Social Organization   144
Callimicos and the Adaptive Radiation of Callitrichids   145
Conservation   146

References Cited   **149**

Index   **167**

List of Figures

Figure 1–1 The Taxonomy of the Platyrrhines   3

Figure 1–2 Anatomical Characteristics of the
    Callitrichids   4

Figure 1–3 Proposed Evolutionary Relationships
    of Callimicos to Other Platyrrhines Based on
    a) anatomical characters as per Hershkovitz 1977;
    b) anatomical characters as per Martin 1990;
    c) anatomical characters as per Ford 1986, and
    d) molecular evidence as per Pastorini et al. 1998   5

Figure 1–4 Map of the Distribution of Callimicos
    and the Rest of the Callitrichids   7

Figure 1–5 A Callimico in the Forests of Bolivia   8

Figure 2–1 Photographs of the Study Species, a) Callimico
    b) Saddle-back Tamarin, and c) Red-bellied Tamarin   14

Figure 2–2 The Distribution Ranges of the Ten Subspecies
    of Saddle-back Tamarins   15

Figure 2–3 The Distribution Ranges of the Two Subspecies
    of Red-bellied Tamarins   17

Figure 2–4 Map of Bolivian Ecosystems   19

Figure 2–5 Map of the Department of the Pando, Bolivia
    and Surrounding Regions   20

Figure 2–6 Monthly Maximum and Minimum
    Temperatures During the Study Period Beginning
    in April, 1998   21

Figure 2–7 Monthly mm of Rainfall During the Study
Beginning in April, 1998   21

Figure 2–8 Map of the Trail System   23

Figure 2–9 The Author Following a Habituated Callimico   25

Figure 3–1 Annual Average Diet for the Callimico,
Saddle-back Tamarin, and Red-bellied Tamarin   36

Figure 3–2 Average Diet in the a) Dry Season and
b) Wet Season for Callimicos, Saddle-back Tamarins,
and Red-bellied Tamarins   37

Figure 3–3 Monthly Mean Frequency of Mycophagy
by Callimicos Plotted with the Abundance
(numbers of fungal fruiting bodies) of Fungi Found
along Botanical Transects   38

Figure 3–4 Fungi Consumed by Callimicos: a) Bamboo
Fungi b) Jelly Fungi   39

Figure 3–5 Monthly Mean Frequency of Nectarivory
for the Saddle-back Tamarin and the Red-bellied
Tamarin   40

Figure 3–6 Fruit and Nectar Abundance along Botanical
Transects, Density Values are the Estimated Number
of Fruits and Flowers Counted Each Month ÷ 10^3 41

Figure 3–7 Flowers Used as Nectar Resources
a) *Ochroma pyrmidales* and b) *Symphonia
globulifera*   41

Figure 3–8 Monthly Mean Frequency of Frugivory for
the Callimico, Saddle-back Tamarin, and
Red-bellied Tamarin   42

Figure 3–9 Monthly Mean Frequency of Gummivory
for the Callimico, Saddle-back Tamarin, and Red-bellied
Tamarin   48

Figure 3–10 Edilio Nacimento Climbing a Tree to Collect
Exudates from the Same Location the Monkeys
Had Eaten   49

Figure 3–11 Monthly Mean Frequency of Insectivory
for the Callimico, Saddle-back Tamarin, and
Red-bellied Tamarin   50

Figure 3–12 Numbers of Orthoptera and Araneida
(all species) Caught Each Month During Sweep Samples   51

Figure 3–13 A Callimico Eating a Grasshopper   52

Figure 3–14 Vertical Stratification in the Forest by
Callimicos, Saddle-back Tamarins, and Red-bellied
Tamarins During Foraging as Averaged for all
Study Months   53

Figure 3–15 Height Classes Used while Eating Fruits
by the Callimico, Saddle-back Tamarin, and Red-bellied
Tamarin   54

Figure 3–16 Diet Overlap among Callimicos and
Saddle-back Tamarins (C - S), Callimico and
Red-bellied Tamarins (C - R), and Saddle-back
Tamarins and Red-bellied Tamarins (S - R) as
Measured by Schoener's Index of Niche Overlap.
Complete Diet Overlap Indicated by Values of 1,
No Niche Overlap Indicated by Values of 0   55

Figure 4–1 Flow Chart Indicating the Influence of
Different Strategies on a Primate's Activity Budget   65

Figure 4–2 Diagram of the Habitat Type Categories
Used in This Study   66

Figure 4–3 Comparison of a) Awakening Times
b) Sleeping Times   69

Figure 4–4 Substrate Use During a) All Activities b) Travel   74

Figure 4–5 Height Class Use by all Three Species   75

Figure 4–6 Habitat Use by Callimicos Across the Year   76

Figure 5–1 The Home Range of One Group of Callimicos   91

Figure 5–2 Species Initiating Mixed Group Activities   92

Figure 5–3 Frequency with which Callimicos' Behavior
Changed According to Association Status and Season:
a) Stream Edge Habitat Use; and b) Primary Forest with
Open Understory Use. Error Bars Show the Standard
Error of the Mean +/– 1.0 SD   94

Figure 5–4 Percentage of Observations Callimicos
Were Found in Each Height Class while Associated vs.
while alone Within Habitat C   95

Figure 5–5 Frequency with which Callimicos' Feeding
Changed According to Association Status and
Season. Error Bars Show the Standard Error of the
Mean +/– 1.0 SD   96

Figure 5–6 The Mean Percentage of Time Callimicos Were in Association with Tamarin Troops, Plotted with: a) The Frequency of Frugivory and Mycophagy; and b) Dietary Overlap Values with Red-bellied Tamarins and Saddle-back Tamarins 98

Figure 6–1 Twin Golden Lion Amarin Infants on an Adult 106

Figure 6–2 Sister Callimicos Born Six Months Apart 109

Figure 6–3 Percentage of Scans Infants Were Carried for Each Month after the Infant's Birth (n = 12,219 Scans) 110

Figure 6–4 Adult Male Carrying an Infant 111

Figure 7–1 Observations of Callimicos Throughout the Pando and Neighboring Areas 126

Figure 7–2 Bamboo Habitat in the Forests Just South of the Acre River and the Indigenous Community of the Yaminahua 130

Figure 7–3 A Rubber Tapper (Seringuero) Cutting a Rubber Tree to Collect its Sap 134

Figure 7–4 The Outer Shells of Brazil Nuts that Were Harvested in the Forest 135

Figure 7–5 The Author with Edilio Nacimento, Rafael, and Orlando, in Front of a Large Mahogany Tree 137

Figure 7–6 A Small Cattle Ranch in the Pando. Notice the Forest that Still Remains in the Background. 137

Figure 8–1 Phyologenetic Tree for the Callitrichids, Including the Divergence of Dietary and Forest Niches among Taxa 147

List of Tables

Table 2–1 The Composition of Study Groups Across the Study Year — 27

Table 3–1 Fruit Consumption by Month for the Study Species — 43

Table 3–2 Plant Species Exploited for Food — 45

Table 3–3 Composition of Food Resources Consumed by Mammals — 59

Table 4–1 Callimicos' Feeding Records Shown as the Number of Records of Each Food Type (#) Used for Analyses and the Food Expressed as a Percentage of the Total Records (%) — 70

Table 4–2 Activity Behaviors for Each Species Shown as the Number of Records Devoted to Each Behavior (#) Used for Analyses and the Behavior Expressed as a Percentage of the Total Records (%) — 71

Table 4–3 Resting Behaviors for Each Species Shown as the Number of Records Devoted to Each Behavior (#) Used for Analyses and the Behavior Expressed as a Percentage of the Total Records (%) — 71

Table 4–4 Seasonal Activity Patterns of Callimicos Shown as Number of Records in Behavioral Category (#) Used for Analyses and Percentage of Total Records (%) — 72

Table 4–5 Locomotor Behavior for Each Study Species Shown as the Number of Records Devoted to Each Behavior (#) Used for Analyses and the Behavior Expressed as a Percentage of the Total Records (%) — 73

Table 4–6 The Proportion of Records that Callimicos, Saddle-back, and Red-bellied Tamarins Were Found in Different Microhabitats Within the Home Range of Tamarin Troop 2   75

Table 4–7 Seasonal Microhabitat Use by Callimicos Shown as Number of Records in Each Microhabitat (#) Used for Analyses and Percentage of Total Records (%)   77

Table 5–1 The Observed and Expected Frequency of Association Between Callimicos and Saddle-back Tamarins Within Test Plots   90

Table 6–1 Maximum Group Sizes for Wild Callimicos in which Age Classes were Observed   113

Table 6–2 Summary of Female Reproduction and Rearing Strategies   115

Table 6–3 Summary of Infant Development in Captive and Wild Callimicos   116

Table 7–1 Summary of Callimico Observations in the Pando, Acre, Brazil, and Madre de Dios, Peru   125

Table 8–1 Comparison of Ecological Specializations among Callitrichids   146

Acknowledgments

The success of my research has required the logistical, academic, and moral support of many people in the United States and Bolivia. Foremost, I would like to thank my guide, site manager, and colleague Edilio Nacimento Becerra (Garoto) for his help with all aspects of my field work. Garoto, with his amazing ability to find, call, track, and even predict the behavior of callimicos, made this research possible. Garoto trained me how to observe callimicos, monkeys that are impossible to study without first learning how to crawl through bamboo, orient oneself in a forest without trails, and spot a little black monkey hidden in the shadows of the understory. He has also served as my medic, chauffeur, research assistant, Spanish and Portuguese teacher, and great friend throughout my field work.

My family has also provided continual and invaluable support of my studies and travels. My parents Edward and Ann Porter provided assistance solving logistical problems throughout my thesis project and have served as my American home base during all my moves and travels throughout North and South America. My mother has also provided helpful comments and suggestions for writing this book. My sister Rebecca Fricke, has supplied me with encouragement throughout my field research, particularly through all the letters she has sent to me in Bolivia.

The data presented here were made possible with the help of two outstanding research assistants, Laura Johnson and Kristin Donaldson. Both Kristin and Laura volunteered an entire year of their lives to help with the collection of this data. They endured six frustrating months of our attempts to habituate callimicos, and fortunately, like me, they were stubborn enough not to give up despite a tedious camp menu, bouts with typhoid fever, and limited company. They also had the patience to collect data when our habituation efforts succeeded: they collected countless hours of observation throughout 1998. Their help with data collection and their companionship in camp were essential for this project.

In addition, I thank Dr. Anita Christen for allowing me to accompany her to Bolivia in 1996, for showing me my first wild callimicos, introducing me to field work in the Pando, and serving as the outside committee member for my doctoral dissertation. My first trip to Bolivia with Dr. Christen and her children Ruth, Kasper, and Tomas was a great pleasure and encouraged me to continue my research.

Several other people came to the field and offered their expertise and friendship during this project. Amy Hanson came to Bolivia to study callimicos for her master's thesis and provided new insights into fungi and the callimicos' diet. Some of her data on fungi distribution and nutrition are discussed in this book. In addition, Vincent Sodaro, the head keeper of the Brookfield Zoo's captive colony of callimicos, provided encouragement for my research and important insights into callimico social behavior. Vince's enthusiasm has been a great incentive for me over the years.

Drs. Paul Garber, Jennifer Rehg, Lesa Davis, and Susan Ford have also been influential in the development of my research as they have made me think about my data in new ways and from new perspectives. Each of them has offered insights into the callimico's evolution, ecology, and anatomy. Paul Garber's collaboration with me in writing an article for *Evolutionary Anthropology* was particularly helpful, as it required synthesizing a large amount of data into a cohesive review of callimicos and their place in platyrrhine evolution.

This book is primarily the result of my doctoral dissertation, completed while a student at Stony Brook University in New York. My thesis committee, Drs. Patricia Wright, John Fleagle, Charles Janson, Diane Doran, and Anita Christen, helped to formulate the hypotheses and methods of this project, and provided suggestions on my thesis in all its various forms and drafts. I am particularly thankful to my advisor Patricia Wright for training me to write grant proposals, introducing me to primate field work, and inspiring me to think about primate conservation. In addition, John Fleagle provided great encouragement for thinking about behavior in an evolutionary framework, and has helped with many versions of grant proposals and articles throughout my graduate and postgraduate career.

Drs. Tim Sullivan and Melinda Pruett-Jones at the Brookfield Zoo also provided tremendous encouragement and support for my research. Following the completion of my doctoral work I was able to work through the Brookfield Zoo as a postdoctoral fellow, conducting research on a second group of wild callimicos at my site in Bolivia. The data I collected as a postdoc allowed me to expand my research on social behavior, some of which is presented in this volume.

Dr. Debbie Moskovitz and her team of conservation biologists, sociologists, and educators at the Field Museum, Chicago, took great interest in my efforts to initiate conservation programs for callimicos. The Field Museum, along with the Brookfield Zoo, sponsored a biological assessment team that collected important data on the flora and fauna of the northwest Pando. Fortunately, both these institutions have continued to develop programs for conservation in Bolivia. One of their achievements has been to help the Universidad Amazonica de Pando establish my field site as the Estación Biologica Tahuamanu, a new facility where Bolivian and international scientists can comfortably conduct research.

I thank my friends and colleagues from graduate school for their help in discussing ideas, editing text, and using statistics, and for teaching me computer programs. In particular, Natasha Shah, Kelly Stevens, Yin Lam, Yoshiko Abe, and Christopher Heesey gave up a lot of their time to make my dissertation a success. In addition, thanks to my friends in Seattle and at the University of Washington that provided encouragement, advice, and friendship while writing this book, particularly Diane and Juan Guerra, Stephanie Cohen, Catherine Ziegler, Joseph Butwin, Andrea Duncan, and Sarah Sterr.

This project would not have been possible without the financial support of several organizations. I received a WJ Fulbright Scholarship, and grants from the National Science Foundation (#9815171), the LSB Leakey Foundation, the Chicago Zoological Society, the Douroucouli Foundation, Primate Conservation, Inc., and the Margot Marsh Biodiversity Foundation to conduct the field work for my dissertation thesis. Funds from the Chicago Zoological Society and the Margot Marsh Biodiversity Foundation made a postdoctoral fellowship possible, and funds from the Research Board of the University of Illinois allowed me to continue the research I started during my postdoc for six additional months. In addition, the Primate Action Fund of Conservation International provided support for my surveys of the Pando to estimate the distribution and densities of callimicos. I thank all these institutions for their support of my research.

Finally, I would like to thank Drs. Natalie Vasey and Robert Sussman for asking me to contribute to this series. Writing this book has provided me the opportunity to reassess my thesis in light of new data I have collected and in consideration of many important research projects and publications that have been completed in the last several years.

"In addition thanks to the Bolivian government for permission to conduct research in the Department of Pando, and the Colección Boliviana de Fauna for their logistical help. Thanks to the Herbario Nacional de Bolivia and Robin Foster of the Field Museum, Chicago for their help identifying plant samples."

1

The Elusive Callimicos

A Swiss zoologist, Emilio Augusto Goeldi, exploring the Brazilian Amazon in 1904, discovered a small, black, shy monkey that had yet to be named scientifically (cited in Heltne, Wojcik, and Pook 1981). The monkeys were given the species name *Callimico goeldii,* meaning "Goeldi's beautiful monkeys." These newly named monkeys were captured and their skins and skeletons were preserved in museums. In subsequent years, other Goeldi's monkeys, hereafter called callimicos, were captured and shipped to zoological gardens around the world where they were bred successfully, and continue to breed to this day. For nearly 100 years, these museum specimens and zoo animals provided all the information that was known of the species.

Superficially, the callimico looks much like the other small monkeys of South America, the callitrichids, which include the marmosets, pygmy marmosets, tamarins, and lion tamarins (hereafter referred to generally as marmosets and tamarins). It was clear from the time of their discovery, however, that several details of the callimicos' anatomy make them distinct from the tamarins and marmosets (Martin 1992). For example, callimicos, unlike the other callitrichids, have three molars rather than two molars, and they produce single rather than twin offspring. These distinctions led many to propose that callimicos were a primitive ancestor of the callitrichids (Hershkovitz 1977). Since nothing was known about their behavior in the field, there was no way of knowing how their unusual anatomy and reproduction corresponded with their behavior and ecology in the wild. Short-term field studies of the monkeys conducted in the late 1970s (Masataka 1981; Pook and Pook 1981), and again in the 1990s (Christen 1999; Christen and Geissmann 1994), provided some clues about the species' natural history, such as their preference for the understory, but the monkeys' diet, habitat preferences, and ranging behavior remained unknown. The goal of this book therefore, is to present data from the first year-long study of callimico behavior and ecology in order to reassess its position in the callitrichid group from an ecological and evolutionary context. In order to understand how callimicos differ from other callitrichids, I chose to study not just the callimico, but also the saddle-back tamarin and red-bellied tamarin. By observing all three species in the same forest, during the same study period, I was able to assess how the callimico differs from these other monkeys.

Callimicos live in the tropical rain forests of the western Amazon basin. They are difficult to find as their distribution is patchy rather than continuous, and their population densities are low (Emmons and Feer 1997). In addition to being rare, callimicos are small in size and timid, making them extremely difficult to observe in the wild (Porter and Garber 2004). Indeed, because of their cryptic nature, local people are often unaware that callimicos live in the forests surrounding their communities (Emmons 1999; Ferrari et al. 1998). Callimicos are found in a few protected areas, such as the Manu National Park in Peru, but their low population densities, and shy nature, make them difficult to observe in the Park, even during intensive studies of the primate community (Terborgh 1983).

Callimicos are considered to be "near threatened" due to their overall rarity (IUCN 2006 Red List: www.redlist.org, May 4, 2006) and the rapid destruction of forests throughout the Amazon basin (Anderson 1990b; Cowlishaw and Dunbar 2000). At present, due to the lack of information on this species, its conservation status and plans for its protection are quite rudimentary. In order to identify areas that would effectively protect callimicos, it is first necessary to determine the species' ecological requirements, such as what foods it eats and its habitats. This book therefore will review the results of my field research on callimicos, and two sympatric species of tamarins, the red-bellied tamarin (*Saguinus labiatus*), and the saddle-back tamarin (*Saguinus fuscicollis*), at a site in northwestern Bolivia. These results make it possible to compare the species diets, habitat needs, activities, and reproductive behaviors, in order to identify what characteristics distinguish callimicos from the tamarins, information that is needed for conservation planning.

CALLIMICO TAXONOMY

Callimicos belong to the infraorder Platyrrhini which includes all the monkeys of Mexico, Central America, and South America. The platyrrhines are generally divided into five families: the Cebidae, which includes the capuchin monkeys and squirrel monkeys; the Aotidae, which includes the nocturnal owl monkeys; the Pithecidae, which includes the saki monkeys, uakaries, and titi monkeys; the Atelidae, which includes the large-sized

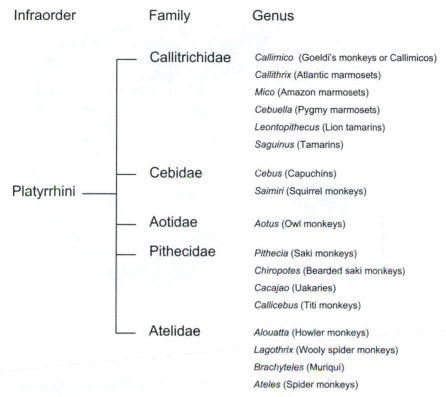

Infraorder   Family   Genus

Callitrichidae   *Callimico* (Goeldi's monkeys or Callimicos)
                  Callithrix (Atlantic marmosets)
                  Mico (Amazon marmosets)
                  Cebuella (Pygmy marmosets)
                  Leontopithecus (Lion tamarins)
                  Saguinus (Tamarins)

Cebidae   *Cebus* (Capuchins)
Platyrrhini   *Saimiri* (Squirrel monkeys)

Aotidae   *Aotus* (Owl monkeys)

Pithecidae   *Pithecia* (Saki monkeys)
                  Chiropotes (Bearded saki monkeys)
                  Cacajao (Uakaries)
                  Callicebus (Titi monkeys)

Atelidae   *Alouatta* (Howler monkeys)
                  Lagothrix (Wooly spider monkeys)
                  Brachyteles (Muriqui)
                  Ateles (Spider monkeys)

Figure 1–1 The taxonomy of the platyrrhines (adapted from Fleagle 1999)

spider monkeys, woolly monkeys, woolly spider monkeys, and howler monkeys; and the Callitrichidae, which includes tamarins (*Saguinus*), lion tamarins (*Leontopithecus*), marmosets (*Callithrix* and *Mico*), pygmy marmosets (*Cebuella*) and callimicos (Rylands et al. 2000; Schneider et al. 1996).

Callitrichids are distinctive from all other monkeys because they have claw-like nails (tegulae) on all digits except their hallux which has a flat nail (see Figure 1–2), and they are small bodied. The pygmy marmosets are the smallest monkeys in the world, weighing only about 100 g (Soini 1993), and the largest callitrichids, the lion tamarins, weigh only 700 g (Rylands 1993). Although the callitrichids used to be referred to as the most primitive monkeys in the world, anthropologists now generally agree that small body size and tegulae are new adaptations of this lineage and not primitive traits inherited from ancient primate ancestors (Porter and Garber 2004).

Most taxonomists currently place callimicos in the subfamily Callitrichidae, but this consensus is new. Over the last thirty years, the evolutionary and taxonomic relationship of callimicos with the callitrichids and the cebids has been the subject of considerable debate. The reasons for

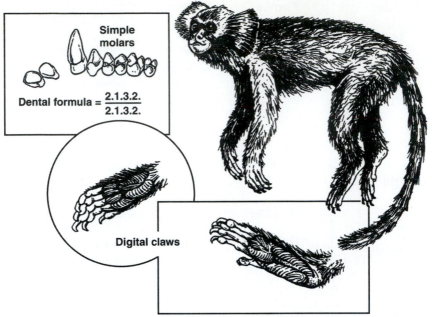

Figure 1–2 Anatomical characteristics of the callitrichids (from Figure 5–19 in Fleagle 1999). Reprinted with permission from Academic Press

this debate are due to the unusual traits that callimicos possess. Although callimicos are small, weighing about 500 g, (Porter and Garber 2004) and have tegulae like other callitrichids (Martin 1992), they resemble squirrel monkeys and capuchin monkeys in their teeth and litter size. Callimicos, like squirrel and capuchin monkeys, have a small third molar, whereas other callitrichids have lost this molar altogether. In addition, while marmosets, tamarins, and lion tamarins regularly have twins, callimicos, like all other monkeys, have single offspring (Tardif 1994).

As a result of these anatomical and reproductive differences between callimicos and the other callitrichids, various phylogenetic trees for these monkeys have been proposed over the last decades. Some trees indicate a long evolutionary split between callimicos and other platyrrhines, with callimicos occupying their own family, Callimiconidae (Hershkovitz 1977) (Figure 1–3a), or their own subfamily, Callimiconinae (Martin 1990) (Figure 1–3b). Alternatively, other trees place callimicos as "basal callitrichids," a lineage of small-bodied monkeys that split from the other callitrichids before twinning and molar loss evolved (Figure 1–3c) (Ford 1986; Ford and Davis 1992; Rosenberger 1981). Most recently, molecular evidence indicates that callimicos are not a distant relative to the other callitrichids, but instead are a close relative of the marmosets (Figure 1–3d) (Claridge et al. 1999; Horovitz and Meyer 1997; Pastorini et al. 1998; Von Dornum and Ruvolo 1999).

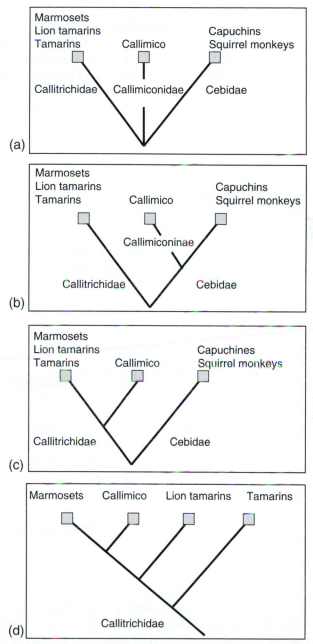

Figure 1–3 Proposed evolutionary relationships of callimicos to other platyrrhines based on: a) anatomical characters as per Hershkovitz 1977; b) anatomical characters as per Martin 1990; c) anatomical characters as per Ford 1986; and d) molecular evidence as per Pastorini et al. 1998

This new molecular data requires a complete rethinking of the callimicos' evolutionary history and the potentially adaptive benefits of their unique morphology and reproductive biology. For example, if callimicos and marmosets are closely related, why did the callimicos revert to the typical monkey litter size of one, while the marmosets have litter sizes of two? Field data can improve our understanding of the ecological factors that have shaped social behavior, diet, density, and distribution patterns in the wild. These data are useful for assessing evolutionary relationships among the callitrichids and the evolution of primate life history traits such as litter size across the primate order.

DISTRIBUTION, BEHAVIOR, AND ECOLOGY OF THE CALLITRICHIDS

The callitrichids are a highly successful group of platyrrhines, with thirty-one species recognized (Fleagle 1999) from Panama southwest through the Amazon basin and southeast through the Atlantic coastal forests of Brazil (Figure 1–4) (Hershkovitz 1977). As many as four callitrichid species may exist in sympatry in some areas of the Amazon basin (Peres 1997). For example, pygmy marmosets (*Cebuella pygmaea*), saddle-back tamarins (*Saguinus fuscicollis*), red-bellied tamarins (*Saguinus labiatus*) and callimicos all live in the tropical forests of northwestern Bolivia.

Many callitrichids show a high degree of regional variation in their appearance, and many subspecies are recognized within their geographic ranges (Rylands 1993). The saddle-back tamarin (*Saguinus fuscicollis*), for example, is comprised of ten subspecies distinguishable from one another by differences in the coloration of their faces and bodies (reviewed in Hershkovitz 1977; Rylands, Coimbra-Filho, and Mittermeier 1993). In contrast, only one species of callimicos, *Callimico goeldii* is currently known, and it shows no regional variation in color throughout its range across the western Amazon—in all areas it is completely black (Rylands 1993) (Figure 1–5).

Callimicos are found only in the western Amazon basin (Figure 1–4) and have a more patchy distribution than other callitrichids (Emmons and Feer 1997), but the reasons for this "patchiness" are unclear. Although callimicos have been described as a bamboo and disturbed forest specialist (Buchanan-Smith 1991a; Ferrari et al. 1998; Izawa 1979), others have reported its presence in mature forests (Christen 1998, 1999; Heltne, Wojcik, and Pook 1981); thus it is unclear if it is restricted to specific patches of habitat. In addition to being "patchy," the population density of callimicos appears to be very low throughout its range in comparison to other callitrichids (Emmons and Feer 1997). For example, a survey of northwestern Bolivia found callimicos at densities of 9.6 individuals/km², whereas sympatric tamarins in the same region were at densities of 16.8–25.2 individuals/km² (Cameron et al. 1989).

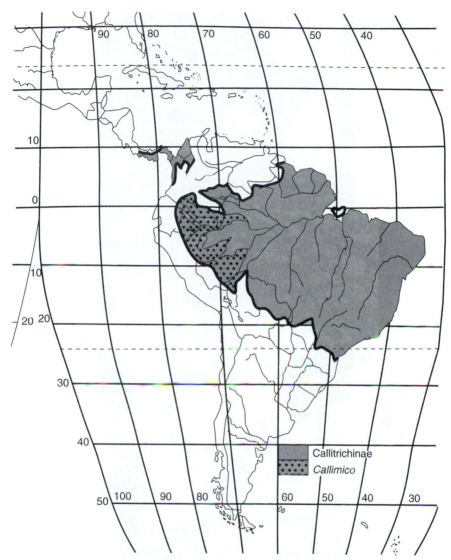

Figure 1–4 Map of the distribution of callimicos and the rest of the callitrichids (redrawn from Figure XIII in Hershkovitz, 1977, used with permission from the University of Chicago Press)

Callitrichids can use a variety of habitats, and many species can successfully colonize secondary forests and disturbed areas (Rylands 1993). Part of the adaptability of the callitrichids results from their diet: callitrichids are omnivores that consume fruits, insects, nectar, small vertebrates, and exudates (Rylands 1993). Marmosets have special procumbent incisors

Figure 1–5 A callimico in the forests of Bolivia (photo by Edilio Nacimento Becerra)

that allow them to scrape holes in trees in order to create exudate feeding sites continuously throughout the year (Fleagle 1999). The callimicos, tamarins and lion tamarins lack these specialized incisors, and therefore must opportunistically forage for exudates on trees damaged by insects, wind and other animals (Heymann and Smith 1999).

Although callitrichids are generally similar in their diets, niche theory predicts that closely related species should establish different diets in order to avoid competing for limited resources (Begon, Harper, and Townsend 1986). Hutchinson (1978) described an ecological niche as an n-dimensional hypervolume within which a species can maintain a viable population. The dimensions of this hypervolume are defined by environmental conditions (such as temperature), as well as the availability of water, food, and sleeping sites. The environmental conditions and resources necessary for a species' survival are collectively called a species' ecological niche.

Animals can avoid competition with one another if they exploit different niches when resources are scarce (e.g., Pianka 1981). For example, sympatric primates within the Manu National Park in Peru have more disparate feeding and foraging strategies in the dry season than they do during the wet season when foods are abundant (Terborgh 1983). Similar studies of primate communities in other parts of the world have further demonstrated niche partitioning among sympatric primates (e.g., Chapman 1987; Cords 1987; MacKinnon and MacKinnon 1980; Overdorff 1993; Vasey 2000).

Heymann and Buchanan-Smith (2000) propose that niche partitioning in callitrichids is accomplished principally through vertical segregation, with species traveling and foraging for insect prey in different levels of the subcanopy and canopy. Callimicos were described as understory specialists in earlier field studies (Pook and Pook 1981), but the details of the species' use of resources within this environment were unknown.

Many callitrichids form stable and highly coordinated mixed-species groups that forage, feed, and travel together (e.g., Buchanan-Smith 1990; Garber 1988a; Norconk 1990; Peres 1992a; Terborgh 1983). These associations between species, called polyspecific associations, occur in a wide variety of animals (for example, ungulates [Fitzgibbon 1990], birds [Munn and Terborgh 1979], fish [Landeau and Terborgh 1986], and spiders [Hodge and Uets 1996]), but are relatively uncommon among primates. Besides callitrichids, only the guenons and colobus monkeys in Africa (e.g., McGraw and Bshary 2002; Nöe and Bshary 1997; Oates and Whitesides 1990; Waser 1982; Whitesides 1989; Wolters and Zuberbuhler 2003) and the capuchin monkeys and squirrel monkeys in South America (Podolosky 1990) are known to form frequent and long-term polyspecific associations.

The first studies of wild callimicos showed that they formed polyspecific associations with two tamarin species, the saddle-back tamarin (*Saguinus fuscicollis*) and the red-bellied tamarin (*Saguinus labiatus*) (Buchanan-Smith 1991b; Christen and Geissmann 1994; Pook and Pook 1982). The frequency and longevity of these associations was not determined in these studies due to their short duration and lack of fully habituated animals. In addition, these studies did not attempt to test hypotheses concerning the benefits callimicos might gain by forming these associations. Studies of other callitrichids show that animals in polyspecific groups improve their ability to find insects and fruits, and to avoid predators (e.g., Buchanan-Smith 1999; Garber 1988a; Heymann 1990; Lopes and Ferrari 1994; Norconk 1990; Peres 1992a, b). Part of my research plan was to determine the benefits that callimicos received while in polyspecific groups.

Travel, foraging, and feeding behaviors may occur within a polyspecific group; however, social activities, such as grooming, infant care, and mating, only take place among individuals of the same species. Callitrichids exhibit a variety of mating systems with monogamous, multimale/multifemale (polygynandrous), and polyandrous mating patterns all reported from the wild (Caine 1993; Garber 1994; Goldizen 1990). Despite the variability in mating strategies all callitrichids exhibit an unusual type of infant care called "communal care" (Garber 1997). Under a communal (or cooperative) care system, all group members help care for infants born in the group. Although communal care is observed in some birds and social carnivores (e.g., Rabenold 1985; Rasa 1994), it is rare among primates (Mitani and Watts 1997).

Communal care is thought to have arisen in the callitrichids due to the high energetic demands of raising twins. A callitrichid mother is unable to both nurse and carry her twin infants because the infants grow rapidly and quickly become too heavy for her to transport both (Dietz, Baker, and Miglioretti 1994; Sanchez et al. 1999; Tardif 1994). For example, pygmy marmoset twins at birth together weigh as much as 25% of their mother's body weight, and quickly increase in weight thereafter (Hartwig 1996). As a result, a callitrichid mother needs help, and has evolved strategies for securing helpers in her group.

Dominant females in tamarin and marmoset groups produce hormones that are usually able to prevent subordinate females from ovulating. This allows the dominant females to maintain exclusive breeding status without using physical aggression to prevent other females from mating. Although subordinate females may mate, they will not become pregnant (Abbott, Barrett, and George 1993). Dominant females in groups of lion tamarins and callimicos do not consistently suppress the hormones of subordinates in captivity (Carroll 1988; Dettling and Pryce 1999; French and Inglett, 1989). Instead, physical aggression among females can lead to disruption of the group and/or death of the subordinates' offspring (Carroll 1988; Hardie 1995). Hormonal studies of callimicos have yet to be conducted in the wild, so the details of reproductive dominance in wild groups are not known. Callimico groups with two breeding females have been observed in the wild, however (Christen 1999; Masataka 1981), suggesting a greater tolerance of multiple breeders than in other callitrichid species.

The small-bodied callitrichids are prey to a wide variety of mammalian, avian, and reptilian predators (Caine 1993), and twinning may provide one mechanism for increasing reproductive output in response to high infant mortality (Caine 1993; Ross 1988, 1991). But, if twinning is a successful strategy for callitrichids, what are the ecological factors that would have made single births a feasible strategy for callimicos? The results of my research help address this question, by providing data on both social behavior and reproduction, as well as ecological data on diet and habitat use.

Understanding a species' dietary flexibility, habitat tolerance, and reproductive potential is essential for developing management plans for its protection. Species that tolerate secondary forest and have a broad diet, for example, are more tolerant of habitat disturbance from agriculture and logging than species that require primary forest habitats and have very narrow diets (Cowlishaw and Dunbar 2000). In addition, knowledge of a species' life history (such as interbirth interval and age at sexual maturity) is important for determining the ability of a species to recuperate from diminished population size due to loss of habitat, famine, disease, and/or predation (Cowlishaw and Dunbar 2000).

In the following Chapters I present data from the first year-long study of callimicos' behavior and ecology and I reassess its distinctive features in an ecological and evolutionary context. In doing so, I hope to present a new perspective on this little understood and little observed monkey, and encourage additional field studies.

2

The General Research Plan: A Comparative Study of Callimicos, Saddle-back Tamarins, and Red-bellied Tamarins

Determining the niche of a species is best done in a comparative study that makes it possible to determine how one species exploits its environment differently than another species living in the same area. Data on the behavior and ecology of primates taken at different study sites cannot easily be compared, as sites generally vary in food and habitat availability. Plant abundance and distribution is affected by soil fertility and rainfall, and may vary considerably across a region (Janson and Chapman 1999). In addition, food availability in one forest can vary annually and affect a primate's diet, ranging, and reproductive strategies (Janson and Chapman 1999), making comparisons of data taken in different years problematic. Therefore, comparative studies of multiple species at the same location and the same time provide the best opportunity for determining the degree to which sympatric species exploit their environments in a different manner.

In northern Bolivia, callimicos are sympatric with two kinds of tamarins, the saddle-back tamarin (*Saguinus fuscicollis weddelli*) and the red-bellied tamarin (*Saguinus labiatus labiatus*) (Christen 1999; Christen and Geissmann 1994; Pook and Pook 1981, 1982) (Figure 2–1), making it possible to conduct a comparative study of the three monkeys at the same time at one study site. In

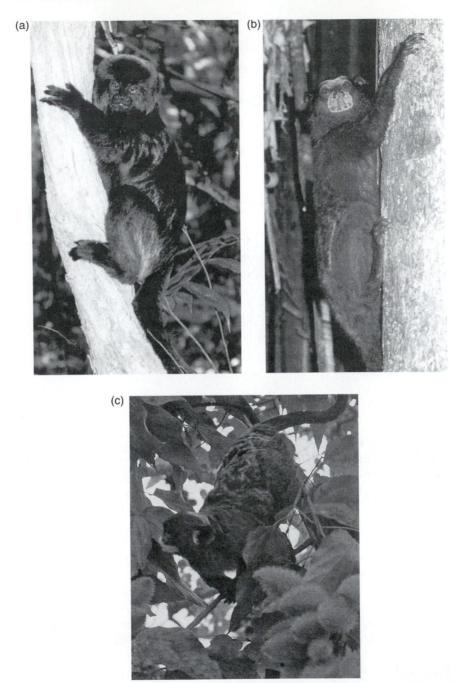

Figure 2–1 Photographs of the study species, a) callimico, b) saddle-back tamarin (photos by Edilio Nacimento Becerra), and c) red-bellied tamarin (photo by the author)

addition, since callimicos form polyspecific associations with tamarins (Pook and Pook 1982), a comparative study provides the opportunity to collect data on the behavior of the monkeys when they are traveling and foraging together as a mixed-species group.

STUDY SPECIES

Saddle-back tamarins and red-bellied tamarins have been the focus of several field studies; thus, many aspects of their behavior and ecology are known. The saddle-back tamarin is one of the smallest tamarins (320–420 g) (Goldizen et al. 1996). At least ten subspecies of saddle-back tamarin are found in the Amazon basin from Colombia south through Brazil, Peru, and Bolivia (Rylands, Coimbra-Filho, and Mittermeier 1993; Figure 2–2).

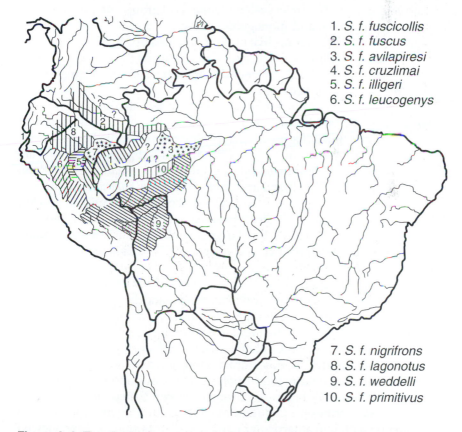

1. *S. f. fuscicollis*
2. *S. f. fuscus*
3. *S. f. avilapiresi*
4. *S. f. cruzlimai*
5. *S. f. illigeri*
6. *S. f. leucogenys*

7. *S. f. nigrifrons*
8. *S. f. lagonotus*
9. *S. f. weddelli*
10. *S. f. primitivus*

Figure 2–2 The distribution ranges of the ten subspecies of saddle-back tamarins (*Saguinus fuscicollis*) (from Figure 1–4 in Rylands 1993, reprinted with permission from Oxford University Press)

Two additional species—*S. fuscicollis melanoleucus* and *S. fuscicollis crandalli*—have been recently recognized (Rylands et al. 2000). The subspecies in Bolivia, *Saguinus fuscicollis weddelli*, is found in the southern region of the species distribution. The saddle-back tamarin is found in both primary and secondary forests throughout its range. It forages in low levels of the canopy or on the ground for insects, often searching for prey in holes and crevices (Yoneda 1984), and in the lower and middle canopy for fruits (Garber 1993). It opportunistically eats gums and saps from insect- or wind-damaged trees, resources that probably provide important nutrients in the dry season when other foods are scarce (Lopes and Ferrari 1994; Terborgh 1983). Saddle-back tamarins generally travel by trunk-to-trunk leaping (Garber and Leigh 2001; Yoneda 1984) in the lower canopy and understory (below 10 m in the forest strata) (Soini 1987). A long-term study of the saddle-back tamarin in the Manu National Park, Peru demonstrates that this species has a flexible social system; while most groups are polyandrous, others are polygynous and monogamous (Goldizen et al. 1996). At some sites, the saddle-back tamarins live at high densities of 3.5–5.5 groups/km^2 (Pook and Pook 1981) with very small home ranges (20–35 ha), while at other sites densities are much lower and home ranges are much larger (over 100 ha) (reviewed in Garber 1993).

The red-bellied tamarin has a much more limited distribution in South America than the saddle-back tamarin, inhabiting only small parts of Bolivia, Peru, and Brazil (Figure 2–3). In contrast to the saddle-back tamarin, which has ten subspecies, only two subspecies of red-bellied tamarins are recognized. *Saguinus labiatus labiatus* is found in a small area of Peru, Bolivia, and southwestern Brazil and *Saguinus labiatus thomasi* is found in a small region of northwestern Brazil (Rylands 1993). An additional species, *S. labiatus refiventer*, has also recently been named (Rylands et al. 2000). The red-bellied tamarin is one of the largest of all the tamarins, weighing 400–610 g (Puertas, Encarnación, and Aquino 1995). It uses the middle and lower-middle layers of the canopy, 15–20 m, for traveling, resting, and insect foraging (Buchanan-Smith 1991b; Pook and Pook 1981; Yoneda 1984). The red-bellied tamarin travels quadrupedally and by branch-to-branch leaping (Yoneda 1984), and forages for insects among leafy branches (Buchanan-Smith 1990). Red-bellied tamarin groups generally contain one breeding female, up to three other females, and up to five adult males (Buchanan-Smith 1991b; Puertas, Encarnación, and Aquino 1995).

The saddle-back tamarin forms polyspecific associations with various other callitrichids (other tamarins: *Saguinus mystax, S. imperator, S. labiatus*; callimicos; and marmosets, *Callithrix emiliae*) depending on which species are sympatric with it in a particular part of its distribution range (reviewed in Heymann 1997; Heymann and Buchanan-Smith 2000). A study of the red-bellied tamarin in Bolivia shows that it may maintain associations with the saddle-back tamarin for as much as 83% of the day, and that groups of each of these species defend a common home range (Buchanan-Smith 1990).

1. *S. l. labiatus*
2. *S. l. thomasi*

Figure 2–3 The distribution ranges of the two subspecies of red-bellied tamarins *(Saguinus labiatus)* (from Figure 1–6 in Rylands 1993, reprinted with permission from Oxford University Press)

Callimicos have been less well studied in the wild than either of these tamarins. Izawa (1979) did a widespread survey across the western Amazon basin and concluded that callimicos were secondary forest specialists that specialized on bamboo forests. Pook and Pook (1981, 1982) collected the first detailed data on diet and habitat use of callimicos in northern Bolivia, observing that they consumed fruits and insects, and that they preferred the forest understory. They also documented that the callimicos formed poly-specific associations with saddle-back and red-bellied tamarins (Pook and Pook 1981, 1982). The Pooks' data were limited however, as the callimicos were not well habituated, and the behavioral study was of only three months in duration. Masataka (1981, 1982, 1983) worked near the Pooks' study site in northern Bolivia, and collected data on vocalizations and social behavior. He was able to collect more detailed social observations of a group of callimicos by luring them to a baited feeding platform. Although Masataka's studies provide some details as to social behavior, they did not focus on ecology. In addition, as he released callimicos into his study group (individuals that had been captured by humans for pets) it is unclear if the group represents a natural social group.

In 1991 and 1996, Christen conducted surveys and behavioral studies at several locations across northwestern Bolivia (Christen and Geissmann 1994). Indeed, in 1996, I was fortunate to accompany Dr. Christen to Bolivia and assist her with her field project. Dr. Christen therefore, provided me with my first opportunity to view wild callimicos and to learn about field work in Bolivia. Like the Pooks, her behavioral data were limited, as her research lasted only two (1991 group) and four months (1996 group), and so the monkeys were not well habituated. Christen's work showed, however, that despite reports to the contrary (Freese et al. 1982; Kohlhaas 1988), callimicos can be found at low densities in many locations in northwestern Bolivia, and that they are not always found in bamboo forests. Indeed, I was with Dr. Christen when she observed a callimico eating a white, rubbery substance, a food item which we could not identify at the time, but which in retrospect we can say was most certainly a fungus.

STUDY AREA

Although Bolivia is best known for the high, arid, flat plateaus found between the peaks of the Andes (the Altiplano), Bolivia has many different ecosystems that contain primates. Bolivian primates are found in the mountainous semihumid forests that slope down from the Andes toward sea level (the Yungas), semihumid lowland forests of the east, semi-arid lowland forests of the south (the Chaco), inundated forests and plains of the northeast (the Pantanal), and the Amazon rainforests of the north (Figure 2–4). The northern region of Bolivia forms the department of the Pando, which is considered part of the Amazon basin and is comprised primarily of rainforest. This study took place in the northwest corner of the Pando near the borders of both the state of Acre, Brazil and the department of Madre de Dios, Peru.

The Pando contains several large rivers that are tributaries of the Amazon (Figure 2–5). These rivers flow from Peru northeast through the Pando where they join other rivers in Brazil, eventually leading into the Amazon to the north. These Pandino rivers contain among the highest density of animal life of all the rivers in the Amazon basin (Chernoff and Willink 1999).

Tropical forests are generally found between the Tropics of Cancer and Capricorn and are characterized by high rainfall (1700–3000 mm/year) and high average mean temperatures (20–28°C) (Goldsmith 1998). The combination of high rainfall and high temperatures make tropical forests optimal environments for plant growth. Plant growth in turn promotes diversification of animal life, making tropical forests the most diverse ecosystems on the planet (Goldsmith 1998). The soil in tropical forests is generally poor in nutrients, and the rivers in northwest Bolivia are considered "white-water"

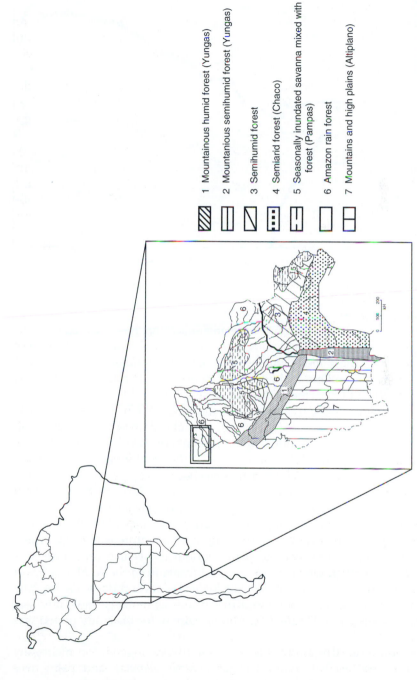

1 Mountainous humid forest (Yungas)

2 Mountainous semihumid forest (Yungas)

3 Semihumid forest

4 Semiarid forest (Chaco)

5 Seasonally inundated savanna mixed with forest (Pampas)

6 Amazon rain forest

7 Mountains and high plains (Altiplano)

Figure 2–4 Map of Bolivian ecosystems (redrawn from Figure 3, Brown and Rumiz 1985). The box outlined with a double line indicates the area shown in Figure 2–5

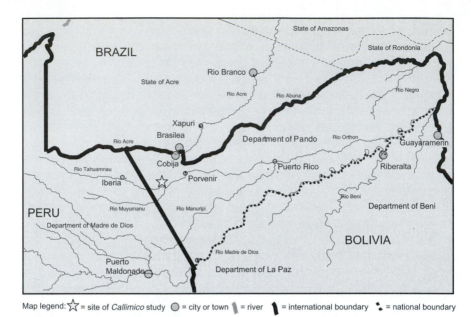

Map legend: ☆ = site of *Callimico* study   ◯ = city or town   ▮ = river   ▮ = international boundary   ⁘ = national boundary

Figure 2–5 Map of the Department of the Pando, Bolivia, and surrounding regions

rivers, as the water contains fine inorganic solids that have entered the river through extensive erosion of soils, which gives them a muddy appearance (Jordan 1985). One of these white-water rivers is the Tahuamanu River, which enters Bolivia from Peru and heads east through the Pando until it joins the Manuripi River to form the Orthon River (see Figure 2–5).

I established a research camp at an abandoned cabin named by its owners "San Sebastian" (11°24' S, 69° 01' W, ca. 280 m elevation; see Figure 2–5). San Sebastian is located 3 km north of the Tahuamanu River, 42 km east of the Peruvian border, and 55 km southwest of the capital city of the Pando, Cobija. Since my study, San Sebastian has been developed into the Tahua-manu Biological Field Station by the Chicago Field Museum, the Brookfield Zoo, and the Universidad Amazonica de Pando, Cobija.

The average maximum temperature during the study (April 1998–March 1999) was 30.0°C and the average minimum temperature was 21.3°C. These temperatures are fairly consistent throughout the year except from May through September, when occasional cold fronts from the south can lower the minimum temperature to 13°C or lower for several days (Figure 2–6). The area experiences pronounced dry (June–September) and rainy sea-sons (October–May) (Figure 2–7). Annual rainfall for the study period was 1970 mm.

The forest at the study site was selectively logged for mahogany (*Swietenia macrophylla*), Spanish cedar (*Cedrela odorata*), and palm trees (*Euterpe precatoria*) one to seven years before the study, by workers associated

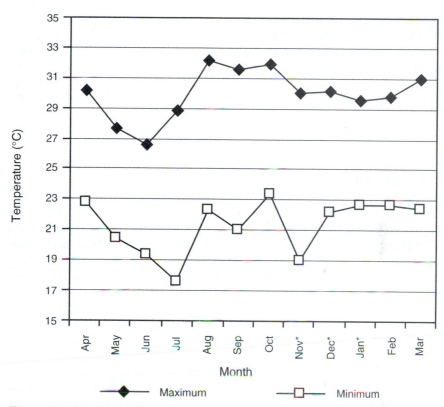

Figure 2–6 Monthly maximum and minimum temperatures during the study period beginning in April, 1998. All temperatures were taken at the research site except for those months indicated with an asterisk, which were taken in the city of Cobija (from the wunderground.com archive database)

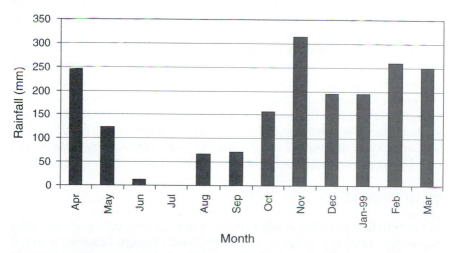

Figure 2–7 Monthly rainfall (in mm) during the study, beginning in April, 1998

with a logging company situated at a camp called Rutina, located along the banks of the Tahuamanu. At the start of my study, Rutina was a functioning lumberyard, but it closed in 1998 and never reopened. In addition to forest disturbance created by the logging operations, small (1 ha) secondary forest patches exist in the area at the sites of an abandoned house and three abandoned agricultural plots. A household (named Callimico) 1 km south of the research camp practices subsistence agriculture (with a 2 ha agricultural plot during the study) and workers collected Brazil nuts from the forest from January–March during both years of the study.

The forest at the site is representative of sandy-clay forests of the south and southwestern Amazonia, and can be described as upland terra firma forest (Alverson, Moskovitz, and Shopland 2000). The forest is remarkable in the great abundance of Brazil nut (*Bertholletia excelsa*) and rubber trees (*Hevea brailiensis*). Flat sections of the forest have high continuous canopy (of 40 m) with a shaded understory, while hilltops have a drier forest with more tree falls and a dense understory. It is estimated that approximately 2,000 species of vascular plants exist in this region of Bolivia (Alverson, Moskovitz, and Shopland 2000).

The primate community consists of callimicos (*Callimico goeldii*), saddle-back tamarins (*Saguinus fuscicollis*), red-bellied tamarins (*Saguinus labiatus*), pygmy marmosets (*Cebuella pygmaea*), brown-capped capuchins (*Cebus apella*), white capuchins (*Cebus albifrons*), Bolivian squirrel monkeys (*Saimiri boliviensis*), titi monkeys (*Callicebus brunneus*), red howler monkeys (*Alouatta sara*), owl monkeys (*Aotus nigriceps*), and the bald-faced saki (*Pithecia irrorata*). The presence of eleven species of primates in the same forest place it as one of the highest density areas of primates in South America.

In addition to primates, thirty-five other large mammals have been observed at the field site (Alverson, Moskovitz, and Shopland 2000). These mammals include herbivores and frugivores such as tapirs, peccary, and deer; insectivores such as the giant anteater and the silky anteater; and carnivores such as the jaguar, puma, and tayras. In addition, 163 species of birds have been documented at the site (Alverson, Moskovitz, and Shopland 2000), and range from the large Harpy eagle, to macaws and parrots, to small canopy birds, and large understory ground birds such as the trumpeter bird (Alverson, Moskovitz, and Shopland 2000). In addition, a variety of amphibians and reptiles have been reported at the site, including tree frogs, turtles, toads, and snakes (Alverson, Moskovitz, and Shopland 2000), including 6 m long anacondas that inhabit the stream that passes by San Sebastian (measured by my guide Edilio Nacimento)!

TRAIL SYSTEM

In order to find potential study groups in the area, we cut small footpaths below the monkeys' arboreal pathways, and through areas with dense

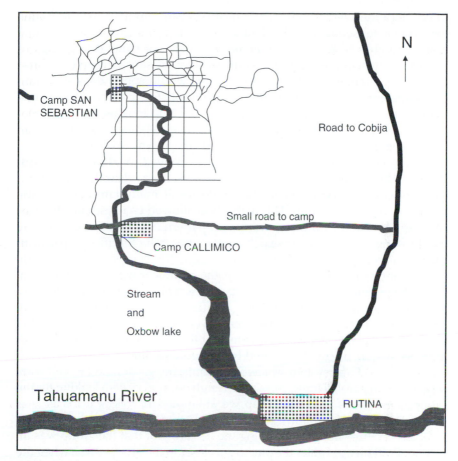

Figure 2–8 Map of the trail system

understory. These footpaths allowed us to follow the monkeys more easily on many of their traveling routes.

In addition, once I decided upon which groups we would habituate, we cut trails at 100 m intervals headed both north-south and east-west within the study groups' home ranges. These trails formed a grid map of 1,300 m × 800 m, with trails delineating 1 ha plots of forest (Figure 2–8). Additional footpaths were added to follow the monkeys within this grid system. As the grid did not cover our callimico study groups' entire home ranges, we continued to use our footpaths as the primary trails in some areas.

STUDY GROUPS

In determining which group of callimicos we should attempt to habituate, we immediately ran into a problem: the callimicos we observed on one day in one location were almost never near or even remotely near the same location on subsequent days. I had assumed that one group of callimicos would roughly have the same home range size of sympatric groups of tamarins. Thus, at the beginning of the study if we saw a group of callimicos with one tamarin group on one day, we would spend days searching that same tamarin group's territory in hopes of seeing callimicos again, a strategy that rarely worked! If, instead, we gave up looking in the original tamarin group's territory and looked in all their neighbors' territories, we would eventually see callimicos again. At first it was unclear if we were observing one group of callimicos that had moved, or different groups. When we began to make accurate group counts, it was clear that the callimicos we were observing across the territories of many tamarins actually belonged to just one group. This realization allowed us to estimate the size of the group's home range, its movement patterns within this home range, and thus made it possible to search more successfully for the group during the habituation process.

In addition to their large home range, the callimicos were also very timid. At the beginning of the study, if we spotted a callimico group we generally had a few seconds to observe them, because as soon as they saw us they would immediately run into the densest vegetation and disappear for the rest of the day. Thus, it quickly became clear that we needed our own habituation technique, a strategy devised by my guide Edilio Nacimento, which required a good trail system. My two assistants, my guide, and I would walk separately, on parallel trails, crossing through our trail system looking for the group. When we found the group we attempted to follow it for as long as possible using the following strategy: first, we would post ourselves as sentinels on three trails surrounding the hectare plot that the group was in; second, Edilio would enter the plot to get closer to the group; third, when the monkeys moved out of that hectare a sentinel would observe their direction of travel; fourth, the sentinel would indicate the monkeys' direction of movement; and fifth, the procedure would start over again in a new parcel of forest. Even with this strategy, the group often would disappear undetected, and once the group was lost it often was not found again for several days.

Finally, after seven months, we were able to follow the callimico group for an entire day (Figure 2–9); after this, we continued to follow them all day, from the time they left their sleeping site in the morning until the time that they retired to a sleeping site at night (hereafter called an "all-day follow"). Once we could conduct all-day follows we began behavioral observations of the group. We conducted these observations for one full year, from April 1998–March 1999.

The saddle-back tamarins were much easier to habituate than the callimicos, as they were less cautious and were not inclined to run and hide at the site of humans. In the seven months we spent trying to habituate the group of callimicos, several saddle-back tamarin groups became accustomed to our presence in their territories. Therefore, we were able to begin

Figure 2–9 The author following a habituated callimico (photo by Edilio Nacimento Becerra)

observations of a saddle-back tamarin group at the same time as the callimicos, in April, 1998. The red-bellied tamarins were a little more wary of us, and so we worked to habituate a study group in April and May, 1998, and were able to begin observations of a group of this species in June, 1998.

As the saddle-back and red-bellied tamarins formed semipermanent polyspecific associations with one another and shared a common home range (see Chapter 5), I will refer to the two groups of tamarin species that shared the same territory with the same number. For example, saddle-back tamarin group 1 and red-bellied tamarin group 1 shared the same home range, and are referred to collectively as tamarin *troop* 1.

Unfortunately, red-bellied tamarin group 1 remained wary of us throughout our observations, and so in October we switched to a neighboring troop of tamarins (troop 2). These tamarins had become well habituated to our presence as the callimicos were often in their home range. Therefore we collected data on saddle-back group 2 and red-bellied group 2 from October 1998–March 1999.

The composition of the callimico and tamarin groups changed throughout the study due to transfers, births, and deaths of group members. The average number of individuals recorded for each group scan for each species during each month is recorded in Table 2–1. As my guide, my two assistants, and I all collected data, we conducted interreliability tests once a month to ensure that our data was comparable. Although we often went in pairs, only a single person took data at a given time.

As we did not mark individuals in the study groups, we could not consistently identify them. We therefore took data on entire groups rather than focal animals. At five-minute intervals throughout the day, we recorded the behavior of all visible individuals during a ten-second scan of the group being followed. An individual monkey's behavior, or an "independent record," formed one part of the total observations of the group at a given interval. For analyses, each independent record was converted into a percentage of the group scan, so that each group scan had equal weight in analyses. This approach is similar to that employed by Milton (1980), Strier (1987) and described by Clutton-Brock (1977b). As callitrichids have been shown to feed and travel in cohesive units (Garber et al. 1993; Peres 2000), the behavior of one individual closely approximates the behavior of other group members, therefore group scans in which some individuals are missing should not greatly differ from samples in which the entire group was observed.

We followed callimicos on seven to fourteen days each month for a total of 957 hours of observations on 111 days (total scans = 11,487). We observed tamarins on five to seven days each month: data on saddle-back tamarins totaled 434 hours on 66 days (total scans = 5,275) and data on red-bellied tamarins totaled 323 observation hours on 57 days (total scans = 3,887). Observations of one group were generally collected on consecutive days each month.

More detailed discussion of behavioral methods will be presented in subsequent chapters, along with the methods used to determine monthly food availability (see Chapter 3). In addition, the specific hypotheses tested will be presented in each chapter, along with the results of data analyses and a discussion of the results.

Table 2–1 The composition of study groups across the study year

Time Period	Callimicos		Red-Bellied Tamarins		Saddle-Back Tamarins	
	Group composition	Average # individuals observed/scan	Group composition	Average # individuals observed/scan	Group composition	Average # individuals observed/scan
April	3f, 3m, 1i	2.72			(1) 2a, 2m, 2f, 2j, 2i	5.33
May	3f, 3m, 1i	2.73			(1) 2a, 2m, 2f, 2j, 2i	4.62
June	3f, 3m, 1i	2.53	(1) 8a, 2j	1.65	(1) 2a, 2m, 2f, 2j, 2i	3.68
July	3f, 3m, 1i	3.14	(1) 8a, 2j	1.58	(1) 2a, 2m, 2f, 2j, 2i	3.23
August	2f, 2m, 1j, 1i	2.96	(1) 8a, 2j	2.55	(1) 2m, 2f, 2j, 2i	2.44
September	2f, 2m, 1j, 1i	3.54	(1) 6a, 2i	1.91	(1) 2m, 2f, 2j, 2i	2.75
October	2f, 2m, 1j, 1i	3.67	(2) 5a	2.79	(2) 2f, 2m, 1j, 1i	3.00
November	2f, 2m, 1j, 1i	4.5	(2) 5a, 2i	2.88	(2) 2f, 2m, 1j, 1i	3.09
December	2f, 2m, 1j, 1i	4.6	(2) 5a	3.05	(2) 2f, 2m, 1j, 1i	3.88
January	1f, 2m	2.6	(2) 5a	2.79	(2) 2f, 2m, 1j, 1i	3.46
February	1f, 1m	1.77	(2) 5a	3.00	(2) 2f, 2m, 2j, 2i	4.24
March	1f, 1m, 1i	1.95	(2) 2f, 2m	3.60	(2) 1f, 2m, 2j	4.39

Group indicated in parentheses (1) or (2)

a = adult, unknown sex

f = adult female

m = adult male

i = infant (age 0–6 months)

j = juvenile (age 6–12 months)

3

Fungi and the Dietary Niche of Callimicos[1]

A species relies on a set of resources within its environment for all its basic needs, including food and substrates for travel, rest, and shelter. When one or more of these resources are limited, niche theory predicts that species living in the same place (sympatric species) should exploit different resources in order to avoid or reduce competition with each other (e.g., Gause 1934; Hutchinson 1959; Pianka 1981). Sympatric species may partition resources in their environment in different ways: through spatial use of their habitat (e.g., Ilse and Hellgren 1995; Vrcibradic and Rocha 1996), the methods they use for foraging (Bergallo and Rocha 1994; Slater 1994), diet choice (Churchfield, Nesterenko, and Shvarts 1999; Luiselli, Akani, and Capizzi 1998), and their activity patterns (Wright 1989). The result is niche partitioning, or niche differentiation, among sympatric species such that no two species use exactly the same set of resources.

Studies of primate communities have shown that primate niches are defined principally through the habitats they use and the foods they choose in those habitats (e.g., Ganzhorn 1988; Tan 1999; Terborgh 1983; Ungar 1995). Dietary niches may be very different, as in the case in which two primate species choose totally different food resources, such as leaves rather than fruits (Clutton-Brock and Harvey 1977), or they may differ in more

[1]A portion of this chapter, as well as the tables and figures, were previously published in "*Callimico goeldii* and *Saguinus:* Dietary differences between sympatric callitrichines in northern Bolivia," *International Journal of Primatology* 22(2001):961–992. From Porter 2001a used with permission from Springer Publishers.

subtle ways. For example, while two primates may both eat fruits, they may choose fruits by different criteria of ripeness, size, acidity, and chemical composition (Conklin-Brittain, Wrangham, and Hunt 1998; Gautier-Hion et al. 1985; Janson 1983; Ungar 1995; Wrangham, Conklin-Brittain, and Hunt 1998), or by the patch sizes and distribution in which the fruits are found (Peres 1996; Terborgh 1983).

Competition among species for food resources is likely to be highest during periods of food shortage, and it is generally expected that species will show the most dietary divergence during this period (Schoener 1974). Many plant species in tropical forests are synchronized in their phenological patterns (the time of year during which they produce fruit), leading to abundant foods in one part of the year and relatively few foods in other parts of the year (e.g., Milton 1980). Primate species may have resources that they use only when preferred foods are scarce; when these "fallback" foods are essential to the species' survival they are called keystone resources. Sympatric primate species generally rely on different keystone resources (Terborgh 1983); however, in some cases primates may choose the same keystone resource, leading to a dietary convergence during food scarcity. In a Brazilian rain forest, for example, two species of tamarins have more similar diets during the dry season when fruits are scarce than during periods of fruit abundance, because the two tamarins resort to eating fruits from the same few plant species (Peres 1996).

Closely related species generally are similar in body size, gut morphology, and locomotor capabilities (Clutton-Brock 1977b; Clutton-Brock and Harvey 1977), and their anatomy limits their ability to exploit different resources. For example, small-bodied primates generally cannot obtain enough energy from leaves to be folivores, and generally consume fruits and insects (Kay 1975; Lambert 1998). Slight anatomical differences between closely related species can influence a species' selection of foods and the habitats where they search for those foods. For example, marmosets have special incisors that permit them to scrape holes in trees: these holes stimulate the tree to produce exudates to seal the damaged bark, thereby creating a feeding site for the marmosets. This ability to create exudate feeding sites enables marmosets to specialize on this resource, a food of limited availability to other callitrichids (Ferrari 1993).

The body size of callimicos is not well established from the wild. Encarnación and Heymann (1998) weighed animals in Peru, and found average body sizes to be 355–535 g. Garber and Leigh (2001) weighed a female at 535 g, and my own data show that an adult male weighed 458 g and an adult female weighed 523 g (unpublished data). Thus, callimicos generally appear to be heavier than the saddle-back tamarin (320–420 g) (Goldizen et al. 1996), and lighter than the red-bellied tamarin (400–610 g) (Puertas, Encarnación, and Aquino 1995). I hypothesized that their diets would not differ dramatically from one another, but rather would be different in subtle aspects of food choice, particularly during times of resource scarcity. Anatomical differences among the three species suggested clues as to how their foraging and feeding strategies would differ.

The morphology of molars can distinguish primates with different diets: molars with high, sharp crests are characteristic of species that are highly folivorous or insectivorous, while molars with low cusps tend to be characteristic of species that are primarily frugivorous (Kay 1975). High shearing crests help insectivores to cut through insects' exoskeletons to access the soft tissue inside, and high crests help folivores shred leaves comprised of complex carbohydrates into small pieces to aid in digestion. Alternatively, ripe fruits are easy to access and easy to digest, thus molar specializations are not required of frugivores.

Body size acts as a major influence on a primates' diet. Small-bodied primates with high metabolic rates cannot obtain sufficient protein from leaves that only provide sufficient nutrition when eaten in large volume whereas large-bodied primates cannot catch enough insects (which are small and dispersed, except for social insects such as termites) to satisfy their protein requirements. Therefore, small-bodied primates tend to obtain their protein from insects, and large-bodied primates tend to obtain their protein from leaves.

The molars of callimicos have higher shearing crests than those of all other platyrrhines (Fleagle, Kay, and Anthony 1997; Kay 1975), evidence that, along with their small body size, was thought to indicate that callimicos are highly specialized for insectivory. This hypothesis is addressed in this chapter, and is not supported.

Hand morphology (size and shape) differs among callimicos, saddle-back tamarins, and red-bellied tamarins, and likely reflects differences in their foraging strategies (Bicca-Marques 1999). The saddle-back tamarin has long, narrow hands and fingers that appear to be best-suited for searching for prey in holes and crevices, whereas the red-bellied tamarin and the callimico have shorter fingers and broader hands. Thus, I hypothesized that callimicos and red-bellied tamarins are less likely to forage for prey concealed in holes and more likely to look for exposed prey. This relationship between hand shape and diet, however, is not always clear. For example, capuchins and squirrel monkeys have foraging strategies opposite of that predicted by their hands: squirrel monkeys have much more gracile hands than the larger-bodied capuchin monkeys (Jouffroy, Godinot, and Nakano 1993), yet it is the capuchins that search for concealed prey (Terborgh 1983). The discrepancy, however, may result from the capuchins' need to pound and break open difficult-to-acquire foods (Terborgh 1983).

The anatomical differences in teeth and hand shape therefore suggest that foraging differences exist among callimicos, red-bellied tamarins, and saddle-back tamarins. In order to look specifically at how their diets differ, I collected feeding and foraging data of the three species during one year of observations. The results will be considered in this chapter, with particular emphasis on how the callimicos' diet differs from the tamarins' diets during periods of food scarcity.

One important discovery of my research is that callimicos rely heavily on fungi, a food resource that is rarely used by primates, and therefore one I had not even considered as a potential component of the callimicos' diet. The consumption of fungi, called mycophagy, is common among some animals, such as Australian marsupials and North and South American rodents (Claridge and May 1994; Claridge et al. 1999), but has been observed rarely among primates. Among most primates for which mycophagy has been observed it appears to be a rare and seasonal event (e.g., Bermejo, Illera, and Sabater Pi 1994; Ruhiyat 1983; Tan 1999). Exceptions include the Yunnan snub-nosed monkeys (*Rhinopithecus bieti*) whose principal food in the temperate forests of China are lichens (fungus and algae) (Kirkpatrick, Long, and Xiao 1998), the Japanese macaques (*Macaca fuscata*) of Yakushima which spend 14% of feeding time on fungi (Hanya 2004a), and the buffy tufted-eared marmoset (*Callithrix aurita*) for which bamboo fungi comprise 12% of its annual diet (Mestre Correa 1995). The implications of this unusual diet will be discussed in greater detail at the end of this chapter.

METHODOLOGY

Behavioral Observations

We collected data on feeding behavior during group scans taken at five-minute intervals (as described in Chapter 2). If we observed an animal eating during a scan, we noted the type of food that was being eaten using the following food categories: fungi, nectar, fruits, plant exudates, arthropods, and vertebrates. We collected and dried samples of all plant and fungus species, and sent voucher specimens of these samples for identification to the Field Museum, Chicago; the National Herbarium of Bolivia, La Paz; and the Department of Plant Pathology, Cornell University. When we observed animals eating arthropods we noted their appearance and collected any discarded wings and legs to aid in identification. Using these plant and arthropod samples, food items were identified to the finest detail possible; for insects generally to the family level, and for plants and fungi generally to the genus or species level.

As feeding data are taken from group scans (see Chapter 2) they are measures of the frequency with which groups feed on food items throughout the day, rather than measures of the absolute proportion of each food item in the diet by volume, or by the actual time spent eating a given food item. I converted group scan data into mean monthly feeding frequencies using the following procedure. First, I selected all scans in which feeding occurred from the data base. Second, if more than one individual was feeding in a scan sample, I converted the food items eaten at that scan into a percentage (e.g., two individuals observed feeding at 8:00, one eating a fruit and one eating an insect, would give a feeding frequency of 50% fruit and 50% insect for this scan). Third, I summed the percentage scan data for each food item (e.g., fruit) for each day within a month, and divided this sum by the total sum of all food items eaten that month (e.g., fruits, insects, nectar, etc.), to give a monthly mean feeding frequency for each food type.

Recording the actual volume of food ingested is a more accurate way of estimating the proportion of different food items in primates' diet (Clutton-Brock 1977a; Kurland and Gaulin 1987; Miller 1997) but is difficult to accomplish with unmarked individuals in a large group. To overcome this problem, I used only scans during which study subjects were feeding for analyses, excluding data on foraging. I defined feeding as the ingestion or manipulation of food items for ingestion, and defined foraging as the search within a substrate for a food item or the visual search of a medium (such as forest leaf litter) for a food object. The exclusion of foraging data for calculating diet should reduce the possibility of overestimating the proportion of invertebrates in the diet, a common problem when combined eating and foraging rates are used, as insect foraging is more time consuming than fruit foraging (Kurland and Gaulin 1987; Miller 1997). Furthermore, since we collected data for all three species using the same methods during the same months, any sampling biases should be the same for all three species, making the dietary calculations of the study species comparable to one another.

To determine the height at which the monkeys fed and foraged I examine all records of individuals in which the animal was feeding or foraging (manipulating a food object, or actively searching in or on the ground or a plant for a food item). Height classes were divided into the following increments: on the ground; ground to 5 m; 5–10 m; 10–15 m; 15–25 m; 25 m or more. For the analyses of height class use while feeding and foraging, I used independent records of individuals feeding on fruits rather than group percentage data (see Chapter 2) as the goal was to determine the height at which an individual monkey fed and foraged specifically o n fruits.

Diet Overlap

Schoener's Index of Niche Overlap (Schoener 1968) was used to calculate diet overlap between each species. Dietary niche overlap (O_{ab}) between species was determined using the formula

$$O_{ab} = 1 - 0.5 \Sigma(|p_{ah} - p_{bh}|)$$

where p_{ah} and p_{bh} are the proportions of food item "h" in the diet of primate species "a" and "b." This index has several benefits, including: it ranges from 1 (complete dietary overlap) to 0 (no dietary overlap) and therefore is easy to interpret; it does not rely on the presence or absence of particular food species in the diets being compared; it can be used with samples of different sizes; and it is not overly sensitive to changes in the use of more common plant species. Its drawback, like that of all similarity indices, is that results cannot be statistically tested (Wolda 1981).

The food categories considered for overlap indices were fruits, nectar, exudates, arthropods, and fungi. Plant items (fruits, nectar, exudates) were considered at the species level in order to determine whether some plants were more important for callimicos than for the tamarins, and vice versa. In contrast, arthropods were grouped as one food type, and fungi as another general food type, thus it was not determined whether there were any differences in the primate species' selectivity of food items within these broad categories. This potentially inflates the obtained diet overlap values for arthropods relative to plants. These biases are the same for all species, thus the maximum diet overlap values for the three species are comparable.

Monitoring Plants, Fungi, and Arthropods

At the end of each month of the study, phenological data of all trees greater than 10 cm diameter at breast height (DBH) (n = 1,342) were recorded from eight (5 m × 500 m) transects (total area sampled = 2 ha), placed in parallel at 100 m intervals in the study area. These transects intersected all major habitat types (see Chapter 4) of the home ranges of the study groups. Each tagged plant was scored for the abundance of flowers, unripe and ripe fruits, and fruits and flowers of plants in the understory (trees less than 10 cm in DBH, and epiphytes and lianas less than 5 m in height) were monitored following the method of Gentry and Emmons (1987).

While walking each transect, we counted the number of individual buds, flowers, or fruits on each fertile plant, or in cases where they were very abundant, we estimated the total number of buds, flowers, and fruits, using the following set of procedures. First, using binoculars, we counted the number of fruits or flowers in the crown of a plant as seen in three separate binocular fields of vision at approximately the same height. We then calculated an average number of fruits (or flowers) for one field of vision. Second, we counted the number of fields of vision necessary to observe the whole fruiting portion of the plant. Third, we took the average number of fruits or flowers/field and multiplied it by the total number of fields of vision, to obtain a rough estimate of the plant's total number of fruits and flowers.

In addition, we monitored fungi growing on dead wood and bamboo along the botanical transects from June 1998–April 1999. We counted the number of fungi growing on dead trees and tree falls, and bamboo stalks and branches along the botanical transects to obtain an estimate of fungi availability. The type of fungi—jelly fungi (*Auricularia*) or bamboo fungi (*Ascopolyporous*)—and the color of the fungi were also recorded.

To monitor changes in insect abundance, we did sweep samples each month, using an insect net to sweep twenty (length 25 m, width 4 m, height 0–2 m) transects placed in parallel every 100 m along trails in the study area. The height was chosen because it represents a common height in which the callimicos regularly forage for insects. These transects run perpendicular to botanical transects and cross all habitats in the study area (see Chapter 4 for details). After sweeping each transect, we emptied the contents of the net and arthropods were sorted and counted by order (Araneida [spiders], Orthoptera [grasshoppers], Homoptera [cicadas], Mantodea [preying mantis], Blattaria [cockroaches], Phasmida [walking sticks], and Lepidoptera [butterflies and moths]). As sweep samples are limited to the understory (from the ground to 2 m in height) they potentially miss many of the important arthropods that live higher in the forest canopy. Thus, the sweep samples should only be considered a rough estimate of the availability of insects actually available to the monkeys throughout the forest strata.

RESULTS

Overall Diet

A comparison of the species' average annual diets is shown in Figure 3–1. The most surprising result was that callimicos ate large amounts of fungi, a resource rarely used by tamarins, or any other primate species yet studied. In addition, the diets of the three species varied between the dry season and the wet season (Figure 3–2). In the dry season callimicos relied on fungi, saddle-back tamarins on exudates, and red-bellied tamarins on nectar. The callimicos consumption of fungi and all other foods will be discussed in detail by food category, along with comparative data for each tamarin.

Fungi

Fungi were an essential component of the callimicos' diet. Callimicos ate two major types of fungi, jelly fungi (*Auricularia*) and bamboo fungi (*Ascopolyporous*). Feeding data across the study period show an increase in fungi consumption (mycophagy) during the months of March–July, with peaks in the months of May, June, and July when fungi comprise 48%–63% of the monthly diet (see Figure 3–3). Thus, although fungus was an important component of callimicos' diet throughout the year, it was particularly important during the dry season. Mycophagy, but not fungi abundance, was highest from May–July (Figure 3–3), indicating that callimicos' consumption of fungi was not limited by its availability.

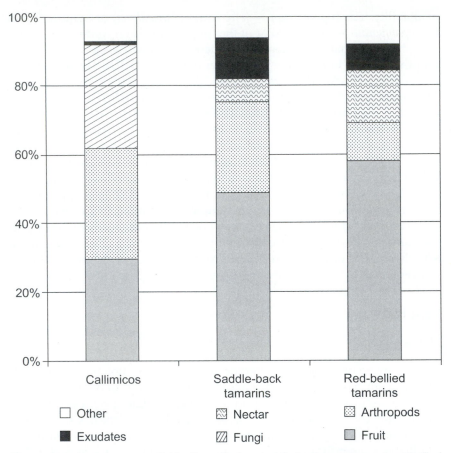

Figure 3–1 Annual average diet for the callimico, saddle-back tamarin, and red-bellied tamarin. From Porter 2001a, used with permission from Springer Publishers

Callimicos ate the fruiting bodies of several different kinds of fungi. Two species of fungi belong to the genus *Ascopolyporous* (*A. polyporoides* and *A. polychorous*), and grow on *Guadua weberbaueri,* the dominant bamboo species in the study area. Both these bamboo fungi have a tough outer layer with a clear gelatinous interior. One type grows on the stalk of the bamboo, is white in color, and grows to be about 2 cm in diameter. The other type grows in the branches of bamboo, is yellowish-brown in color, and can grow as large as 5 cm in diameter (Figure 3–4a).

Callimicos also consumed at least three kinds of jelly fungi (*Auricularia delicate* and at least two other species of *Auricularia* whose identity remains uncertain), which grow on decaying wood or dying tree branches. Callimicos foraged for this type of fungi near the ground on fallen tree limbs, or on decaying but upright tree trunks (Figure 3–4b).

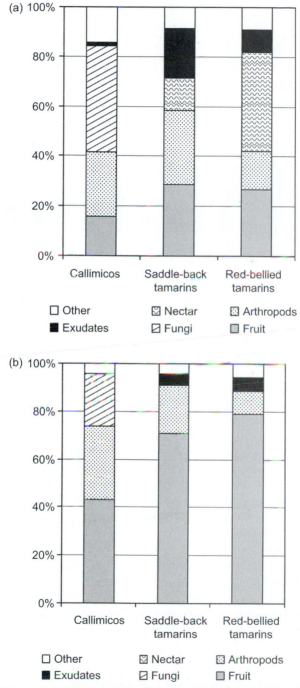

Figure 3–2 Average diet in the a) dry season and b) wet season for callimicos, saddle-back tamarins, and red-bellied tamarins

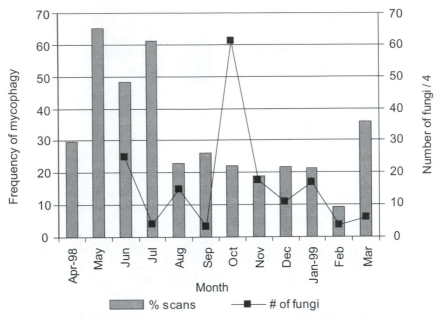

Figure 3–3 Monthly mean frequency of mycophagy by callimicos plotted with the abundance (numbers of fungal fruiting bodies) of fungi found along botanical transects. From Porter 2001a, used with permission from Springer Publishers

These types of fungi are thin and rubbery; of brown, tan, or purplish color; and grow up to 25 cm in diameter.

Bamboo fungi occurred at low densities throughout the forest, and were most often found in very small stands of bamboo in primary forest with dense understory. Bamboo fungi were most abundant along transects in the month of January, at a density of 1 patch/20 m^2 with an average patch containing five fruiting bodies. Jelly fungi were also patchily distributed in the forest, but in contrast to the bamboo fungi, jelly fungi were often abundant on a single decaying trunk or branch. For example, seventy-three fruiting bodies of jelly fungi were present on a single trunk during the month of October.

The red-bellied tamarin occasionally ate bamboo fungus in the branches of bamboo, but overall, fungi accounted for less than 1% of its diet. The saddleback tamarin was never observed to eat fungi. Callimicos therefore do not compete with tamarins for fungi, and more importantly fungi provide a food that is available during the dry season when other foods are scarce.

Nectar

Just as mycophagy distinguishes callimicos from tamarins, nectarivory distinguishes tamarins from callimicos. Although the annual average

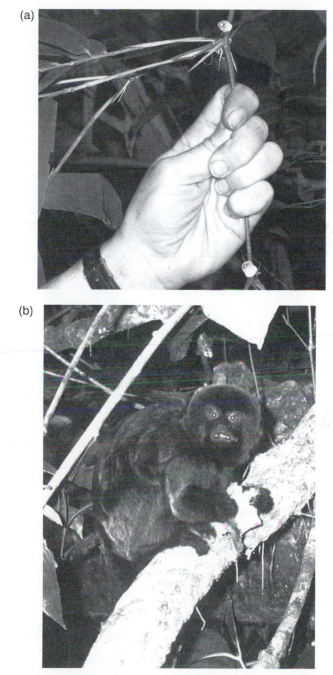

Figure 3–4 Fungi consumed by callimicos: a) bamboo fungi, and b) jelly fungi (photos by Edilio Nacimento Becerra)

percentage of nectar in the tamarins' diet was low (red-bellied tamarin 15%, saddle-back tamarin 7%), it was an important food source during the dry season months of June, July, and August. In these months nectar consumption was 15%, 18%, and 44% of the monthly diet of the saddle-back tamarin, and 22%, 82%, and 55% of the monthly diet of the red-bellied tamarin (see Figure 3–5). Phenology data indicates that these were not the months of highest flower abundance (and thus inferred nectar abundance) in the forest (see Figure 3–6). This discrepancy can be explained as tamarins principally exploited the nectar of only two plant species, *Symphonia globulifera* and *Ochroma pyrmidale* (Figure 3–7), which flowered at the end of the dry season before the peak of other flowers. A single *Symphonia globulifera* tree and a patch of *Ochroma pyrmidale* trees may contain hundreds of flowers, thereby providing a highly localized but abundant source of nectar. The saddle-back tamarin additionally exploited nectar from flowers of one species of *Mabea*.

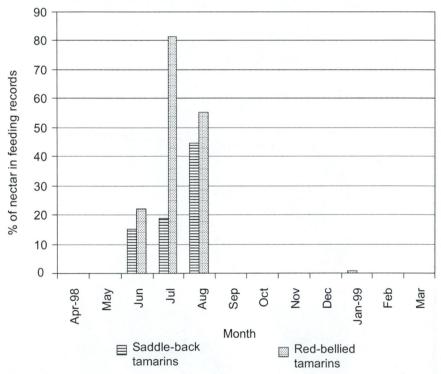

Figure 3–5 Monthly mean frequency of nectarivory for the saddle-back tamarin and the red-bellied tamarin. From Porter 2001a, used with permission from Springer Publishers

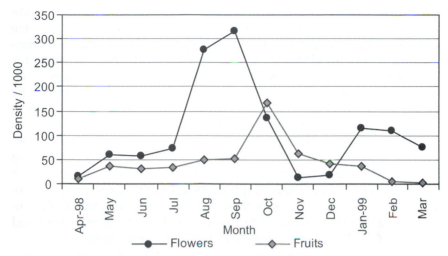

Figure 3–6 Fruit and nectar abundance along botanical transects, density values are the estimated number of fruits and flowers counted each month ÷ 10^3. From Porter 2001a, used with permission from Springer Publishers

Figure 3–7 Flowers used as nectar resources a) *Ochroma pyrmidales*, and b) *Symphonia globulifera* (drawings by the author)

Fruits

Fruit was an essential component of the diet of all three species (annual mean percent of fruit in the diet: callimico 29%; saddle-back tamarin 49%; red-bellied tamarin 58%) particularly from October–March (Figure 3–8). The months in which fruit comprises the highest percentage of the callimicos' and tamarins' diets correspond with months when botanical transect phenology records show fruit densities were declining (Figure 3–6).

This discrepancy between high fruit intake and low fruit density appears to result from the primates' use of only a few select fruiting species which are not abundant along botanical transects or throughout the forest. For example, the fruit species *Inga thibaudiana* comprised 55% of all feeding records for callimicos for the month of February (see Table 3–1). *Inga thibaudiana* was represented by only seventy-seven trees on botanical transects (6% of all transect trees), and of these only eleven individuals (less than 1% of all transect trees) were fruiting in February. Thus *Inga thibaudiana* contributed little to the monthly fruit abundance estimate, despite its importance in the monkeys' diets.

Although callimicos were the least frugivorous of the three species, fruit composed 73% of feeding time in the month of February (see Figure 3–8),

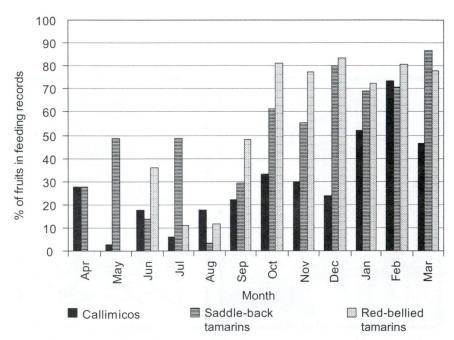

Figure 3–8 Monthly mean frequency of frugivory for the callimico, saddle-back tamarin, and red-bellied tamarin. From Porter 2001a, used with permission from Springer Publishers

Table 3–1 Fruit consumption by month for the study species[1]

Month	Callimicos				Saddle-back tamarins				Red-bellied tamarins			
	# fruit species eaten	Primary fruit species	% of fruit in diet	% of primary fruit in diet	# fruit species eaten	Primary fruit species	% of fruit in diet	% of primary fruit in diet	# fruit species eaten	Primary fruit species	% of fruit in diet	% of primary fruit in diet
Apr. 1998	4	Celtis iguanea	28	11	11	Cissus sp.	28	6	X	X	X	X
May	1	Celtis iguanea	30	30	5	Philodendrum sp.	49	6	X	X	X	X
Jun.	3		17	*	2	Celtis iguanea	14	14	4	Undetermined Sp. #64	36	18
Jul.	3		6	*	3	Celtis iguanea	49	16	2	Pseudolmedia laevis	11	3
Aug.	6	Cecropia scyodaphylla	18	8	1	Cecropia scyodaphylla	4	1	2	Cecropia scyodaphylla	11	6
Sep.	13	Cecropia scyodaphylla	22	13	11		29	*	8	Pseudolmedia laevis	48	12
Oct.	21	Pourouma sp.	33	5	9	Pseudolmedia laevis	61	16	9	Pourouma sp. 2	81	28
Nov.	15	Microphilis sp.	30	14	12	Pourouma sp 2	55	15	8	Helicostylis sp.	77	22
Dec.	8	Pourouma minor	24	14	11	Pourouma sp 1	80	30	11	Pourouma minor	83	24
Jan. 1999	3	Inga thibaudiana	52	47	14	Inga thibaudiana	69	37	11	Inga thibaudiana	72	40
Feb.	6	Inga thibaudiana	73	55	11	Inga thibaudiana	71	15	14	Inga thibaudiana	81	31
Mar.	4	Leonia glycycarpa	46	35	7	Leonia glycycarpa	87	61	5	Leonia glycycarpa	78	62

X = no data from these months

* = several fruits are equal

[1]From Porter 2001a, used with permission from Springer Publishers.

43

but dropped to only 3% of the diet at the start of the dry season in May. The greatest fruit abundance recorded on botanical transects occurred during the month of October, and is also the month callimicos had the greatest fruit diversity in their diet, with at least twenty-one species of fruits consumed.

The saddle-back tamarin relied heavily on fruits throughout the year (see Figure 3–8), except during the dry season. From October–March, fruits comprised more than 50% of the diet. The saddle-back tamarin, like the callimico, relied heavily on a few fruit species during some months. For example, during March, the saddle-back tamarins' total diet was 61% *Leonia glycycarpa* fruits (see Table 3–1). Unlike the callimico, the saddle-back tamarin consumed the greatest variety of fruits (fourteen species) in January, rather than October.

Of the three species, the red-bellied tamarin was the most frugivorous. From October–March, fruits comprised over 70% of its feeding time. It was only during the dry season months of July and August that fruit consumption dropped to below 12% of its diet (Figure 3–8). As with the callimico and the saddle-back tamarin, the red-bellied tamarin diet was dominated by just a few species during some months of relative fruit scarcity (Table 3–1).

In total, the three primate species consumed at least ninety-five different fruit species (Table 3–2). Ripe fruits with abundant fruit crops were eaten by all three species. Fruits in the understory generally were not eaten by the red-bellied tamarin. For example, although both saddle-back tamarins and callimicos ate *Hirtella racemosa*, red-bellied tamarins did not. Fruits in emergent trees like *Castilla ulei* were eaten by tamarins in the canopy whereas callimicos ate only fallen fruits of this tree that they were able to collect from the ground.

Exudates

Plant exudates also provided an important food resource for the tamarins and to a lesser degree for callimicos. The monkeys ate exudates that appeared to have been produced as a result of natural or animal damage, or from trees such as *Parkia pendula* that produce exudates around their fruit pods. Exudates composed more than 50% of the saddle-back tamarin diet in April and 25% of the diet in May, and it was observed eating exudates in all other months except December (Figure 3–9). Exudate eating (gummivory) was highest for the red-bellied tamarin during September when exudates were 25% of its monthly feeding time (see Figure 3–9). The red-bellied tamarin was observed eating exudates in all months except December and July (no observations of the red-bellied tamarin were collected in either April or May). Callimicos were also observed eating exudates at low levels from June through February except for the month of

Table 3–2 Plant species exploited for food[1]

	Family	Common name	Exploited by	Food type
Abuta grandifolia	Menispermaceae	Piton pequeño	C	Fr
Abuta sp.	Menispermaceae	Piton de liana	S,R	Fr
Annona ambotay	Annonaceae	Ata	C	Fr
Annona hypoglauca	Annonaceae	Ata	C,S,R	Fr
Bactris major Jacq.	Palmae	Marayau	S	Fr
Bellucia sp.	Melastomataceae	Jambre	R	Fr
Brosimum lactescens	Moraceae	Nui	S,R	Fr
Capirona decorticans	Rubiaceae		R	Fr
Casearia pitumba	Flacourtiaceae	Huevo de perro	C,S	Fr
Casearia sp.	Flacourtiaceae	Huevo de perro sp.3	C	Fr
Cecropia sciadophylla	Moraceae	Ambaibo	S,R,C	Fr
Celtis iguanea	Ulmaceae		C,S,R	Fr
cf. Licania	Chrysobalanaceae	Ata brava	S,R	Fr
Cissus sp.	Vitaceae		S,R	Fr
Clarisia racemosa	Moraceae	Mururé	C,S,R	Fr
Clavija weberbaueri	Theophrastaceae		C,S	Fr
Combretum sp.	Combretaceae		S,R	Ne
Cordia nodosa	Boraginaceae	Huevo de gallo	C,S	Fr
Cordia sp.	Boraginaceae	Fre Jorge	S,R	Fr
Cordia sp.	Boraginaceae	Loro	S	Fr
Curarea toxicofera	Menispermaceae		C	Fr
Dialium guianense	Leguminosae	Tamarindo		Fr
Eugenia	Myrtaceae	Uva de monte	S,R	Fr
Euterpe precatoria	Palmae	Asai	C,S	Ex
Ficus sp.	Moraceae	Bibosi	S,R	Fr
Guarea glabra	Meliaceae		S,R	Fr
Guarea sp.	Meliaceae		C	Fr
Gurania sp.	Cucurbitaceae	Liana banana	C,S	Fr
Gustavia hexapetala	Lecithydaceae	Umbligo de buey	C,S,R	Fr
Helicostylis sp.	Moraceae	Pama caucho	C,S,R	Fr
Herrania sp.	Stericuliaceae	Cacao jacare	C,S	Fr
Hirtella racemosa	Chrysobalanaceae	Macucu	C,S	Fr
Hirtella sp.	Chrysobalanaceae	Caripe		Fr
Inga thibaudiana DC	Leguminosae	Pacay	C,S,R	Fr
Iriartella retisera	Palmae	Patchobiña	S,R	Ex
Iryanthera juruensis	Myristicaceae	Sangre de torro	C,S,R	Fr
Leonia glycycarpa	Violaceae	Piton grande	C,S,R	Fr
cf. Licania	Chrysobalanaceae	Ata brava	S,R	Fr
Mabea sp.	Euphorbiaceae	Seringuerita	S	Ne
Mayna odorata	Flacourtiaceae			Fr
Mayna sp.	Flacourtiaceae		C	Fr

(Continued)

Table 3–2 (Continued)

	Family	Common name	Exploited by	Food type
Mendoncia sp.	Acanthaceae		C,S	Fr
Mendoncia lindawii	Acanthaceae		C,S	Fr
Miconia nervosa	Melastomataceae		C	Fr
Miconia sp.	Melastomataceae	Pelusa morado	C,S	Fr
Miconia sp.	Milastomataceae		S	Fr
Micropholis sp.	Sapotaceae	Abioletra	C,S,R	Fr
Monstera cf. Spruceana	Araceae		C,S	Fr
Mouriri	Melastomataceae	Miudao amarillo	C,S	Fr
Mouriri	Melastomataceae	Miudin	C	Fr
Moutabea sp.	Polygalaceae		C,S	Fr
Myrcia sp.	Myrtaceae	Uva de barbecho	C,S,R	Fr
Myroxylon balsamum	Leguminosae	Balsamo	S,R	Ex
Ochroma pyrmidale	Bombacaceae	Balsa	S,R	Ne
Ouratea sp.	Ochnaceae	Masarandubiña	R	Fr
Ouratea sp.	Ochnaceae		S	Fr
Palmae	Arecaceae	Maho	S,R	Ex
Palmae	Arecaceae	Pona	S,R	Ex,Fr
Parkia pendula	Mimosaceae	Tocoblanco	S,R	Ex
Parkia velutina	Mimosaceae	Tococolorado	S,R	Ex
Perebea xanthochyma	Moraceae	Quechu	S,R	Fr
Philodendrum sp.	Araceae		S	Fr
Philodendrum sp.	Araceae	Tripa de gallina	C,S	Fr
Pourouma cecropiifolia	Moraceae	Toren uva	C,S,R	Fr
Pourouma minor	Moraceae	Toren	C,S,R	Fr
Pourouma sp.	Moraceae	Toren	C,S,R	Fr
Pourouma sp. 2	Moraceae	Toren ambaibo	C,S,R	Fr
Protium sagotianum	Burseraceae	Isigo	S,R	Fr
Pseudolmedia laevis	Moraceae	Nui	C,S,R	Fr
Pseudolmedia macrophylla	Moraceae	Pama pequeña	C,S,R	Fr
Psychotria sp.	Rubiaceae		S,R	Fr
Quararibea witti cf.	Bombacaceae	Piraquina blanca	C,S,R	Fr
Randia c.f.calycina	Rubiaceae		C,S	Fr
Rollinia sp.	Annonaceae	Ata	C,S,R	Fr
Ryania speciosa	Flacourtiaceae	Huevo de perro verde	C	Fr
Salacia sp.	Hippocrateaceae	Xixuaxa liana	C,S	Fr
Siparuna decipiens	Monimiaceae	Palo de agua	C,S,R	Fr
Siparuna sp.	Monimiaceae	Caricuara negra	C,S,R	Fr
Sloanea sp.	Elaeocarpaceae		S,R	Ex
Soracea sp.	Moraceae		S	Fr
Stericulia apeibophylla	Stericulaceae		S,R	Ex

Table 3–2 (Continued)

	Family	Common name	Exploited by	Food type
Symphonia globulifera	Guttigerae	Floro rojo	S,R	Ne
Syngonium podophyllum	Araceae		C,S	Fr
Tapirira cf. Guianensis	Anacardiaceae		C,S,R	Fr
Tapirira sp.	Anacardiaceae		S,R	Fr
Tetragastris altissima	Burseraceae	Isigo	C,S,R	Fr
Theobroma cacao	Sterculiaceae	Cacao	C,S,R	Fr
Tocoa sp.	Melastomataceae	Pelusa morado	C	Fr
Trichilia sp.	Meliaceae	Isigo mashishi	S,R	Fr
Xylopia sp.	Annonaceae	Piraquina estrella	S,R	Fr
?	Hippocrataceae		S	Fr
?	Lauraceae	Palta de monte	C,S,R	Fr
?	Menispermaceae		S	Fr
?	Myrtaceae		C	Fr
?	Rubiaceae		C,S	Fr
?	Rubiaceae		C,S,R	Fr
?	Sapotaceae		S,R	Fr
?	Annonaceae	Ata	C,S,R	Fr

Key to symbols: C = callimico, S = saddle-back tamarin, R = red-bellied tamarin, Fr = fruit, Ne = nectar, Ex = exudate

[1]From Porter 2001a, used with permission from Springer Publishers.

December. Callimicos most frequently consumed exudates in June and August, when exudates were respectively 5% and 2% of the monthly diet (Figure 3–9). On average, exudates comprised only 1% of the callimicos' annual diet.

Arthropods

Callimicos consumed arthropods slightly more than the saddle-back tamarin and much more than the red-bellied tamarin. Arthropods formed up to 51% of the callimicos' feeding time (this does not include foraging time) in December, and formed at least 10% of feeding time in all other months of the year (Figure 3–11). The general term "insectivory" will be used throughout this book to describe this food category as the majority of the arthropods the monkeys consumed were insects (class Insecta), even though this dietary category actually includes a small portion of spiders and scorpions (class Arachnida). Results of sweep samples showed a rise in orthopteran abundance during the rainy season months of December and January (Figure 3–12). There were no discernable patterns in the abundance

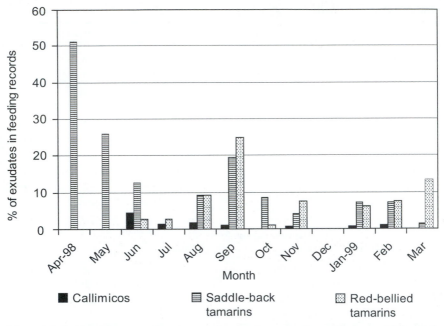

Figure 3–9 Monthly mean frequency of gummivory for the callimico, saddle-back tamarin, and red-bellied tamarin. From Porter 2001a, used with permission from Springer Publishers

of spiders (Araneida) captured throughout the year (Figure 3–12). Other arthropods were insufficiently sampled using the sweep sample method to calculate changes in abundance over time (total individuals sampled in ten months: cockroaches [Blatteria] n = 2, walking sticks [Phasmida] n = 2, cicadas [Homoptera] n = 2, mantids [Mantodea] n = 1, moths [Lepidoptera] n = 9).

Although callimicos ate a wide variety of arthropods, orthopterans formed the majority of the arthropod diet (41% of all insect feeding records) (Figure 3–13). Walking sticks were the second most commonly eaten arthropod (7% of total insect records) and eggs, larvae, and pupae of unknown taxa formed 5% of the diet. The remaining arthropods that were eaten comprised less than the 5% each of the total insect feeding records: scorpions (Scorpionida), spiders, cicadas, mantids, cockroaches, and moths. The presence of venom in scorpions and large venomous spiders did not deter callimicos from catching or eating them.

Orthoptera caught by callimicos were generally large in size, ranging from 2.5–6 cm in body length, with the largest orthopteran weighing about 6 g. Orthoptera wings and legs were generally not consumed by the monkeys, and a collection of these discarded wings showed that at least nineteen different kinds of orthopteran were eaten.

Figure 3–10 Edilio Nacimento climbing a tree to collect exudates from the same location the monkeys had eaten (photo by the author)

Callimicos foraged for arthropods in the understory (see below) on thin flexible branches and beneath leaf litter on the forest floor. Callimicos also searched in leaves for eggs and larvae, sometimes hanging from small vertical supports to retrieve spiders, and grabbing insects while anchored to a support by their feet. Callimicos were never observed to search in holes or crevices like the saddle-back tamarin.

Both tamarin species also consumed a great quantity of arthropods. The saddle-back tamarin ate arthropods most during June, August, September, and November when insects made up more than 20% of the monthly diet (Figure 3–11). The saddle-back tamarin was observed eating a wide variety of arthropods, but was seldom seen eating spiders (Araneida) and never seen

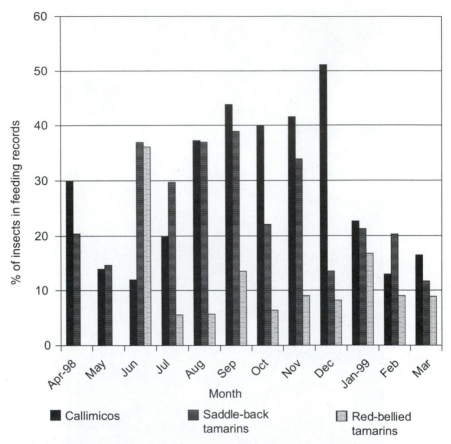

Figure 3–11 Monthly mean frequency of insectivory for the callimico, saddle-back tamarin, and red-bellied tamarin. From Porter 2001a, used with permission from Springer Publishers

eating adult moths or butterflies (Lepidoptera). Orthopterans accounted for at least 58% of the saddle-back tamarins' total insect feeding records.

Saddle-back tamarins foraged in the lower canopy and understory, often searching for large prey items in cracks, holes, and crevices in large trunks and branches. It was not uncommon for them to enter large holes or to reach into holes with their arms to search for hidden prey items. They also occasionally descended to the ground to look for hidden prey under leaf litter, or to retrieve fallen prey items.

Insectivory was higher for the red-bellied tamarin in June (35% of the monthly diet) than in all other months (17% or less) (Figure 3–11). The importance of arthropods in the red-bellied tamarin diet may be underestimated to some degree due to the difficulty of determining if they successfully caught

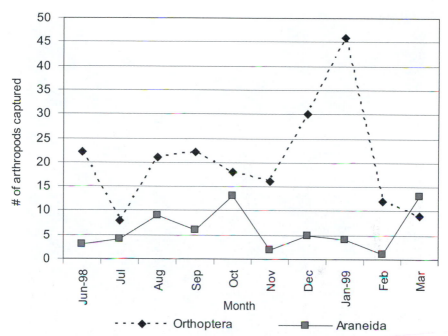

Figure 3–12 Numbers of Orthoptera and Araneida (all species) caught each month during sweep samples. From Porter 2001a, used with permission from Springer Publishers

arthropods during their foraging searches in leafy branches where they were concealed from view. It was also difficult to identify the types of arthropods being eaten by the red-bellied tamarin, as we were able to retrieve only a few discarded wings floating down from the canopy. These wings were all from Orthoptera (n = 6), suggesting Orthoptera were its major arthropod food source.

Vertebrates

Vertebrates formed a small part of the callimico diet. Callimicos were observed eating frogs and toads (approximately 5–6 cm body length), birds' eggs from nests found in the trees and on the ground, and small lizards. Vertebrates were consumed most during August (9% of the total feeding time) and May (6% of the diet). Vertebrates comprised 3% of the diet in April, 2% in September and November, and 1% in June, July, October, and December. Unfortunately, we did not collect specimens of these vertebrates so the particular species that were eaten are unknown.

Vertebrates appear to be a particularly prized food item. Intergroup aggression for food items was only observed for vertebrate prey (n = 10).

Figure 3–13 A callimico eating a grasshopper (photo by Edilio Nacimento Becerra)

One juvenile callimico was particularly aggressive for vertebrate food items, and was observed on several occasions harassing an adult until she acquired part or the entire prey item. Vertebrate prey items were eaten entirely, beginning with a bite to the head.

The saddle-back tamarin was occasionally seen eating frogs, but was never seen eating other vertebrates, and vertebrates formed less than 1% of their total diet. The red-bellied tamarin was never observed eating vertebrate prey.

Vertical Stratification: Height Class Use

Callimicos, saddle-back tamarins, and red-bellied tamarins had distinct patterns of height class use during foraging for all types of foods (Figure 3–14). Callimicos were the understory specialists, with 84% of all foraging occurring in the understory (0–5 m). The saddle-back tamarin also foraged in the understory extensively (62% of all scans) but used the lower, middle, and upper canopy with greater frequency than the callimico. The red-bellied tamarin foraged principally in the lower canopy (10–15 m, 40%) but also used the middle canopy (30%) and the understory (5–10 m, 22%) frequently.

The heights at which fruits were eaten differ from the generalized foraging pattern. As the callimico, saddle-back tamarin, and red-bellied tamarin ingest fruits on or near the branch where the fruits are found, it is possible to use "height while eating fruits" as an approximation of the height at

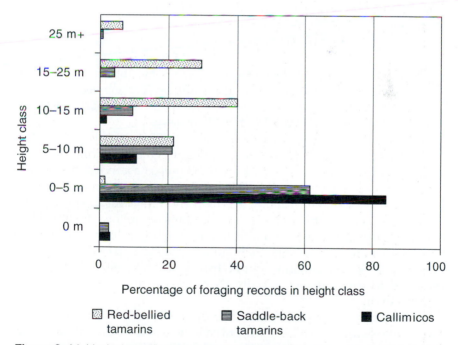

Figure 3–14 Vertical stratification in the forest by callimicos, saddle-back tamarins, and red-bellied tamarins during foraging as averaged for all study months. From Porter 2001, used with permission from Wiley-Liss Publishers

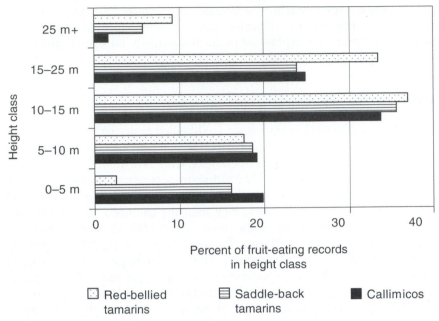

Figure 3–15 Height classes used by the callimico, saddle-back tamarin, and red-bellied tamarin while eating fruits. From Porter 2001, used with permission from Wiley-Liss Publishers

which the monkeys are locating their fruit sources. Height while eating fruit varied between the three species (Figure 3–15). Fruit eating heights among callimicos (C), saddle-back tamarins (S), and red-bellied tamarins (R) were statistically significant (Mann-Whitney U Test results: C-S, $Z = -2.572$, $p < 0.01$; C-R, $Z = -9.906$, $p < 0.001$; S-R, $Z = -8.475$, $p < 0.001$).

Comparing overall foraging height (Figure 3–14) to fruit ingestion height (Figure 3–15), demonstrates that callimicos ascended trees to eat fruits that were easily accessible (25% of fruits are eaten from 15–25 m), but did not remain in the canopy to search and forage for food items (0% of foraging occurs from 15–25 m). Callimicos followed red-bellied tamarins during mixed troop movements, allowing callimicos to remain below in the understory while their tamarin counterparts located fruiting trees above. When tamarins found fruit resources, callimicos quickly ascended to eat, and then rapidly descended to the understory again before moving on.

All three monkey species found the majority of their fruits in the lower and middle canopy (from 10–25 m), but callimicos and saddle-back tamarins fed more on fruits in the understory and less on fruits in the upper canopy than red-bellied tamarins. Thus, the potential for fruit feeding competition appears to be greatest between saddle-back tamarins and callimicos.

Diet Overlap

Comparisons of diet overlap between the three species demonstrate that callimicos had greater diet overlap with saddle-back tamarins than with red-bellied tamarins. Additionally, saddle-back tamarins and red-bellied tamarins had greater diet overlap with each other than either had with callimicos (Figure 3–16). All three species had greater diet overlap from January–March as all three primates ate large quantities of a few select abundant fruit species. In the dry season, the callimicos' reliance on fungi lowered its dietary overlap with the saddle-back tamarin and the red-bellied tamarin, as callimicos never concentrated on nectar or exudate resources like the tamarins.

Feeding Competition

Although the tamarins showed the highest diet overlap, red-bellied tamarins appeared to avoid interference competition with saddle-back tamarins through its dominant status. The larger-bodied red-bellied tamarin was clearly the dominant species and was never challenged by the callimico or the saddle-back tamarin for food resources. In fact, members of callimico and

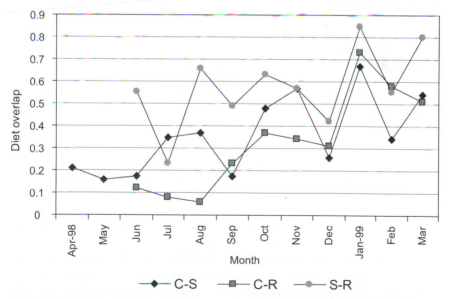

Figure 3–16 Diet overlap among callimicos and saddle-back tamarins (C-S), callimico and red-bellied tamarins (C-R), and saddle-back tamarins and red-bellied tamarins (S-R) as measured by Schoener's Index of Niche Overlap. Complete diet overlap indicated by values of 1, no niche overlap indicated by values of 0. From Porter 2001, used with permission from Wiley-Liss Publishers

saddle-back tamarin groups appeared to avoid confrontations with the red-bellied tamarins by moving out of the way to let them pass or feed. Although callimicos and saddle-back tamarins occasionally had aggressive interactions, these were infrequent. Aggressive interactions between callimicos and saddle-back tamarins occurred on 44 of 111 observation days, but on only six of these days were these aggressive interactions clearly over food resources. On these six days, both callimicos and saddle-back tamarins defended and challenged fruit resources from each other.

DISCUSSION

Although the callimico, saddle-back tamarin, and red-bellied tamarin all consumed many of the same fruits and arthropods, several important distinctions among these species were found including: the height at which they forage; their foraging techniques; and their dry-season foods. Understanding these foraging and dietary differences allows us to understand the dietary niche of each species.

Insects are a common source of protein for small-bodied primates such as the callitrichids (Kay 1984). The callimico was predicted to be the most insectivorous of the three species; however, callimicos and the saddle-back tamarins showed similar levels of insectivory. This suggests that either callimicos in other areas are more insectivorous, or that their high shearing crests are indicative of other dietary specializations (as discussed below).

In previous studies of callitrichids, vertical stratification during insect foraging (Buchanan-Smith 1999; Nickle and Heymann 1996; Peres 1992b; Yoneda 1981), and differences in insect foraging techniques (Nickle and Heymann 1996; Peres 1992b; Yoneda 1984) were suggested to be the major mechanisms by which associated species partition arthropod (particularly orthopteran) prey. Similar results were found for this study. Callimicos were never observed to forage in holes and crevices like saddle-back tamarins, and instead used pounce and capture techniques like red-bellied tamarins. Callimicos, unlike the red-bellied tamarins, searched in the understory rather than in the canopy. These differences in insect foraging techniques are reflected in the hand morphologies of the three species, with the saddle-back tamarin having more narrow fingers than the other species (Bicca-Marques 1999).

Fruits are an important component of all three species' diets. As in other studies (Soini 1987; Terborgh 1983), fruits from a few select species dominated the monkeys' diets each month, resulting in a taxonomic change in the fruits consumed across the year. During the start of the wet season, from October–December, a larger number of fruit species were consumed by the primates, including more understory fruits, allowing the three primate species to reduce dietary overlap. Toward the end of the wet season, from January–March, when fruits were less abundant, all three primate species focused on a few abundant fruiting species, resulting in greater dietary overlap than in other months.

In the dry season, the two tamarins—but not callimicos—frequently ate nectar. Primate studies in other localities have shown that nectar is a major plant resource used by tamarins in the dry season (Buchanan-Smith 1991; Garber 1988b; Janson, Terborgh, and Emmons 1981; Lopes and Ferrari 1994; Terborgh 1983). The nectar of the large flowers of *Ochroma pyrmidales* and *Symphonia globulifera* were the two main nectar sources used by both species of tamarin in this study. The red-bellied tamarin consumed nectar more frequently than saddle-back tamarins.

In contrast, the saddle-back tamarin consumed exudates more than the other two species. Feeding on exudates (gummivory) is not common among mammals, but is found among several groups of primates including callitrichids, many strepsirrhines, and some African cercopithecines (Nash 1986; Power and Oftedal 1996). The tegulae, or claw-like nails, of callitrichids allow them to feed on exudates of large trunks and branches, a resource unavailable to other platyrrhine primates (Garber 1980). Although tamarins and callimicos lack the specialized dentition found in marmosets to actively stimulate exudate flow, most (if not all) tamarin species opportunistically forage for exudates where trees have received wind or insect damage (Ferrari 1993).

Tamarins primarily consume exudates of a few select species (reviewed in Garber 1993) during the dry season (Lopes and Ferrari 1994; Norconk 1986; Soini 1987; Terborgh 1983), but exudates may provide an important source of calcium for reproductive females at other times of year (Garber 1984). In this study, exudates comprised more than 50% of the saddle-back tamarin diet during the dry season month of April, and gummivory continued at low levels throughout the year. Red-bellied tamarins consumed exudates most frequently in September (25% of feeding records), whereas callimicos only rarely consumed exudates throughout the year.

Callimicos were observed to consume vertebrates more often than either species of tamarin. Frogs, toads, lizards, and birds eggs can be a high source of protein for the small-bodied callitrichids, and callimicos appear to find these vertebrates in the understory more than their tamarin counterparts traveling at higher levels in the forest. Due to the high levels of chasing, begging, and aggression that were associated with capture of vertebrate prey, these food items appear to be the most prized of all the callimicos' food items.

The callimico is distinct from both tamarin species and virtually all other known primates in the extensive use of fungi as a fallback resource during the dry season. Among other callitrichids, some populations of marmosets and lion tamarins also eat fungi as a dry season food resource: fungi formed 12% of dry season diet in a study of the buffy-tufted-ear marmoset,

Callithrix aurita (Mestre Correa, 1995), and in a study of the black-faced lion tamarin, *Leontopithecus caissara*, fungi was the most common item in the diet for three months of the dry season (Prado, as cited in Raboy and Dietz, 2004). The reason that this resource is scarcely used by primates likely results from its low nutritional value. Studies have shown that an animal's ability to digest the total energy and nitrogen found in fungi is dependent on their digestive system: animals with foregut fermentation (such as chambered stomachs) can better digest fungi than animals with hindgut fermentation (such as enlarged ceaca), while specialized hindgut fermenters can digest fungi better than moderate hindgut fermenters (reviewed in Hanson, et al. 2006). Stomach chambers and enlarged ceaca provide havens for microbes that can digest the fungi, leaving the by-products, primate-digestible molecules for the gut to absorb. Fungi eaten by mammals can be high in protein and carbohydrates, and also may contain organic compounds such as steroids and phenols, vitamins such as niacin and riboflavin, and minerals such as copper, zinc and calcium (Claridge and May, 1994).

Callitrichids, including callimicos, do not have a multi-chambered stomachs (Hill 1966), thus they are probably not as efficient at digesting fungi as some other mycophagous mammals. Marmosets do however, have compartmentalized caecums that aid in the digestion of exudates (Ferrari, et al. 1993; Ferrari and Martins 1992). Given the possible close phylogenetic relationship between the marmosets and callimicos, Hanson and colleagues (Hanson et al. 2006) suggest that it is possible that callimicos may also be capable of caeco-colic fermentation. If they are, callimicos may be able to digest fungi better than primates that lack this digestive adaptation, including the tamarins which have simple guts (Ferrari and Martins 1992).

Hanson and colleagues (Hanson et al. 2006) analyzed the nutritional composition of both jelly and bamboo fungi and found them to be high in fiber, low in sugar, low in fat, and low in starch (Table 3–3). Crude protein values ranged from 5.5–13.4%, indicating that fungi may serve as a protein source, although since most of this protein is in the form of nitrogen locked in cell walls and spores, it is unclear how much of this crude protein callimicos are able to digest.

Mycophagous mammals, such as the long-nosed potoroos of Australia, consume fungi that are similar in nutritional content to those eaten by callimicos (Table 3–3). In comparison to other primate food items that are used as sources of protein, such as leaves and invertebrates, the protein values of fungi eaten by callimicos are low (see Table 3–3) and suggest that fungi is not a high-quality food source. It is likely, therefore, that callimicos have some digestive adaptations for mycophagy to increase the nutrition they are able to obtain from this resource. In addition to possible hindgut adaptations, Hanson and colleagues (Hanson et al. 2006) suggest

Table 3–3 Composition of food resources consumed by mammals[†]

Food type	Mammal known to consume food type	Fiber*	Fat*	Crude protein*	Energy Kcal/g dry weight
Fungi— Ascopolyporus Auricularia	Callimico	66.2–83	0.9–1.6	5.5–13.4	4.08–4.31
Fungi— Mesophillia	Long-nosed potoroo Potorus tridactylus	46.2		10.2	5.98
Crickets— Acheta domestica	Captive primates	19.1	22.8	64.4	NA
Leaves— 8 species	Western lowland gorilla Gorilla gorilla gorilla	46.1	0.6	64.2	NA

*listed as the percentage of dry matter

[†]Adapted from Hanson et al. 2006

that the high shearing crests on the callimicos' molars may serve to break fungi into small pieces to improve digestion. Digestibility studies are necessary to determine the manner in which callimicos are capable of digesting fungi and how many nutrients they provide.

The fungi eaten by callimicos contain minerals also found in other primate foods, such as fruits, leaves, exudates, and arthropods. Hanson et al. (2006) found that bamboo and jelly fungi have low levels of calcium, a mineral hypothesized to be an important resource for lactating females, and probably acquired by eating tree exudates (Garber 1984). In contrast, they found bamboo and jelly fungi to be high in potassium, but this is a mineral found in many food items, and therefore is unlikely to be the reason callimicos are mycophagous.

Although the nutritional benefits of fungi for callimicos remain to be determined, it is clearly an important dry season resource for callimicos when fruits are scarce. During this study, callimicos survived the dry season consuming fungi, while tamarins survived the dry season by eating exudates and nectar. Saddle-back tamarin populations consume more exudates in areas where less nectar is available (Ferrari 1993), and similarly, callimicos may consume more exudates in areas where less fungi are available. Studies of other populations of callimicos are necessary to determine the extent of mycophagy and gummivory across the species' range, as a primate species' diet may vary between different areas (Chapman and Fedigan 1990; Crandlemire-Sacco 1986).

Rehg (2003), studying callimicos in Brazil, found that fungi comprised 19% of the callimicos' diet, and 0% of the tamarins' diets, while exudates formed 5% of the callimicos' diet, 15% of the saddle-back tamarins' diet, and 9% of the red-bellied tamarins' diet. Rehg's data, therefore, are consistent with the hypothesis that fungi is used exclusively by callimicos, but it also suggests that callimicos' reliance on fungi as a food resource varies across populations or by season.

Callimicos, saddle-back tamarins, and red-bellied tamarins exhibit several differences in their foraging strategies that result in dietary niche differentiation, particularly during the dry season. These differences appear to reduce competition for food resources and allow the three species to coexist in the same forest.

Rylands (1996) suggests that marmosets and tamarins evolved specializations to exploit gums and insects in secondary forest, and that their social and reproductive behaviors are best suited for these habitats. Before the arrival of humans in South America, secondary forest was likely of limited availability; thus, the marmosets and tamarins evolved a social system in which subordinates were inhibited from reproducing, and offspring were allowed to remain in their natal group as helpers. This system allows individuals to remain in the safety of a group while waiting for a suitable habitat to become available.

Rylands (1996) did not have sufficient data on the diet and habitat preference of callimicos to comment on the evolution of its social behavior; however, in the proceeding chapters I attempt to show that many aspects of callimicos' behavior are related to its unusual diet including its habitat use (Chapter 44), ranging patterns and interactions with other species (Chapter 5), reproductive strategies (Chapter 6), and population density and distribution (Chapter 7). These factors all need to be examined in order to understand callimicos' ecological niche, and the role these monkeys play in their ecosystem.

4

Habitat Use and Activity Budgets[1]

As demonstrated in Chapter 3, callimicos have a dietary niche that is different from either saddle-back or red-bellied tamarins, particularly during the dry season. Callimicos are the only species of the three to consume large quantities of fungi, and to forage predominantly in the understory. Given these differences in diet and foraging, it is important to consider what other behaviors and ecological specializations distinguish these species from one another. In this chapter I compare use of habitat, locomotor style, and activity budgets among callimicos, red-bellied tamarins, and saddle-back tamarins.

HABITAT SPECIALIZATION

Many different types of vegetation exist within a tropical rainforest and these differences create a variety of microhabitats even within the same forest. This diversity of microhabitats provides animals with the potential to either narrow or broaden their pattern of resource use. For example, within a primary forest, the size and orientation of trunks and branches varies considerably at different heights: the understory is dominated by large vertical tree trunks, whereas the middle canopy has many medium-sized, horizontal branches. In addition, the quantity and number of plants

[1]From "Differences in forest utilization and activity patterns among three sympatric callitrichines: *Callimico goeldii, Saguinus fuscicollis* and *S. labiatus*," *American Journal of Physical Anthropology* 124(2004):139–153, used with permission from Wiley-Liss Publishers.

may vary among forest levels, with lianas more prevalent in the canopy, and small shrubs and herbs more prevalent in the understory. Additional habitats may be created in the forest by tree falls that create gaps in the canopy and allow sun-loving plants to prosper, and by meandering streams that provide habitats for plants specializing on wet or inundated soils. In areas where several primate species coexist, species may restrict their pattern of habitat use to different layers and/or plant communities as a strategy of avoiding competition with one another.

Given that callimicos occupy the same forests as red-bellied and saddle-back tamarins, I predicted that the three species would show preferences for different layers of the forest as a means of defining their own distinct niches. Anatomical evidence provides one means of predicting the habitat to which a primate is adapted, as a primate's forelimbs and hindlimbs show adaptations for moving on substrates regularly encountered within their preferred habitat (Fleagle 1999). Although the intermembral index—the ratio of the length of the forelimb divided by the length of the hindlimb—has been used as a simple measure of predicting locomotor behavior, Davis (2002) found the intermembral index to be a poor predictor of locomotor behavior among callitrichids. For example, she found that although the moustached tamarin (*Saguinus mystax*) is reported to leap infrequently in the wild, it has similar limb proportions to the callimico, which is reported to leap from trunk to trunk frequently in the wild (Garber and Leigh 2001). In a detailed analysis of the limb bones, however, Davis (2002) did find anatomical traits that indicate that callimicos are one of the more specialized leapers of the callitrichids. For example, callimicos have long tibias, and elbows and ankles more specialized for vertical leaping than other callitrichids (Davis 1996, 2002). Thus, these anatomical traits suggest that callimicos would spend more time moving in the understory—where vertical supports are abundant—than either saddle-back or red-bellied tamarins.

Studies of locomotor behavior have indicated that callimicos move differently than tamarins. Garber and Leigh (2001) showed that callimicos engage more frequently in hind-limb dominated bounding along horizontal supports, and trunk-to-trunk leaping between vertical supports than tamarins. Garber, Blomquist, and Anzenberger (2005) found that when callimicos leap between vertical supports, they land hand-first, and can jump farther than marmosets in the same experimental setting. Garber, Blomquist, and Anzenberger (2005) use the phrase "trunk-to-trunk leaping" to describe this forelimb-first landing pattern, which is different from the hind-limb first landing pattern observed in many (but not all) prosimians, which is called vertical clinging and leaping.

An animal's postcranial skeleton is not just designed for locomotion, but must also be adapted for foraging. Thus, an animal's skeleton should allow it to travel on frequently encountered supports and to move and maintain itself in positions needed to obtain food. Small body size and claw-like nails (tegulae), for example, are proposed to have evolved among callitrichids as specializations for the exploitation of foods (exudates and insects) found on large trunks and branches (Garber 1980; Hamrick 1998; Sussman and Kinzey 1984). Claws may facilitate grasping large vertical supports during trunk-to-trunk leaping (Cartmill 1974; Ford 1986), but since only a small number of species of callitrichids frequently move by means of trunk-to-trunk leaping (Davis 2002) it is more likely that claws evolved first as a foraging adaptation.

As shown in Chapter 3, callimicos did not frequently eat exudates, nor did they search for arthropods on large vertical supports, thus callimicos were rarely seen clinging to vertical supports during foraging and feeding. If callimicos do not often engage in large trunk foraging, it is therefore important to consider whether claws are used for other activities. In this chapter, I look at callimicos' locomotor patterns, and how they use different strata of the forest and different habitats during all of their activities. A better understanding of how callimicos use their environment for traveling, foraging, feeding, and resting, can provide essential information for understanding the adaptive significance of claws for this species and the callitrichid family in general.

Primates have many reasons for moving around their habitats, including searching for food and resting sites; avoiding predators; patrolling territories; and monitoring, searching for, or defending mates. The total area used by a group is therefore directly influenced by the distribution and abundance of resources such as food, mates, and sleeping sites (Barton et al. 1992), and is called the home range (Burt 1943). For example, abundant sleep sites throughout a groups' habitat could allow for reduced travel in the evening before the group enters its night resting area.

Groups or individuals that are territorial must patrol the boundaries of their home range frequently in order to prevent the intrusion of neighbors. Thus, territorial groups have home ranges small enough that animals can frequently check their borders, and fight off intruders if necessary (Mitani and Rodman 1979). Saddle-back and red-bellied tamarins are known to be territorial, with frequent intergroup encounters and border disputes among neighboring groups (Buchanan-Smith 1991b; Norconk 1990; Peres 1989; Peres 1992a). Prior to beginning this study it was unclear if callimico groups, like tamarin groups, also spent time patrolling the boundaries of their home ranges from neighboring groups.

ACTIVITY BUDGETS

Activity budgets provide one means of characterizing the amount of time a group or individual engages in different behaviors (such as rest, forage, and travel) in order to compare energy expenditure among different animals, groups, or species. Primates and other animals living in cold temperatures may need lots of energy just to maintain their body heat (thermoregulation) (Dunbar 1992). Athough callimicos live in the tropics, some nights and days can be cool (see Chapter 2); thus, thermoregulation is likely to be one significant source of energy expenditure for callimicos and tamarins, as has been demonstrated for other callitrichids (Thompson et al. 1994). In addition to energy required for thermoregulation, animals must have energy to maintain their basal metabolic rate, digest food, grow, reproduce, and engage in other activities (Karasov 1992). In primates, these other activities include: fleeing from predators, searching for food, finding mates, and transporting their offspring.

The energy required for these activities is acquired by eating food, and the time required to eat sufficient food to meet daily energy requirements is dependent upon the distribution of food, food quality, food abundance, and the speed that food can be consumed (reviewed in Hanya 2004b). The abundance and distribution of food in turn affects travel behavior (Oates 1986). For example, if a primate uses a microhabitat that is widespread and contains a plentiful supply of food resources, it may be able to rest frequently and move little. If the time spent feeding, foraging, and moving between food sites is substantial, these behaviors may restrict the amount of time available for other activities, such as social behaviors. For example, Dunbar and Dunbar (1988) demonstrated that the amount of time gelada baboons engaged in social behaviors is negatively related to the amount of time they spent feeding.

Thus, the combination of strategies used to satisfy energy requirements, avoid predators, find mates, and care for infants, all influence the habitat (or habitats) a primate uses, and the distances a primate needs to travel in a day. The combination of all these factors will therefore shape a primate's activity budget (Figure 4–1). The goal of this chapter, therefore, is to compare the activity budgets and habitat use of callimicos, saddle-back tamarins, and red-bellied tamarins. Given that the three species have different foraging strategies, particularly in the dry season (Chapter 3), these data allow for an understanding of how their diets influence other aspects of their behavior. This in turn provides a more detailed view of the different ecological niches of these species.

METHODOLOGY

In order to calculate home range size, I counted the number of hectare quadrats used by the monkey groups (on more than three occasions) over the course of the study. In the case of points that were outside of the grid trail system, I used a Global Positioning System (GPS) to determine coordinates, and used a computer-triangulating program to calculate the area defined by these coordinates.

On each observation day, we recorded the time that groups left their sleeping sites in the morning and retired to a sleeping site in the afternoon

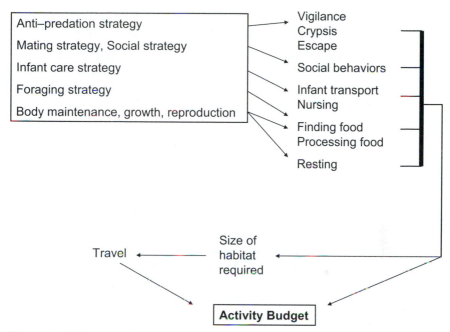

Figure 4–1 Flow chart indicating the influence of different strategies on a primate's activity budget

or evening. I compared these times with sunrise and sunset data obtained from the U.S. Naval Observatory (22 Nov. 2002. www.aa.usno.navy.mil/data/docs/RS_One Year.html) to determine if activity patterns were affected by variation in day length across the year.

Groups were followed all day (see Chapter 2) and data on the behavior of group members were collected at five-minute intervals. For each of these scan samples, we recorded the following data: general and specific behavior, height class, and habitat type. General behavioral categories included forage and feed (defined in Chapter 3), rest, travel, and other (play, aggression, and sexual activities). Specific behavioral categories provided more detailed descriptions of these general activities. Travel, for example, included quadrupedal movement (including walking and running), branch-to-branch leaping, trunk-to-trunk leaping, and vertical ascent and descent. Resting included scanning the environment, investigating objects (at close range), grooming and being groomed, and sitting (not actively looking at an object or around the environment). Height classes were used to define the vertical distance from the forest floor to a study animal, and are defined in Chapter 3.

The habitat type was also recorded during each scan using a coded system for microhabitats within the region. These microhabitats are defined by the height of canopy, visibility criteria, and the dominant plant species present in a 10 m³ space around each observed animal. Visibility was determined by noting the maximum observable distance at eye level for which a monkey could be seen. The following criteria were used to define habitats:

A = primary forest, canopy > 15 m, visibility at eye level > 20 m
B = *Heliconia* dominant plant species, canopy > 15 m, visibility < 20 m
C = primary forest, canopy > 15 m, visibility at eye level < 20 m
D = bamboo dominant plant species, canopy < 15 m, visibility at eye level < 20 m
E = secondary forest, canopy < 15 m, visibility < 20 m
F = stream edge habitat, canopy > 15 m, visibility < 20 m, dominant plants are ferns and stilt root palms.

Figure 4–2 provides a diagram of the vegetation found on 25 m transects taken within each habitat type.

More detailed data on the locomotion and substrate use of callimicos were collected during the last two months of the study. At each scan the substrate used by the animal (bamboo stalk or stem, vine, tree branch, or tree trunk) was recorded, as well as its size (small trunk or branch diameter < 8 cm; medium trunk or branch diameter 8–24 cm; large trunk or branch diameter at breast height > 24 cm) and its orientation (horizontal = 0°–15°; oblique 16°–74°; vertical 75°–90°).

Analyses

To compare feeding records I counted the number of feeding records devoted to fruit, fungi, insects, and other foods, between the hours 8:00–9:00, 12:00–13:00, and 16:00–17:00. Because an animal never fed on the same food item or in the same food location for three hours in a row, these sample periods ensured that they were independent of one another. The number of feeding records for each food type was compared to the

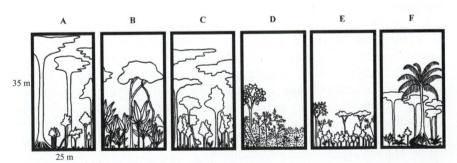

Figure 4–2 Diagram of the habitat type categories used in this study. From Porter 2004, used with permission from Wiley-Liss Publishers

total feeding records for that food type for all hours (6:15–18:15) using the Chi-squared test for independence (Hinton 1995). For example, between 8:00–9:00, 44 feeding records were of fungi and 164 records were of other foods, whereas for the whole day 953 records were of fungi and 1,489 records were of other foods.

Behavioral differences (general and locomotor) among callimicos, saddle-back tamarins, and red-bellied tamarins were also compared using the Chi-squared test for independence. For these analyses, the total observations of each behavioral category were compared among species. I compared microhabitat use data only during the months when callimicos were within tamarin troop 2's territory, and when data on troop 2 was collected. Thus, data on habitat use were compared among eleven days from two months (October and November) when data were available on all three species in territory 2. In this way I controlled for differences between the availability of microhabitats between tamarin troop territories, and for differences in microhabitat use over time. These daily averages were compared using the Wilcoxon Signed Rank Test. Chi-squared tests for independence were done to determine whether callimicos' behavior and microhabitat use varied between the wet and dry season (wet season: October–March; dry season: April–September).

To compare height class usage, I compared the average daily height used each day for each species. These average daily heights were calculated by taking the proportion of daily observations recorded for each height class value (e.g., 80% of observations were between 0–5 m) and multiplying them by the middle point value of that height class (e.g., 80% × 2.5 m). Height class five (25 m and above) has no middle point, so a value of 25 m was used in daily calculations. These daily average heights were compared between callimicos and each tamarin species, and between the two tamarins using the Kolmogorov- Smirnov test (Sokal and Rohlf 1995).

RESULTS

Home Range Size and Density

The home range size of the callimico group was found to differ dramatically from those of the saddle-back tamarin and red-bellied tamarin groups. The two tamarin species frequently formed polyspecific associations (see Chapter 5) and shared and defended common home ranges of about 30 ha. In contrast, the home range of the callimicos was nearly 150 ha, and overlapped completely with six troops of tamarins, and partially with two others. As callimico group sizes are similar to the tamarin species, the density of callimicos within the study area was estimated as one fifth that of either tamarin species.

This callimico study group seldom encountered neighboring groups of callimicos, and it did not regularly patrol the boundaries of its home range. Callimicos, therefore, unlike the tamarins, do not actively defend their home range, a topic which will be discussed in further detail in Chapters 5 and 6.

Sleeping Sites

Callimicos, saddle-back tamarins, and red-bellied tamarins repeatedly used their own set of sleeping sites. The same sleeping site was almost never used on two nights in succession. The tamarins slept in holes in tree trunks and branches, and used eleven to thirteen different sleeping sites located throughout their territories. Saddle-back tamarins occasionally slept in the dense fronds of palm trees. The callimicos were never observed sleeping in tree holes, but rather chose tangles of vines and leaves above 10 m as their sleeping sites. In total, the callimico group used at least twenty-two sleeping sites throughout its range during the study period.

Activity Period

For each month I compared the mean times at which callimicos, saddle-back tamarins, and red-bellied tamarins left their sleeping sites in the morning and retired to their sleeping sites in the afternoon with the average time of sunrise and sunset for that month. All three species generally emerged from their sleeping sites one to two hours after sunrise, between 6:15–7:30 (mean monthly times groups emerged from their sleeping sites are plotted in Figure 4–3a).

Red-bellied tamarins were generally the first to retire to their sleeping sites in the afternoon—between 16:00–16:30 (mean monthly retirement times for each species are plotted in Figure 4–3b); saddle-back tamarins generally retired soon after red-bellied tamarins (16:30–17:00). Callimicos, on the other hand, usually continued to travel slowly, with occasional bouts of foraging until at least 17:00 and often until nearly 18:00. Unlike the tamarins that quickly entered their sleeping sites upon arrival, callimicos would rest and scan beneath the intended sleeping tree until dark with their tails curled beneath their bodies, only climbing to their intended sleeping site just before sunset.

To determine whether the callimico's extended activity period was used for specialized foraging, I compared feeding records devoted to different food types among three one-hour periods. If there were no diurnal variations in diet, the distribution of feeding records (hourly diet) for each food type within a sample period would have matched the total daily distribution of feeding records (Table 4–1), but they did not. Fungi was eaten more in the afternoon and less in the morning than expected (X^2 = 16.32, X^2 = 26.1

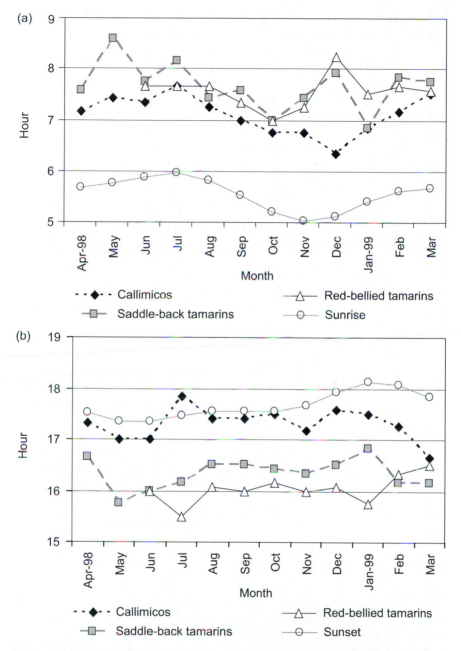

Figure 4–3 Comparison of a) awakening times and b) sleeping times. From Porter 2004, used with permission from Wiley-Liss Publishers

Table 4–1 Callimico feeding records shown as the number of records of each food type (#) used for analyses and the food expressed as a percentage of the total records (%)[1]

Time period	Fungi		Fruit		Insects		Other	
	#	%	#	%	#	%	#	%
8:00–9:00	44	21	92	44	57	28	15	7
12:00–13:00	87	33	71	28	91	36	7	3
16:00–17:00	120	57	43	21	43	20	5	2
Day (6:15–18:15)	953	39	729	30	658	27	102	4

[1]From Porter 2004, used with permission from Wiley-Liss Publishers.

respectively, $df = 1$, $p < 0.001$). Fruit was eaten less in the afternoon than expected ($X^2 = 9.55$, $df = 1$, $p < 0.001$) and insects were eaten more at midday and less in the afternoon than expected (12:00–13:00, $X^2 = 8.47$, $df = 1$, $p < 0.01$, 16:00–17:00, $X^2 = 8.57$, $df = 1$, $p < 0.01$). Thus, there was temporal variation in diet: fungi were eaten more and fruit was eaten less during the late afternoon after the two tamarins retired to their sleeping sites.

General Activity Budget

General behaviors were analyzed in pair-wise comparisons between species (Table 4–2). Chi-squared tests show that there were significant differences in behavior among callimicos (C), saddle-back tamarins (S), and red-bellied tamarins (R) in all pair-wise comparisons (forage: C-S $X^2 = 71.3$, C-R $X^2 = 153.1$, R-S $X^2 = 10.27$; feed C-R $X^2 = 16.00$, R-S $X^2 = 9.31$; rest C-S $X^2 = 289.73$, C-R $X^2 = 580.00$, S-R $X^2 = 82.34$; travel C-S $X^2 = 122.49$, C-R $X^2 = 433.70$; S-R $X^2 = 9.31$, $df = 1$, $p < 0.001$ for all tests) except for feeding, which was similar between callimicos and saddle-back tamarins ($X^2 = 0.39$, $df = 1$, $p = 0.53$). Callimicos rested more and traveled and foraged less than either tamarin species. Red-bellied tamarins traveled, foraged, and fed more than the other two species. It is important to note that if it was unclear what a monkey was looking at, the behavior was recorded as rest/scan. As it was generally unclear what a monkey was looking for as it scanned its surroundings, all visual searches were recorded as resting and scanning. This category, therefore, likely includes scanning for predators and visually searching for food items in substrates not in the monkey's immediate vicinity. This procedure likely increased the amount of resting and scanning recorded for all species.

A particular group of saddle-back tamarins associated exclusively with one group of red-bellied tamarins (and vice versa) and were found in physical association with one another during 67% of all observations. Callimicos associated with eight troops of tamarins throughout its range. Callimicos were observed in association with both tamarin species at the

Table 4–2 Activity behaviors for each species shown as the number of records devoted to each behavior (#) used for analyses and the behavior expressed as a percentage of the total records (%)[1]

Behavior	Callimicos		Saddle-back tamarins		Red-bellied tamarins	
	#	%	#	%	#	%
Feeding	892	9	563	8	558	10
Foraging	654	6	646	10	637	12
Resting	7140	66	3508	54	2559	46
Travel	1790	17	2559	22	1689	31
Other	324	2	340	6	57	1

[1]From Porter 2004, used with permission from Wiley-Liss Publishers.

same time, with only saddle-back tamarins, and with only red-bellied tamarins, during 22%, 22%, and 7% of observations respectively (see Chapter 5 for more details). Thus, although the three species were often in association, they were not together all the time, and this explains why it is possible for them to have slightly different activity patterns.

Closer examination of resting behaviors shows that there were significant differences among species (Table 4–3). Pair-wise comparisons using Chi-squared tests show that callimicos scanned more than either tamarin species (C-S X^2 = 379.32, C-R X^2 = 409.04, df = 1, $p < 0.001$), and saddle-back tamarins scanned more than red-bellied tamarins (X^2 = 11.83, df = 1, $p < 0.001$). Red-bellied tamarins groomed (including grooming another animal, receiving grooming, and self [allo] grooming) more than either saddle-back tamarins or callimicos (R-S X^2 = 28.00, R-C X^2 = 487.52, df = 1, $p < 0.001$) and saddle-back tamarins groomed more than callimicos (X^2 = 341.74, df = 1, $p < 0.001$). Investigating and sitting were rarely observed in any of the three species.

Table 4–3 Resting behaviors for each species shown as the number of records devoted to each behavior (#) used for analyses and the behavior expressed as a percentage of the total records (%)[1]

Behavior	Callimicos		Saddle-back tamarins		Red-bellied tamarins	
	#	%	#	%	#	%
Scanning	6448	87	1912	71	913	66
Grooming	774	11	677	25	458	33
Sitting	110	1	91	3	15	1
Investigating	55	1	21	1	7	0

[1]From Porter 2004, used with permission from Wiley-Liss Publishers.

Table 4–4 Seasonal activity patterns of callimico shown as number of records in each behavioral category (#) used for analyses and percentage of total records (%)[1]

	Forage		Feed		Rest		Travel		Other	
Season	#	%	#	%	#	%	#	%	#	%
Wet	234	5	400	8	3207	67	761	16	187	4
Dry	485	7	558	8	4517	66	1141	17	193	3

[1]From Porter 2004, used with permission from Wiley-Liss Publishers.

Changes in Callimico Activity by Season

To determine whether season affected activity patterns I compared callimico behaviors during the dry and wet seasons (dry season April–September; wet season October–March: Table 4–4). In the dry season animals foraged slightly more (7%) than during the wet season (5%; $X^2 = 22.59$, $df = 1$, $p < 0.001$). There were no differences in feeding, resting, or travel, although "other" behaviors increased in the wet season ($X^2 = 10.96$, $df = 1$, $p < 0.001$). As troops of tamarins observed in the dry season were not the same as those observed in the wet season, I did not compare activity patterns between seasons for either tamarin species.

Locomotion

The three species show significant differences in their locomotor activities (quadrupedal, branch-to-branch leaping, trunk-to-trunk leaping, vertical ascent, and vertical descent; Table 4–5). The frequency of vertical descent by saddle-back tamarins and callimicos was significantly different ($X^2 = 5.09$, $df = 1$, $p < 0.05$) but vertical ascent was not ($X^2 = 1.64$, $df = 1$, $p < 0.05$). All other pair-wise comparisons were significant ($X^2 > 10.82$, $df = 1$, $p < 0.001$). Callimicos traveled by means of trunk-to-trunk leaping more than either saddle-back or red-bellied tamarins. Red-bellied tamarins traveled by quadrupedal walking and running and branch-to-branch leaping more than either saddle-back tamarins or callimicos.

Callimico Substrate Use

Data on callimicos' substrate use were recorded during the last two months of the study. If substrate use during all behaviors is summed (Figure 4–4a), small branches are found to be the predominant substrate used, and small tree trunks and vines are also commonly used. The orientation of these substrates was found to be horizontal during 54% of scans, vertical during 34% of scans, and oblique during 12% of scans. During travel (Figure 4–4b),

Table 4–5 Locomotor behavior for each study species shown as the number of records devoted to each behavior (#) used for analyses and the behavior expressed as a percentage of the total records (%)[1]

Behavior	Callimicos		Saddle-back tamarins		Red-bellied tamarins	
	#	%	#	%	#	%
Vertical ascent	163	8	126	10	41	4
Vertical descent	94	5	87	7	18	2
Quadrupedal leap	108	6	137	11	317	27
Quadrupedal	669	35	626	49	751	64
Trunk-to-trunk leap	850	45	285	22	39	3
Other	4	0	4	0	1	0

[1]From Porter 2004, used with permission from Wiley-Liss Publishers.

small tree trunks and small branches were most frequently used. Vines were used less frequently, and medium branches, bamboo, and large trunks were used rarely during travel.

Height Class Use

The three species exploited distinct parts of the forest (Figure 4–5), and average daily height used (during all behaviors) was significantly different among species (C-S $Z = 4.7$, $p < 0.001$; C-R $Z = 6.0$, $p < 0.001$; R-S $Z = 4.9$, $p < 0.001$: $n = 108$, 66, and 56 for callimicos, saddle-back, and red-bellied tamarins respectively). Callimicos were the understory specialists and were found on average at a height of 4 m, while red-bellied tamarins almost never used the understory and were found most frequently in the lower canopy (average height 14 m). Saddle-back tamarins used both the understory and the lower canopy (average height 7 m). The upper canopy (25 m and above) was occasionally used by red-bellied tamarins, rarely used by saddle-back tamarins, and never used by callimicos. The tamarins would ascend to these heights only to forage and feed on fruits or exudates from legume pods (see Chapter 3).

Microhabitat Use

To compare habitat use between species, I examined microhabitat use by saddle-back tamarins and red-bellied tamarins in troop 2, and by callimicos when they were in troop 2's territory. During October and November, data for tamarin troop 2 were available and the callimico group was frequently in troop 2's territory. In this way I was able to control for potential differences between seasons and for differences in habitat availability

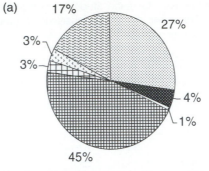

(a)

□ sm trunk   ▨ med trunk   □ lg trunk   ⊞ sm branch
⊟ med branch   ▨ bamboo   ▨ vine

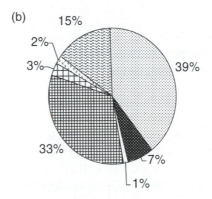

(b)

□ sm trunk   ▨ med trunk   □ lg trunk   ⊞ sm branch
⊟ med branch   ▨ bamboo   ▨ vine

Figure 4–4 Substrate use during a) all activities and b) travel. From Porter 2004, used with permission from Wiley-Liss Publishers

between territories. The proportions of observational records within each microhabitat, along with estimates of the availability of each microhabitat within the home range are presented in Table 4–6. Habitat C, primary forest with dense understory—the most common habitat type within the home range—was also the most frequently used by all species. Red-bellied tamarins were found more in Habitat C (98.7% of observations) than callimicos (95.6%) and although this is statistically significant ($Z = -2.38, n = 11, p < 0.05$), the difference is small. Callimicos were found in habitat F, stream edge habitat, slightly more than either tamarin species (although the difference was only statistically significant between callimicos and red-bellied tamarins, $Z = -2.201, n = 11, p < 0.05$).

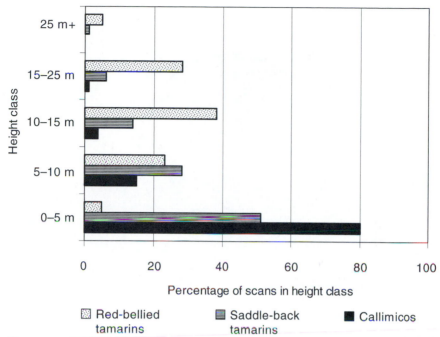

Figure 4–5 Height class use by all three species. From Porter 2004, used with permission from Wiley-Liss Publishers

Table 4–6 The proportion of records that callimicos, saddle-back, and red-bellied tamarins were found in different microhabitats within the home range of tamarin troop 2[1]

Habitat type	Availability[2]	Callimicos	Saddle-back tamarins	Red-bellied tamarins
C – 1° dense	75	95.6	97	98.7
D – Bamboo	0	1	0.5	0
F – Stream	14	2.7	0.5	0.7
Other	11	.7	2	.6

[1]From Porter 2004, used with permission from Wiley-Liss Publishers.
[2]Availability data taken from Hanson 2000.

Seasonal Changes in Microhabitat Use

Yearly habitat use records show that callimicos spend most of their time in primary forest with dense understory (Figure 4–6). To determine whether season affected habitat use I compared microhabitat use during the dry and

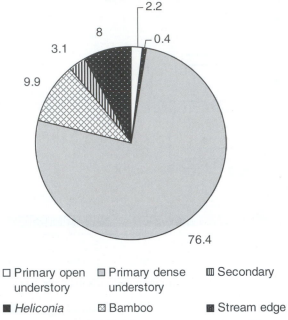

○ Primary open   ▤ Primary dense   ▥ Secondary
   understory   understory

■ *Heliconia*   ⊠ Bamboo   ▦ Stream edge

Figure 4–6 Habitat use by callimicos across the year. From Porter 2004, used with permission from Wiley-Liss Publishers

wet season (dry season April–September; wet season October–March: Table 4–7). In the dry season, *Heliconia* and bamboo microhabitats were used more, and primary forest with dense understory was used less when compared to the wet season ($X^2 = 24.36$, $X^2 = 44.31$, $X^2 = 68.92$, respectively, $df = 1$, $p < 0.001$). During drier months when fruits were scarce, callimicos appeared to search for alternative foods (fungi and insects) leading to a change in habitat use: fungi are found in bamboo microhabitats, and insects are found in the leaves of *Heliconia* plants. Seasonal changes in *Saguinus* study groups were not performed as groups observed in the dry season were not the same as those observed in the wet season, and these groups had different home ranges with different microhabitat availability.

DISCUSSION

As predicted by niche theory (Pianka 1981; Walter 1991), callimicos, saddle-back tamarins, and red-bellied tamarins have evolved different specializations with which they exploit a common environment. As shown in Chapter 3, each species differs in their foraging strategies, foraging height, dry season food selection, and foraging techniques. In addition, in the present chapter, we find that the three species are vertically stratified, differ in

Table 4–7 Seasonal microhabitat use by callimicos shown as number of records in each microhabitat (#) used for analyses and percentage of total records (%)[1]

	A-Primary open		B-Heliconia		C-Primary dense		D-Bamboo		E-Secondary		F-Stream edge	
Season	#	%	#	%	#	%	#	%	#	%	#	%
Wet	127	2	27	1	4355	79	428	8	199	3	365	7
Dry	117	2	208	3	4466	73	704	12	199	3	461	7

[1]From "Differences in forest utilization and activity patterns among three sympatric callitrichines: *Callimico goeldii, Saguinus fuscicollis* and *S. labiatus*," *American Journal of Physical Anthropology* 124(2004):139–153, used with permission from Wiley-Liss Publishers.

their locomotor styles and activity budgets, and use available habitats with different frequencies.

All three species have a unique set of sleeping sites. Callimicos prefer dense vegetation tangles, while both tamarin species generally choose sleeping holes. Studies of sleeping site use for other sympatric callitrichids, however, have showed that tamarins do not always choose tree holes at other sites (e.g., Dawson 1979; Day and Elwood 1999; Heymann 1995). As in other studies (Coimbra-Filho 1977; Day and Elwood 1999; Heymann 1995), each species used its set of sleeping sites repeatedly throughout the year. A site was rarely used two nights consecutively, a strategy that likely serves to reduce predictability and thereby lower predator risk (reviewed in DiBitteti et al. 2000).

All three species left their sleeping sites shortly after dawn, but callimicos entered their sleeping sites later than the tamarins. This longer activity period may have provided callimicos extra time to search and consume fungus, the most common food type eaten during this evening hour. Mycophagy may not be entirely compatible with tamarin foraging strategies, as it is found in microhabitats (e.g., bamboo stands and decaying trees) that do not contain many tamarin foods, and it may be easier for callimicos to forage and feed on fungi when they are alone. Additionally, the early evening consumption of fungi by callimicos may be a strategy for increasing digestion time of this food source, which is composed of complex carbohydrates (Claridge and May 1994). Mycophagous mammals can greatly improve digestion of complex carbohydrates if the carbohydrates are first broken down by microbial fermentation in the gut (Claridge et al. 1999; McIlwee and Johnson 1998), a similar digestive strategy to that used by folivores and some gummivores (Lambert 1998). Although not all studies show the same dietary temporal patterns, many show that folivorous and gummivorous primates consume leaves and gums before resting (e.g., chimpanzees [Wrangham 1977]; howler monkeys [Estrada et al. 1999; Milton 1980]; owl monkeys [Ganzhorn and Wright 1994]), a strategy that may allow primates to maximize digestion time (Milton 1980) and avoid traveling with their stomachs full of bulky foods

(Chapman and Chapman 1991). The latter strategies appear to be employed by callimicos for mycophagy.

Callimicos' daily activity periods were longer throughout the year, not just in the dry season when fungi comprised a greater portion of the diet (Chapter 3). It is therefore possible that these longer activity periods are influenced by other factors. For example, it may be that callimicos use these late-afternoon hours to move between tamarin troop territories, making it more likely that in the morning it will encounter a neighboring troop. This possibility will need to be explored in future studies.

Callimicos, like some other primates (e.g., tamarins [Pook and Pook 1982] and titi monkeys [Kinzey et al. 1977]) eat fruits more in the morning and eat insects more in the middle of the day. It is suggested that fruits are eaten early in the morning to meet the high energetic demands of an animal beginning its daily activities after a long night without food (Clutton-Brock 1977b). In addition, Dawson (1979) suggests that orthopterans (the principle arthropod food source of callimico; see Chapter 3) are not active during early morning hours, making them more difficult to find. One or more of these factors may influence the callimicos' daily feeding rhythm.

Although all three species formed frequent associations with each other (see Chapter 5), their activity budgets differed. Red-bellied tamarins traveled, fed, and foraged more than the other two species, and callimicos rested and scanned more than either tamarin species. Based on dietary comparisons of the three species, it appears that these behavioral differences are related to differences in their diets and foraging strategies (Chapter 3). Red-bellied tamarins eat more fruits and nectar than either of the other two species, thus the greater travel most likely is a result of their frequent movement between fruiting and flowering trees.

As discussed in Chapter 3, arthropods were eaten more by callimicos and saddle-back tamarins than by red-bellied tamarins. Saddle-back tamarins and callimicos were distinguished from one another by their arthropod foraging techniques: saddle-back tamarins were more active foragers, searching for prey in tree holes and crevices, while callimicos were more passive foragers, slowly moving through the understory, scanning and listening for prey. As passive foraging is virtually indistinguishable from scanning (visual search for non-food items) it is likely that the high rates of scanning reported in this study for callimicos are reflective of its arthropod foraging technique (and the periods of rest in the late afternoon under its sleeping sites).

Differences in antipredation strategies also likely contribute to the differences in resting behaviors among species. Callimicos are entirely black, unlike the tamarins, which have white facial markings and red pelage on their bellies (red-bellied tamarins) and backs (saddle-back tamarins) (Chapter 2). This inconspicuous coloration, combined with frequent resting behavior, makes callimicos difficult to detect (as anyone who has tried to locate a group can attest) and likely serves as an important means of avoiding predators.

Callimicos, red-bellied tamarins, and saddle-back tamarins also show significant differences in their spatial use of the forest. In Chapter 3, it was shown that the three species differed in the heights they used for foraging and feeding, and this same basic pattern is apparent when we compare overall height class use for all activities: callimicos showed the most intensive use of the understory. Saddle-back tamarins used the understory extensively, but used other forest levels (5–25 m) more frequently than callimicos. Red-bellied tamarins, in contrast to the other two species, rarely used the understory, and instead were found most frequently in the lower canopy (10–15 m) and middle canopy (15–25 m). Similar height use by the tamarins was reported in earlier studies (Buchanan-Smith 1990, 1991b, 1999; Yoneda 1984).

The differences in vertical stratification between the three study species are reflected in their locomotor styles. Primates that travel in the understory generally move by leaping between vertical supports (trunks) as there are few branches available to cross the gaps between one tree and another (Demes et al. 1995). The results of this study, like those of Pook and Pook (1981), show that callimicos almost always travel below 5 m. This preference for the understory environment across activities is not surprising given the callimicos' foraging strategies. By traveling near the ground, callimicos likely are able to move and search for foods simultaneously as fungi and arthropods are both resources found at low densities throughout the forest understory.

Callimicos used trunk-to-trunk leaping as their primary form of locomotion in this study (46% of all travel). Saddle-back tamarins were also observed traveling frequently by trunk-to-trunk leaping (22%), but to a lesser extent than callimicos. Yoneda (1984), however, reports that 44% of travel by saddle-back tamarins is by trunk-to-trunk leaping, nearly the same that is reported in this study for callimicos. The discrepancies among locomotor patterns reported for the same species during different studies may reflect differences in the definitions researchers used to classify locomotor behavior. Alternatively, they may reflect differences in habitat structure among sites, particularly in the amount of horizontal supports available in the understory.

Callimicos showed the greatest preference for small vertical supports while they were traveling. When support use during all activities was examined, small branches were used the most frequently of all substrate types, with small trunks and vines used less often. Saddle-back tamarins have also been shown to rely heavily on vertical supports (Buchanan-Smith 1999; Crandlemire-Sacco 1986). Thus, saddle-back tamarins and callimicos have more similar locomotor styles, and have greater overlap in the substrates they use than either species has with red-bellied tamarins.

Although claws are suggested to be adaptations for large branch foraging (Garber 1992; Sussman and Kinzey 1984), callimicos rarely used large supports when searching for or eating food. In the present study, callimicos rarely ate exudates, and those exudates it did eat were from small palms (Hanson and Porter 2000). Callimicos did use their claws for one type of foraging: they usually clung to vertical supports in the understory while looking for arthropods on the ground and in understory vegetation. Thus, small vertical supports were used as foraging platforms from which arthropod searches were made (Chapter 3). Although callimicos' claws assist with leaping between, and grasping, small vertical supports in the understory, it is likely that callimicos have claws simply because they are recent ancestors of other clawed, large-branch-foraging callitrichids.

Small-bodied primates that use the middle and lower canopy generally travel quadrupedally and use branch-to-branch leaping to cross gaps between tree branches (Cannon and Leighton 1994; Fleagle and Mittermeier 1980). These locomotor patterns are suitable for moving along and between thin horizontal supports in the lower and middle canopy. Indeed, red-bellied tamarins, which were found predominantly in the middle canopy, relied mostly on quadrupedal walking and running and branch-to-branch leaping and rarely performed trunk-to-trunk leaps. Saddle-back tamarins, which used the lower canopy and understory frequently, relied on a combination of quadrupedal movement, leaps between terminal branches, and leaps between trunks in the understory. Thus the saddle-back tamarin's locomotor pattern indicates their willingness to use a wide variety of substrates in their environment. Callimicos, as predicted, engaged in trunk-to-trunk leaping in the understory more than either species of tamarin. The callimicos' morphology indicates they are specialized for this type of movement, with relatively longer legs than the tamarins (Garber and Leigh 2001) and specialized joints in the ankle, shoulder, and forelimb, adaptations that permit efficient travel between vertical supports (Davis 1996).

Primary forest with dense understory, the most common microhabitat type within the home range, was also the most frequently used by all species. There were differences between callimicos and red-bellied tamarins, however, with callimicos showing a slightly greater preference for stream-edge habitats. If data were available simultaneously for callimicos and all the tamarin troops in its range, a broader comparison of habitat use would be possible. In Chapter 5, comparisons of callimicos' patterns of habitat use while in and out of association with tamarins will be discussed in order to further address species differences in habitat use.

Callimicos used bamboo, stream edge, and secondary forest habitats during 18–20% of observations throughout the year (dry season: bamboo 11%, stream edge 8%, secondary 3%; wet season: bamboo 8%, stream edge 7%, secondary 3%). Hanson (2000) showed that these habitats contain more fungi than primary forest habitats, and it may be that callimico groups require that some portion of their home range contains wet and bamboo areas. As callimicos rely on fruits and arthropods in addition to fungi (Chapter 3), it is likely that callimicos prefer areas that contain a mixture of habitats in which to find these foods: forests with dense understory, wet microhabitats, and patches of bamboo.

Although callimicos, saddle-back tamarins, and red-bellied tamarins are sympatric, each species has its own manner of traveling and resting within its environment, activities that are linked with their different foraging and antipredation strategies. Callimicos are different from all other callitrichids in their specialized use of the understory, their preference for wet habitats, and their frequent inactivity. These behaviors allow them to remain in areas that are most likely to contain fungi, and allow them to rely on crypsis as an antipredation strategy. Thus, as is expected, callimicos use their environment in a manner distinct from the sympatric tamarins.

With a better understanding of the differences and similarities in foraging strategies, habitat use, and activity budgets among callimicos, saddle-back, and red-bellied tamarins, it is now possible to assess why, when, and for what purpose the three species interact with one another during the course of their daily activities. Previous studies indicated that callimicos join groups of saddle-back and red-bellied tamarins to form large mixed-species troops (Pook and Pook 1982), but the frequency and duration of these associations were unknown. As demonstrated in this chapter, some of the callimicos' activities are not compatible with those of the tamarins', and the callimico group's home range was significantly larger than any of the tamarin troops. Thus, although saddle-back tamarins and red- bellied tamarin groups can form permanent associations with one another, callimicos form more ephemeral relations with several groups of tamarins. Details of the frequency and duration of polyspecific associations among the tamarins and callimicos, as well as their potential benefits to callimicos, are discussed in the next chapter.

5

Polyspecific Associations[1]

POTENTIAL COSTS AND BENEFITS
OF POLYSPECIFIC ASSOCIATIONS

Among the unusual characteristics of the marmosets and tamarins is their tendency to form stable, long-lasting polyspecific associations (e.g., Garber 1988a; Heymann 1990; Norconk 1990; Peres 1992a). Saddle-back tamarins and red-bellied tamarin groups, for example, have been shown to spend up to 83% of their time together, and defend a common territory from their neighbors (Buchanan-Smith 1990). The first studies of wild callimicos showed that they associated with groups of saddle-back and red-bellied tamarins (Christen and Geissmann 1994; Pook and Pook 1982), but the frequency and longevity of these associations remained uncertain due to the short duration of these investigations and lack of fully habituated animals.

Polyspecific associations are not likely to occur between species with disparate behavior. In order to spend time together, associated species must have some degree of ecological similarity that allows them to coordinate group activities (Terborgh 1983). Unfortunately, with increasing ecological similarity comes a potential increase in feeding competition if individuals in the mixed-species troop consume the same foods, and if

[1]From "Benefits of polyspecific associations for the Goeldi's Monkey (*Callimico goeldii*)," *American Journal of Primatology* 54(2001):143–158; used with permission from Wiley-Liss Publishers.

these foods are limited in supply. Some studies of competition among group members of the same species suggest that an increase in group size correlates with an increase in feeding competition among group members (Janson 1988; Janson and Goldsmith 1995); however, in other studies this correlation was not found (Sussman and Garber 2004).

Given that some data suggest that competition increases as interspecies group size increases, it is also possible that feeding competition will be high among individuals of different species that travel together and eat similar foods under specific conditions: if foods are in small, spatially restricted patches; if these patches are rare; if the foods can be consumed rapidly by a few individuals; and if access to alternative resources are not available (Podolsky 1990; Terborgh 1990).

Groups of species in polyspecific associations need to balance the benefits gained through joining another species' group with costs associated with feeding competition, and with modifying travel to accommodate companions with slightly different foraging strategies. Polyspecific associations are found in a variety of animals other than callitrichids, such as ungulates (Fitzgibbon 1990), birds (Munn and Terborgh 1979; Popp 1988), fish (Landeau and Terborgh 1986), and spiders (Hodge and Uets 1996). No single factor can universally explain why these associations occur, as differences between species living in closed versus open habitats (such as forests versus savannas), the types of predators present, and resource distribution all appear to influence association patterns and their formation (Chapman and Chapman 1996; Cords 1990a; Fitzgibbon 1990; Terborgh 1990).

The goal of this chapter is to identify the benefits that callimicos gain from associating with tamarins. In order to address what benefits associations might provide callimicos, it is first necessary to refute the null hypothesis (Waser 1982, 1984; Whitesides 1989) that polyspecific associations among groups of callimicos and tamarins are merely chance encounters that result from groups using the same habitats and/or feeding on the same food resources. If this null hypothesis can be rejected, than it is possible to propose alternative hypotheses to explain their occurrence, including reduced predation risk, improved location of food resources, and improved insect foraging.

Polyspecific associations may improve monkeys' abilities to avoid attacks by predators. The threat of predation is thought to be very high for small-bodied callitrichids, which are prey to a variety of mammalian, avian, and reptilian predators (Peres 1993). Although published accounts of predation on callitrichids are scarce (Oversluijs Vasquez and Heymann 2001), there is increasing evidence that primates are an important part of the diet of terrestrial and aerial predators (e.g., Boinski 1987; Goodman, O'Conner, and Lagrand 1993; Isbell 1990; Mitani et al. 2001; Wright 1998).

Increasing group size through polyspecific associations can result in several potential antipredation benefits. Large polyspecific troops may reduce the probability that any one individual in the troop will be preyed upon, thereby reducing an individual's risk of predation (Roberts 1996). Predator avoidance may further improve if associated species are active at different heights in the forest, leading to a wider spread of vigilant individuals than is found in a monospecific group: with greater vigilance spread, the troop can more rapidly detect predators (Caine 1993; Hardie and Buchanan-Smith 1997; Peres 1993; Pook and Pook 1982). Some studies of African primates support the antipredation hypothesis, showing that polyspecific associations increase in frequency when predation risk is highest (Holenweg, Nöe, and Schabel 1995; Nöe and Bshary 1997; Oates and Whitesides 1990).

If polyspecific associations improve the ability to avoid predators, callimicos should have increased survival rates while associated with tamarin groups as compared to when they are alone. This hypothesis can only be tested with long-term data on group demographics and predation rates, data which is not available for callimicos. It is possible, however, to assess whether associations improve predator avoidance through other indirect measures. The group-size effect (Pulliam 1973) predicts that individuals in large groups can reduce vigilance behaviors because the group as a whole can maintain a high vigilance rate. Callitrichids use scanning to look for predators (Caine 1984; Ferrari and Lopes Ferrari 1990; Koenig 1998), and scanning comprises a large part of their daily activities (Ferrari and Lopes Ferrari 1990; Koenig 1998; Savage et al. 1996). Scanning was shown to be a large part of the activity budgets of callimicos, saddle-back, and red-bellied tamarins, and was particularly high for callimicos (Chapter 4). A reduction in scanning can lead to an increase in the amount of time available for other activities such as foraging and feeding, if these activities are time limited. The group-size effect has been supported by studies of polyspecific association among some species (Cords 1990b; Hardie and Buchanan-Smith 1997) but not for others (e.g. Garber and Bicca-Marques 2002; Treves 1998; Rose and Fedigan 1995). I predicted that if callimicos benefit from the group-size effect they would spend less time scanning for predators and more time eating during associations with tamarin groups than while they were alone.

In addition to antipredation benefits, it has been suggested that some species form mixed-species groups in order to exploit the resource knowledge of their associates, with one species using another species to lead it to food. During experimental field studies, emperor tamarins were found to improve their foraging efficiency on small food patches while associated with saddle-back tamarins (Bicca-Marques 2003). These benefits were one-sided, as the foraging efficiency of saddle-back tamarins during these associations declined (Bicca-Marcques and Garber 2003). Similarly, squirrel monkeys in the Amazon follow tufted capuchin monkey groups around their territories in order to parasitize the capuchins' knowledge of fruit resources, but capuchins do not seem to benefit from the squirrel monkeys (Podolsky 1990; Terborgh 1983). Cords (1990a) also found that one species of forest guenon, *Cercopithecus ascanius*, uses another forest guenon, *Cercopithecus mitis*, as a guide to food resources in areas where they have comparable diets. If callimicos are found to follow at least one tamarin species, and if callimicos gain from the tamarins' knowledge of resource location, I predicted that feeding would account for a greater percentage of the activity budget while callimicos were associated with tamarins than while they were alone.

Finally, improved insect foraging may occur in polyspecific associations as a result of one species flushing insects from the middle and upper canopy to another species traveling below (Munn and Terborgh 1979; Terborgh 1990). This has been shown to be one advantage that saddle-back tamarins gain from associations with moustached tamarins (*S. mystax*) (Peres 1992b). If callimicos benefit from insect flushing from tamarins, I predicted that callimicos would forage for insects at lower levels in the forest than at least one tamarin species, and have increased insect feeding rates while associated with tamarins than while they were alone.

METHODOLOGY

Interspecific associations including both physical proximity and vocal contact were noted using one:zero sampling during five-minute intervals. One:zero sampling simply records whether a behavior occurred during a time interval (regardless of frequency or duration) or did not occur. Groups of two species were recorded as being "in association" for a five-minute sample interval if at any point during the interval the groups satisfied the association criteria. To be in "physical association," at least one individual of one species needed to be within 15 m of another individual of a different species. Although other studies have used greater distance criteria to define physical association (e.g., 20 m [Cords 1990b], 25 m [Nöe and Bshary 1997], and 50 m [Buchanan-Smith 1990; Chapman and Chapman 1996; Wachter, Schabel, and Nöe 1997]), I chose 15 m for this study as callimicos were in dense understory forest (with visibility less than 20 m) during the majority of observations (see Chapter 4). Thus, a distance criterion of 15 m ensured that association data were recorded accurately, although more strictly than previous studies.

Two species were considered to be in "vocal association" if contact calls, feeding calls, or alarm calls of one species were audible by the observer following a group of a different species. The use of one:zero sampling allowed for the recording of vocal associations, behaviors that are rare and short in duration but very important for group movement and cohesion (Pook and Pook 1982). The use of one:zero sampling should not overestimate association duration (Martin and Bateson 1993) as the typical association was generally long-lasting and uninterrupted for much longer periods of time than the sample interval used (five minutes).

Data on leadership within mixed-species groups were recorded on fourteen days. The leader was defined as the species that physically (for travel, feeding) or temporally (for long-call communication) began an activity that one or more associated species followed. The initiator of an association was defined as the species that moved toward another group, with the result that they traveled to within 15 m of one another. The species initiating the change was noted every time there was a change of activity. Travel was noted as having begun if one or more individuals of a species left its resting, feeding, or foraging site and then was/were followed by the rest of the group. No leader was noted if there was no species clearly leading the group, or if an activity change was ambiguous.

Analyses

Location data recorded during observations allowed for an assessment of the area of the forest the callimicos used each day. The callimicos' home range included the core areas of eight tamarin troops (composed of both saddle-back and red-bellied tamarins). The location data therefore allowed for an assessment of the time callimicos spent within the territory of each tamarin troop—while they were by themselves and while they were with the tamarin troop that "belonged to" that forest area.

To determine whether callimicos associated with tamarins more than expected by chance, I performed two types of analyses. Using a model developed by Waser (1982, 1984) it is possible to estimate the expected proportion of time that two groups will be found in proximity if these encounters are not planned. The model treats primate groups as molecules moving in an ideal gas, thus the model is generally referred to as Waser's Gas Model. Under this premise, formulas can be developed to predict the expected frequency that groups will run into each other, and how long the encounters will last, if the encounters are due to chance alone (see Box 5–1). Although this method has been used frequently in primate studies of polyspecific associations (e.g., Cords 1987; Podolsky 1990; Whitesides 1989), the model has several drawbacks. First, it is not possible to test whether observed association rates are statistically different from the expected value. Second, the model assumes that animals use all parts of their range equally, an assumption that is clearly violated for most primates who adopt travel routes to efficiently exploit available resources

Box 5–1 Waser's Gas Model

Encounter Rate Z

$$Z = 2 \times (v_i^2 + v_j^2)^{1/2} \times P_j \times (r_i + r_j + d)$$

Where:

v = mean velocity of groups of species i and species j
P_j = density of groups of species j per unit area
r = mean radius of group spread
d = criterion distance for association

Mean Duration of an Encounter K

$$K = \frac{2 \times s}{4 \times (v_i^2 + v_j^2)^{1/2}}$$

Where:

$$s = r_i + r_j + d$$

Expected Proportion of Time in Association T

$$T = Z \times K$$

From Waser (1982) and Whitesides (1989)

(Milton 2000). I therefore conducted an additional test to examine whether callimicos and tamarins associate more than predicted by chance.

I calculated the percentage of observational scans callimicos occupied nineteen (1 ha) plots of forest within tamarin troop 1's home range (see Chapter 2), and the percentage of observations that saddle-back tamarins in troop 1 used these same nineteen plots. Using these plot-use data, I then calculated the probability the two species would have occupied the same plot at the same time (callimicos' percent plot use multiplied by saddle-back tamarins' percent plot use). This represents the expected percentage of time the species would have been together if their proximity were a result of chance encounters in a commonly used area. The expected rate was then compared to the actual association rate (based on the much more conservative criteria of 15 m proximity) using a pair-wise t-test (SPSS® 9.0 for Windows) to assess whether associations were due to chance alone.

Data collected on behavior, diet, and habitat use (as described in Chapters 3 and 4) were used to test additional hypotheses concerning the benefits of associations. All percentage data (behavior, diet, and habitat use) were arcsine transformed before analyses: this transformation is recommended for comparisons of percentage data as it stretches out both tails of a distribution and compresses the middle of the distribution, so that the data approximates a normal distribution. Using the entire data set, monthly differences in association rates were compared using a Standard Factorial ANOVA with unbalanced sample sizes (SPSS 9.0 for Windows). A Model 1 Step-wise Multiple Regression (SPSS 9.0 for Windows) was then used to test which of the following variables best predicted monthly changes in association frequency: group size, dietary overlap, and the frequency of feeding, insectivory, frugivory, and mycophagy.

For comparison of callimicos' behavior in and out of association, subsamples of the data were selected from four one-hour periods (between 8:00–9:00, 10:00–11:00, 12:00–13:00, and 14:00–15:00) across the entire data set to control for possible temporal variation in behaviors. Hourly averages of the occurrence of specific behaviors from these subsamples were used for analyses. Hours during which callimicos were alone (100% of all five-minute samples for that hour show no polyspecific associations) were compared to all hours that it was associated (groups were associated with one or more species during at least 83% of five-minute sample intervals for that hour). In all associated samples a five or ten-minute lapse in association was immediately followed by at least one hour during which the groups were continuously associated, thus these brief lapses were not indicative of a splitting of the polyspecific troop. Interactions between association status (alone or associated) with season (dry season, May–October, or wet season, November–April) and time of sample were examined for all analyses. Unless otherwise stated, interactions among these fixed factors (time of day, season, and association status) were not statistically significant.

To test for differences in height use during sample periods, the Kolmogorov-Smirnov test (Sokal and Rohlf 1995) was used to compare the average height used during hours associated versus during hours alone. The middle point of each height class (see Chapter 4) was used for calculations (e.g., the middle point of height class 0–5 m = 2.5 m).

RESULTS

Patterns of Associations between Callimicos and Tamarins

Callimicos were found within tamarin troop 1's home range during 20% of all observations. From these observations, grid location data were available for 47% of scans (n = 1,224). Location data for saddle-back tamarins in troop 1 were available for 30% of scans (n = 1,145). These location data were used as an estimate of the total frequency that plots were used. Using these frequencies, I calculated the expected percentage of time the two species would occupy any given plot at the same time if associations were due to chance (callimicos' percent plot use multiplied by saddle-back

Table 5–1 The observed and expected frequency of association between callimicos and saddle-back tamarins within test plots[1]

Plot #	Observed %	Expected %
1	0.13	0.02
2	0.66	0.13
3	0.6	0.05
4	0.1	0.01
5	0.8	0.14
6	0.1	0.01
7	0.6	0.02
8	0.4	0.02
9	0.7	0.04
10	0.21	0.01
11	1	0.09
12	1	0.05
13	0.25	0.02
14	0.03	0.02
15	1	0.07
16	0.47	0.01
17	0.25	0.00
18	0.03	0.00
19	1.4	0.09

[1]From Porter 2001b, used with permission from Wiley-Liss Publishers.

tamarins' percent plot use) (Table 5–1). The observed rate was significantly different than the expected rate ($df = 18$, $t = 5.56$, $p < 0.001$), thus associations were not due to chance alone.

In addition, using Waser's model (1982, 1984) I found that callimicos spent more time with tamarins than expected. For this model, the following values were used: average group speed = 1.02/km/day, radius of a group = 10 m, density of tamarins = 4 groups/km², density of callimicos = 0.66 groups/km² (based on home range of 150 ha), association criterion = 15 m, and a daily activity period of 12 hours. Using these values in Waser's formula (see Box 5–1), callimicos are expected to be in physical association with a *Saguinus* group during 3% of observations. In contrast, callimicos were observed in physical association with saddle-back tamarins during 44% of observations and with red-bellied tamarins during 24% of observations, much more often than expected by chance.

Association data were examined for all observations of callimicos taken throughout the year. Callimicos were found within 15 m of both tamarin species at the same time during 22% of observations. Callimicos were found within 15 m of only saddle-back tamarins during 22% of observations, and within 15 m of only red-bellied tamarins during 2% of observations. Callimicos were in vocal association with tamarins during 7% of observations. Callimicos were alone (not within 15 m of, or vocal contact with either tamarin species) 47% of the time.

In contrast, data from troop 2 tamarins shows that saddle-back tamarins were in association with red-bellied tamarins during 72% of all records (67% within 15 m and 5% in vocal contact) and with callimicos during 21% of all records (20% within 15 m and 1% in vocal contact).

Callimicos, unlike tamarins, do not maintain association with only one group of another species. The home range of the callimico study group, with an area of 150 ha, included the entire home ranges of six tamarin troops, and parts of two other troops (Figure 5–1). Callimicos spent the most time within the home range of troop 2, smaller amounts of time with troops 1, 3, 4, 5, and 6, and only brief periods with troops 7 and 8. The percentage of time that callimicos associated with tamarin troops in these areas are indicated in Figure 5–1. Associations with a particular tamarin troop (1–8) were maintained for as little as a half an hour, and as long as several days.

Three patterns of association transfers were recorded during forty sequences when callimicos moved from one tamarin territory into another. First, callimicos switched directly from one tamarin troop to another when the

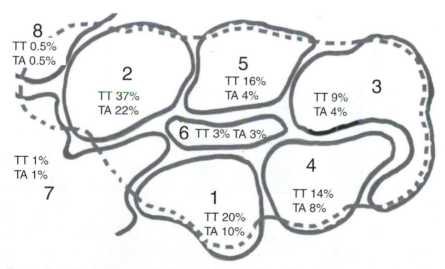

Figure 5–1 The home range of one group of callimicos (dashed line) in relation to the home ranges of eight tamarin troops. The total proportion of time callimicos spent in each range (TT) and the proportion of that time spent in association with each tamarin troop (TA) is listed below each group number. For simplicity, only the core areas of a tamarin troops, and not overlapping boundary areas, are shown. From Porter 2001b, used with permission from Wiley-Liss Publishers

troops met at their territory boundary (n = 11). Second, callimicos simply abandoned their tamarin associates when they were near a tamarin territory boundary. The callimicos would then travel by themselves in the new territory giving long calls intermittently until it encountered a new troop; this encounter often happened on the same day of the transfer (n = 11) or after an entire day or several days spent traveling alone (n = 7). Third, callimicos also would leave one tamarin troop at their sleeping sites in the late afternoon, but then would continue to travel out of the troops' territory, so that in the morning the callimicos began their day in a different territory and with a different troop (n = 11).

Callimicos generally initiated associations (66% of records), as they were usually the first to start contact calls to locate tamarin troops. All three species responded to each other's contact calls, and their calls often made it possible for them to form polyspecific groups immediately after they descended from their sleep trees, and to coordinate their activities throughout the day. Once the polyspecific group had formed, red-bellied tamarins almost always led group travel and feeding at common food resources, and it was generally the species that initiated resting bouts (Figure 5–2). Neither callimicos nor saddle-back tamarins were observed directing aggression (charging or chasing) at red-bellied tamarins. Callimicos and

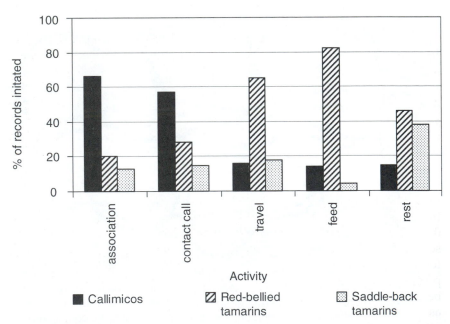

Figure 5–2 Species initiating mixed-group activities. From Porter 2001b, used with permission from Wiley-Liss Publishers

saddle-back tamarins engaged in aggressive interactions with each other on 39% of observation days, but as these episodes were brief, they formed less than 1% of observations during their association. Thus, feeding competition by aggression consumes little energy or time for any of the study species.

Effects of Polyspecific Associations on the Behavior of Callimicos

Habitat use by callimicos varied with association status and by season. The mean frequency with which stream-edge habitats (habitat F) were occupied by callimicos was higher while they were alone than while they were associated ($F_{[1, 180]}$ = 10.64, $p < 0.001$) and higher in the dry season than the wet season ($F_{[1, 180]}$ = 3.92, $p < 0.05$) (dry season [alone 12%, associated 3%], wet season [alone 5%, associated 0%], Figure 5–3a). In contrast, use of primary forest with open understory (habitat A) was highest during the wet season during associations (wet season [associated 8%, alone 0%], dry season [associated 2%, alone 0%], $F_{[3, 178]}$ = 5.58, $p < 0.05$, Figure 5–3b).

The mean frequency with which callimicos used bamboo forest (habitat D) was higher when alone (16%) than when in association with tamarin troops (3%) regardless of season ($F_{[1, 180]}$ = 15.10, $p < 0.001$). In contrast, the mean frequency with which callimicos used primary forest with dense understory (habitat C) was higher while callimicos were associated (88%) than while they were alone (67%), regardless of season ($F_{[1, 180]}$ = 18.68, $p < 0.001$).

Height use varied with association status in habitat C. By using data only from habitat C, I controlled for potential differences in the height at which an animal travels in habitats with different vegetation profiles. Callimicos were found at higher heights (average 3.96 m) while associated than while alone (average 3.14 m) within habitat C (Z = 1.43, $p < 0.05$). These data are shown in Figure 5–4 as the percentage of observations callimicos were observed in each height class: the callimicos spent 10% more time above 5 m when they were associated as compared to when they were alone.

I also examined scanning within habitat C to test for possible benefits through the group effect. If data from all height classes are combined, scanning is significantly less when callimicos were part of a polyspecific group (mean 53%) than when they were alone (mean 62%) ($F_{[1, 98]}$ = 10.77, $p < 0.001$). As it was not always possible to determine whether monkeys were scanning for predators, group members, or other distant objects (such as food), it is possible that scanning for objects other than predators forms a portion of this behavior. In this analysis I do not attempt to distinguish between different types of scanning, but assume that the majority is done as vigilance for predators.

If scanning rates from the same height class are compared (height class 1: 0–5 m), however, to control for potential differences in scanning rates in

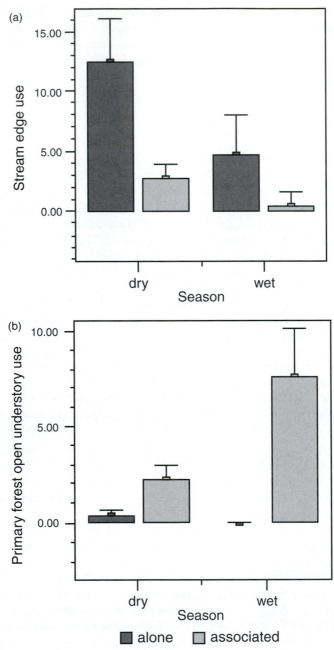

Figure 5–3 Frequency with which callimicos' behavior changed according to association status and season: a) stream-edge habitat use; and b) primary forest with open understory use. Error bars show the standard error of the mean +/− 1.0 SD. From Porter 2001b, used with permission from Wiley-Liss Publishers

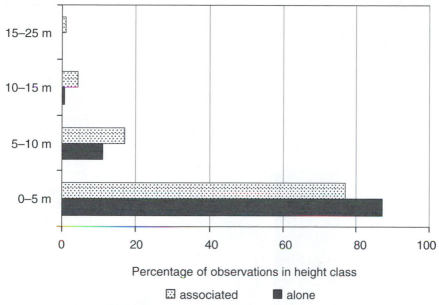

Percentage of observations in height class

☒ associated ■ alone

Figure 5–4 Percentage of observations callimicos were found in each height class while associated versus while alone within habitat C

different height classes (in which predators and predation risk may vary), there is no significant difference in scanning while associated versus while alone. Although on average callimicos scanned less during associations (57%) than when alone (65%) ($F_{[1, 29]} = 2.26, p < 0.14$), this difference is not significant. Thus, callimicos continue to scan the environment frequently within height class 1 regardless of association status.

Although not significant, there was a trend toward increased frequency of travel by callimicos when they were in association (14% of observations) in comparison to when they were alone (11% of observations) ($F_{[1, 98]} = 3.46$, $p < 0.07$). As we did not measure the distance groups traveled each day, it is not certain if increased travel frequency corresponds with increased day ranges. Increased travel may be indicative of increased feeding competition within a polyspecific troop; therefore, I also looked at the affects of associations on feeding behaviors.

Feeding frequencies were compared between times when callimicos were alone to times when they were associated using samples collected only within habitat C. In this way, the analysis controlled for potential differences in food availability between habitats. Feeding rates were significantly higher during the wet season while callimicos were associated (13%) than while they were alone (2%), whereas feeding rates varied little in the dry season between times when they were associated (7%) and while they were alone (8%) ($F_{[3, 96]} = 13.31$, association × season $p < 0.001$; Figure 5–5).

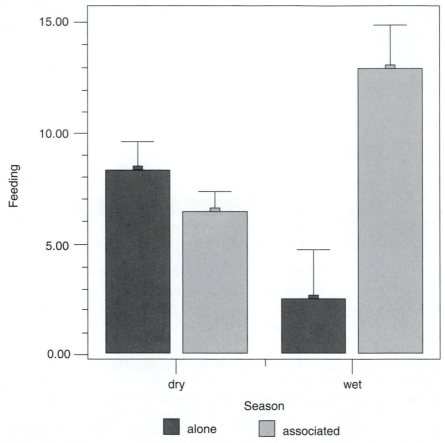

Figure 5–5 Frequency with which callimicos' feeding changed according to association status and season. Error bars show the standard error of the mean +/− 1.0 SD. From Porter 2001, used with permission from Wiley-Liss Publishers

Thus, callimicos do not appear to suffer from feeding competition within mixed-species troops, as they eat more while in association than they do while they are alone.

I examined the types of food eaten during samples in habitat C (in which feeding occurred) to determine if associations affected the frequency with which different types of food were consumed. First, I examined whether arthropod foraging was affected by flushing of arthropods by one species to another. Using the height at which arthropods were eaten as an approximation of the height at which they were captured, I found that red-bellied tamarins captured insects at higher heights than the other two species (mean insect-eating heights: callimicos 2.94 m; saddle-back tamarins 3.88 m; red-bellied tamarins 11.78 m). Therefore, as the red-bellied tamarin is the species that potentially flushes insects to callimicos, I compared arthropod feeding only during hours when callimicos were in association with both red-bellied and saddle-back tamarins to hours in which callimicos were alone. The proportion of feeding time devoted to insects did not differ significantly between hours associated versus hours alone ($F_{[1, 63]}$ = 1.38, $p <$ 0.25). Thus, although red-bellied tamarins potentially flush insects from the lower and middle canopy to callimicos in the understory, its proximity does not result in significant increases in insectivory.

Just as there were no significant increases in insectivory, there were no significant increases in the frequency of frugivory or mycophagy when callimicos were associated as compared to when they were alone. Thus, associations appear to result in a general increase in feeding behaviors in the wet season, rather than an increase in consumption of any particular food type.

Although there were no significant changes in the types of food consumed by callimicos while in polyspecific associations as compared to when they were alone when compared by season, I also tested whether monthly feeding behaviors were linked to polyspecific association rates. I tested, through multiple regression analyses, whether time spent feeding on different food types was a good predictor of association rates. Using data from Chapter 3 on monthly dietary overlap (with saddle-back and red-bellied tamarins), and monthly consumption of fruits, fungi, and insects, for the multiple regression analyses, I found that the percentage of fruit feeding records (frugivory) was the best predictor of monthly association rates ($F_{[5,11]}$ = 6.08, $p <$ 0.05; Figure 5–6a). It can also be seen that although frugivory was the best predictor of association rates, mycophagy was roughly inversely proportional to association rates, and that monthly dietary overlap with both tamarins roughly parallels monthly association rates (Figure 5–6b). Thus, overall, there does not appear to be evidence of feeding competition when callimicos were part of a mixed-species troop, and instead, foraging compatibility likely shapes association patterns.

DISCUSSION

Groups of saddle-back tamarins in this study, as in previous studies (Buchanan-Smith 1990, 1999; Peres 1992b), maintain associations exclusively with one group of red-bellied tamarins (and vice versa), sharing common home ranges, and defending common territories. In contrast, callimicos have a home range approximately five times larger than the tamarins, and move between different tamarin troops over time. This is similar to association patterns described for squirrel monkeys with capuchin monkeys (Podolsky 1990; Terborgh 1983), with one squirrel monkey group associating with multiple capuchin groups throughout its large home range. Associations were generally initiated by callimicos through contact calls, and the calls were responded to by both tamarin species.

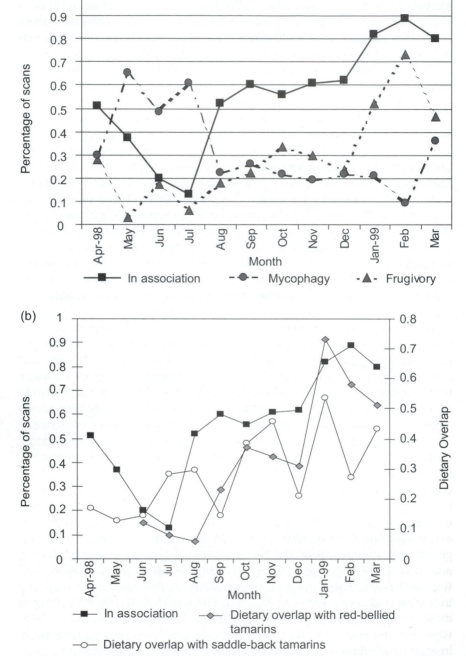

Figure 5–6 The mean percentage of time callimicos were in association with tamarin troops, plotted with: a) the frequency of frugivory and mycophagy; and b) dietary overlap values with red-bellied tamarins and saddle-back tamarins. From Porter 2001b, used with permission from Wiley-Liss Publishers

Once together, red-bellied tamarins led group activities, such as travel and feeding, and initiated resting bouts.

One cost of polyspecific associations for callimicos may be increased competition with the tamarins for limited food resources. Callimicos were subordinate to red-bellied tamarins, as indicated by the callimicos' movement out of a red-bellied tamarin's path, and the callimicos' abandonment of feeding sites on the red-bellied tamarins' approach. This subordinate role of callimicos to red-bellied tamarins was also noted in a study of polyspecific associations in Brazil (Rehg 2003). In contrast, callimicos and saddle-back tamarins appeared to be of more equal status, and although infrequent, they were occasionally observed chasing each other from feeding sites. These displacements and interspecies aggressive events were rare, suggesting that in general the three species feed cooperatively.

Associations between callimicos and tamarin troops occurred much more frequently than expected by chance. On average, callimicos were found in association with tamarins during 53% of observations. Monthly association rates varied from 89% of observations in the wet season month of February to 13% in the dry season month of July. Multiple regression analyses showed that association frequency was best predicted by the frequency of fruit feeding: months of high frugivory were also the months of high association rates (Figure 5–6a). In addition, dietary overlap rates roughly parallel association rates. This suggests that polyspecific associations are linked closely with foraging compatibility. In a study of callimicos, saddle-back, and red-bellied tamarins in Brazil, Rehg (2003) found similar results: the three species formed mixed-species groups with lower frequency in the dry season when non-fruit foods were eaten. Thus, it appears that the pattern of associations I have described here is common across forests where callimicos and tamarins are present.

Foraging compatibility has been proposed to constrain polyspecific associations among other primate species. Cords (1990a) found that species of forest guenons associated more frequently at a site where they had higher dietary overlap than at a site where dietary overlap was low. Furthermore, Chapman and Chapman (2000) found that food availability and interspecific feeding competition limited associations between red colobus groups and groups of other primate species. The data from the present study suggest that differences in foraging and feeding strategies among callimicos and tamarins during periods of fruit scarcity reduces their compatibility with one another, thereby reducing association rates. My data does not indicate that feeding competition occurs between callimicos and tamarins; during the wet season callimicos ate more often while in associations than while they were alone, and during the dry season there were no differences in callimicos' feeding rates by association status.

As shown in Chapter 3, during fruit scarcity tamarins eat nectar and exudates while callimicos eat fungi. My data show that fungi are eaten by callimicos throughout the year, particularly in the dry season, but fungi are rarely eaten by tamarins. Fungi are patchy and ephemeral resources that are found more often in stream-edge and bamboo habitats (Hanson 2000): these habitats, however, may contain little food for tamarins. Indeed, callimicos used habitat differently depending on their association status and season. Callimicos used both stream-edge and bamboo habitats more while alone than while associated, and used stream-edge habitats more in the dry season when mycophagy was highest. These patterns of habitat use suggest that foraging for fungi limits callimicos' associations with tamarins who forage on other resources (exudates and nectar) found in other habitats.

Callimicos, on average, were found almost one meter higher during associations than while alone, and their use of the middle and upper canopy increased by 10%. This increase in height use appears to allow callimicos to expand the area in which they forage and feed, a benefit that appears to have been particularly important during the wet season when callimicos fed more during polyspecific associations than while alone. During the wet season, fruits were the principle food resource for callimicos and 89% of these fruits were consumed above 5 m from the ground (see Chapter 3). During months when fruits are available callimicos benefit most from increasing height use to forage in the middle and upper canopy where these fruits are most abundant.

Similar results of increased use of different forest layers were found for monkeys in polyspecific associations in Africa. During associations among terrestrial mangabeys (*Cercocebus atys*) and arboreal monkeys (*Cercopithecus diana* and *Cercocebus atys*) (McGraw and Bshary 2002), the arboreal monkeys exploited foods in the understory more while in association with mangabeys than without them. As mangabeys form large groups and are understory specialists, they are likely to be highly vigilant for ground predators, thereby providing relaxed ground predation pressure for arboreal monkeys during associations. Similarly, Diana monkeys and Campbell's monkeys (*Cercopithecus diana* and *C. campbelli*) change their use of forest strata while in association: Diana monkeys descend lower in the forest strata while Campbell's monkeys move higher in the forest strata during associations (Wolters and Zuberbuhler 2003).

Although many studies have reported decreased scanning rates during associations (e.g., Wolters and Zuberbuhler 2003), callimicos during this study showed no reduction in scanning behavior if habitat type and height were controlled for in the analysis. It should be noted that in my study, it was impossible to distinguish scanning for predators from scanning for food resources or conspecifics; thus, although I assume that all scanning was done with the goal of predator detection, a portion of scanning time may have been for other motives. It is possible, therefore, that scanning for predators may have decreased during polyspecific associations, but scanning for food or conspecifics increased. If this was the case, scanning rates would not change by association status even though the motive of scanning while alone or associated may have been different. Testing this possibility is difficult in the field however, where it is often unclear what a monkey is looking for during a scan.

Although my data do not support for the group effect (associations did not permit a decrease in scanning rates), overall predation risk is likely to be lower in polyspecific groups due to decreased probability of capture (Roberts 1996) and increased number and spread of vigilant individuals in a larger group (Caine 1993; Hardie and Buchanan-Smith 1997; Peres 1993). Increased predator avoidance in the mixed group is likely to explain why callimicos leave their preferred habitats (the dense understory), for more exposed habitats (primary forest and the lower and middle canopy) more frequently while in the presence of tamarins. Indeed, this is supported by anecdotal observations: if callimicos arrived at a fruiting tree before tamarins, they would wait under the tree until tamarins arrived before climbing into the canopy to feed together (Porter and Hanson, personal observations).

As callimicos follow red-bellied tamarins while in associated groups, it is possible that callimicos use red-bellied tamarins as guides to fruit resources in the canopy, thereby increasing the height at which they forage and feed. Parasitic relationships, in which one species increases food consumption by following a species with greater fruit resource knowledge, have been demonstrated in experimental field studies with tamarins (Bicca-Marcques and Garber 2003), with captive tamarins (Prescott and Buchanan-Smith 1999), with squirrel monkeys and capuchin monkeys (Podolsky 1990; Terborgh 1983) and in forest guenons (Cords 1990a). In this study, although associations led to an increase in feeding during the wet season and associations were more frequent during months of high fruit feeding, they did not specifically lead to an increase in frugivory. These results could occur if the callimicos learned the location of fruit resources from the tamarins, but then later returned to the fruit sites on their own: this scenario would increase frugivory both while callimicos were alone and associated. This possibility will need to be tested by carefully monitoring which species is first to find fruit trees when their fruits first begin to ripen.

Rehg's study (2003) of callimicos, red-bellied tamarins, and saddle-back tamarins in Brazil indicates that callimicos may have small home ranges in some areas. Rehg estimated that her study group of callimicos had a home range of about 48 ha, a home range similar in size to the tamarins with which they associated frequently (67% of observations). In areas where callimicos have small ranges it is unlikely that they benefit from the resource knowledge of tamarins, as the callimicos would likely know their home range equally as well as the tamarins.

While associations improve general feeding and foraging, callimicos do not appear to gain from associations with tamarins through improved insectivory. Studies show that orthopterans (grasshoppers), the principal type of arthropods eaten by callimicos and tamarins, are at very low abundance and sparsely distributed in tropical forests (Penny and Arias 1982), making it unlikely that tamarin troops lead callimicos to orthopterans. Given the differences in the foraging height of red-bellied tamarins and callimicos, red-bellied tamarins could potentially flush orthoptera down to callimicos traveling in the understory, but there were no significant increases in insectivory for callimicos during polyspecific associations.

Improved foraging through increased niche expansion therefore appears to be the principal benefit that callimicos gain from polyspecific associations. Given recent evidence suggesting that polyspecific associations can vary considerably over small spatial and temporal scales (Chapman and Chapman 2000), it is important that further studies be conducted in order to compare association patterns from this study with those of callimicos in other areas. It is particularly important to more closely assess the role that callimicos and tamarins have in predator detection in the understory and canopy. The high rates of scanning by callimicos regardless of their association status suggest that one reason that tamarins may actively maintain associations with callimicos is that callimicos provide good sentinels for understory predators.

Just as food and predation shape polyspecific associations, these same factors influence social organization (Janson 1992; van Schaik 1983) and life history strategies (Ross 1988, 1991). Although callimicos, like tamarins and other callitrichids, are small-bodied, there are several important differences in their reproductive strategies. The consistent production of twin offspring by marmosets and tamarins is distinctly absent in callimicos, which produce single offspring—a distinction that may correspond with different predation pressures. In addition, the ability to produce twins biannually is thought to be possible only when resources are consistent across the year. Thus, resource availability and abundance as well as predation risk are likely to have major influences on callimicos' reproductive strategies and social organization. Reproductive ecology is the subject of the next chapter where these ideas will be discussed in more detail.

6

Social Organization and Reproductive Strategies of Callimicos[1]

OVERVIEW OF THE SOCIAL ORGANIZATION OF CALLITRICHIDS

The social system of callitrichids is highly variable as compared to other South American monkeys. Wild callitrichid groups of virtually all combinations of breeding adults have been observed, including polyandrous, polygynous, multimale multifemale, and monogamous (Garber 1994; Goldizen 1990; Nievergelt et al. 2000). Physiological and ecological differences between genera, and habitat differences among populations of the same species, all appear to influence the frequency with which these social systems are expressed (Ferrari 1993; Garber 1994; Goldizen et al. 1996).

Callitrichids are also distinct from other monkeys in the extensive care that group members (including adults and juveniles of both sexes) provide to infants, a system referred to as communal (or cooperative) care (Garber 1997). Infant care by nonmothers (also called allocare) is thought to be essential for the survival of callitrichid infants, but varies in intensity and duration between species, and even among groups in the same population (Bales et al. 2000).

---

[1]From "Social organization, reproduction and rearing strategies of *Callimico goeldii:* New clues from the wild," *Folia Primatologica* 72(2001):69–79, used with permission from Karger AG Publishers.

Although callimicos are best maintained in monogamous groups in captivity (Beck et al. 1982; Carroll 1988; Sodaro 2004), short-term field studies indicate that callimico groups more often contain two breeding females than do tamarin and lion tamarin groups, and may be comparable with common marmoset groups in which 33–50% contain multiple breeding females (reviewed in Digby and Saltzman, in prep). Callimico groups with two same-aged offspring have been reported in all populations observed in the wild (Christen 1998; Encarnación and Heymann 1998; Masataka 1981; Pook and Pook 1981). The presence of two breeding females in many callimico groups may be due to differences between callimicos and other callitrichids in their hormones, litter sizes, and the distribution and abundance of food resources.

In tamarins and marmosets, polyandrous groups are affected by a dominant female who can prevent subordinate females from ovulating solely through hormonal and behavioral reproductive suppression (Abbott, Barrett, and George 1993). Hormonal suppression allows a dominant female to maintain reproductive control of her group without expending energy required on mate guarding, aggression, or physical inhibition of mating among other group members. Hormonal suppression may not always be effective (Lottker, et al. 2004), however, and polygynous groups of marmosets and tamarins are sometimes observed in the wild (Digby and Ferrari 1994; Goldizen et al. 1996). When hormonal suppression fails, dominant females may use infanticide as a means of eliminating subordinate females' infants from the group, thereby eliminating competition for caregivers (infanticide has been observed in both wild and captive groups) (Digby 1995; Saltzman 2003; reviewed in Digby and Saltzman, in prep.). Occasionally two breeding females do successfully reproduce, and are thought to be mother-daughter pairs (Goldizen and Terborgh 1989). In addition, in tamarin and marmoset groups with two breeding females, the infants are more likely to survive if their mothers give birth asynchronously, apparently because the group avoids the energetic burden of transporting and feeding two litters simultaneously (Goldizen and Terborgh 1989; Digby, 1995). In species in which the birth season is narrowly confined to one part of the year, such as with golden lion tamarins, asynchronous births may not be possible (Dietz and Baker, 1993).

In contrast, female callimicos and lion tamarins generally suppress reproduction of subordinate females through behavioral means, namely through aggression (Carroll 1988; French and Inglett 1989; Hardie 1995), as they lack the hormonal mechanisms of other marmosets and tamarins (Dettling and Pryce 1999; but see Abbott, Barrett, and George 1993; Carroll et al. 1990). Behavioral suppression by dominant females appears to be variable in its success in controlling reproduction, particularly in large groups with multiple adult females. For example, in a study by Dietz and Baker (1993), 10% of lion tamarin groups contained two breeding females, although these groups tended to be unstable and seldom lasted more than two years. Captive studies of callimicos (Pryce et al. 2002; Sodaro 2005) indicate that just as in lion tamarins, callimico groups with two breeding females are not stable. Pryce and his Colleagues (2002) suggest, therefore, that females that breed together in a single group are relatives, as relatives may have greater tolerance for one another than unrelated females. This hypothesis is similar to that proposed for tamarin and marmoset groups that contain two breeding females (Goldizen et al. 1996). Both hypotheses are based on the concept of kin selection and fitness. If fitness is achieved by passing down one's genes to subsequent generations, then an individual's fitness will increase not only through production of it's own offspring, but also by helping rear the offspring of its relatives. This is because an individual and their relative's offspring will have some genes in common.

Callimicos, unlike any other callitrichid, give birth to single rather than twin offspring (twin births in captivity are extremely rare, Warneke 1992), a strategy that reduces infant rearing costs for callimico mothers. It has been argued that callitrichid mothers with twins would not have sufficient energy to both lactate and transport their offspring, making communal care necessary for infant survival. Twins at birth are very heavy (together weighing between 12–25% of their mother's body weight) (Garber and Leigh, 1997; Hartwig 1996), and therefore are very energetically costly to carry (Figure 6–1). For example, in common marmosets, an individual carrying two newborn infants leaps distances that are 17% shorter than when it is unburdened (Schradin and Anzenberger 2001a). Thus, infant transport likely makes travel and escape from predators difficult. As callimico mothers have single offspring weighing about half that of other callitrichid litters (reviewed in Porter and Garber 2004), they may be under less pressure to maintain exclusive breeding access in a group than marmoset and tamarin mothers.

In captivity, allocare in groups of callimicos does not begin immediately after an infant's birth, but it still comprises an essential part of the infant rearing strategy (Beck et al. 1982; Carroll 1982). Group members in other species of callitrichids help to transport infants from the day the infants are born, whereas callimico group members in captivity help to transport infants only in the third week after their birth (Schradin and Anzenberger 2001b). Masataka (1981) collected data from one group of callimicos in the wild, and found that infant transfer occurred between eleven and fifteen days, earlier than after birth reported from captivity. One of the goals of this project was to determine if infant transfer consistently occurs earlier in wild groups than in captive groups, and to compare these data with other callitrichids.

In common marmosets, larger mothers with greater energy reserves are more successful at raising twin infants and have shorter interbirth intervals than lighter mothers, indicating that female health influences long-term reproductive success (Tardif et al. 2002). Furthermore, captive-born

Figure 6–1 Twin golden lion tamarin infants on an adult (photo by Vincent Sodaro)

females have shorter interbirth intervals than wild-born females that have been captured and bred in captivity, even when both are provided the same nutrition in their captive environment, indicating that health during development affects female reproductive success more than health as an adult (De Vleeschouwer, Leus, and Van Elsacker 2003). These data suggest that single callimico infants that do not need to share maternal and allo-care with a sibling during their development may have greater lifetime reproductive success.

In this chapter I examine how field data on group composition, mating behaviors, and infant development contributes to our understanding of callimicos' reproductive and rearing strategies. As these results are based on detailed observations of one group and only three infants, and opportunistic observations of two groups, they are preliminary, but they provide the opportunity to propose hypotheses linking callimicos' ecology with callimicos' life history and reproductive and social strategies.

METHODOLOGY

In addition to the data reported in earlier chapters, I also collected data on infant-care behaviors. During group scans (at five-minute intervals), I noted if an adult was carrying an infant. If an infant was independent (not riding on an adult) during a scan, the infant's behavior was noted. All-occurrence sampling (the behavior was noted whenever it was observed, not just at five-minute intervals) was used to record the following behaviors: mating, nursing, infant transfers, and food sharing between individuals. Although nipple contact and nursing are not necessarily the same, it was impossible to distinguish when an infant was suckling versus simply in contact; therefore, all nipple contact was considered nursing during this study. Nursing frequency reported in this study therefore, may be inflated. It was not always possible to identify individual adults during these observations, so detailed data on which adults provided allocare were not collected.

RESULTS

Breeding Females

The focal group of callimicos contained one breeding female throughout the study period, suggesting the group was either polyandrous or monogamous. One neighboring group was comprised of two adults (sex not determined) and one juvenile, suggesting it was a monogamous pair and their offspring, or that some individuals of this group had recently died or emigrated. A second neighboring group contained two breeding females, as indicated by the presence of two infants in the group during the month of February; however, the exact sex composition of the group was not determined.

Breeding Males

Throughout the month of September when copulations were observed, one male often traveled very close to the breeding female, apparently guarding her from other group members. Data on proximity between group members was not recorded, however, so it is not certain that distances between group members changed significantly during this month.

Males were rarely observed mounting females during the year of observations (n = 10). Five of these behaviors occurred in September, only three weeks after the birth of the last infant, and appeared to involve only the dominant male and female. Another three mating attempts were observed in October, all of which were with the juvenile female who was then only eight months old, and at least one (and probably all) mating attempts were initiated by a subordinate male.

Predation and Dispersal

From March–July, the group was at its maximum size, with six adults (three females, three males) and one infant female (see Table 2-1). In August, the group was missing one adult female and one adult male; it is not known whether they emigrated or died. In January, the group was missing one female, the juvenile, and the infant. Although it is possible that the missing adult female emigrated to a new group, it is unlikely that the juvenile and infant transferred to a new group at their young age, thus they most likely were killed by predators or disease. Group size diminished further in February, when the dominant male disappeared.

Due to the large size of callimico group home ranges (150 ha), group encounters occurred during only 3% of all observation days. In contrast, saddle-back and red-bellied tamarins have smaller home ranges (30 ha) and encounter neighboring groups more frequently (saddle-back 19%, and red-bellied 38% of observation days: Chapter 5). The low encounter rates between callimico groups are likely to make group transfers more difficult for callimicos than for tamarins.

Birth Season

The focal group's breeding female had three infants during the course of the study. The first infant (a female) was born before the group was fully habituated, and was first observed on February 12. Based on her size and behavior in April when the group was well-habituated (visual assessment by Vince Sodaro), she is thought to have been born just before she was seen in February. The second infant (a female) was born on the night of August 21. The third infant (a female) was born between the dates of February 26 and March 8. These births occurred at the end of the dry season (August) and the second half of the rainy season (mid-February to early March) (see Chapter 2).

Interbirth Interval

The interbirth interval of the breeding female was approximately six months (Figure 6–2). Given the gestation length in captivity of 147–157 days

Figure 6–2 Sister callimicos born six months apart (photo by Edilio Nacimento Becerra)

(Buchanan-Smith et al. 1996; Carroll 1982; Jurke and Pryce 1994), the female conceived only one month after parturition. Indeed, while mating behavior was generally rare, the majority of mating behaviors with the dominant female occurred in the month of September, the month following the birth of the second infant.

Infant Development

The first infant was observed nursing until she was estimated to be five months old, and the second infant was observed nursing until she was 3.5 months old (before her disappearance). The second infant was first seen walking on a branch when she was twenty-six days old. The infants only began to walk independently when adults began to forcefully remove them from their backs. Infants are increasingly treated in this manner, forcing them to move independently for longer and longer periods of time. At 2.5 months infants willingly left the adult that was carrying them to walk and play alone. Data on the third infant was collected only during the first month after her birth. Carrying rates of the three infants are shown in Figure 6–3.

Communal Care

Although the mother carries and feeds the infant exclusively during the first days after the baby's birth, all group members then aid in rearing offspring by helping to transport and feed infants and juveniles (Figure 6–4). A group member transported the second infant born during the study when she was older than four days in age but younger than twenty days (unfortunately no observations were taken between the fourth and twentieth days after her birth). The third infant was transported by an adult male sometime between

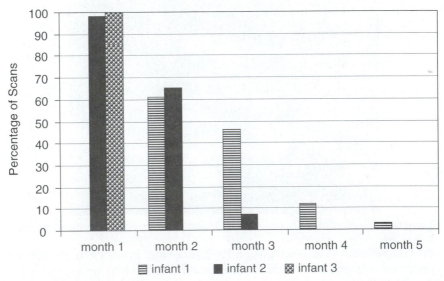

Figure 6–3 Percentage of scans infants were carried for each month after the infant's birth (n = 12,219 scans). From Porter 2001c, used with permission from Karger AG Publishers

the time she was two and ten days old (the group was not observed during intervening days, thus exact dates are not possible).

The juvenile female at seven months old was keenly interested in the second infant. On three occasions the juvenile approached her sister in

Figure 6–4 Adult male carrying an infant (photo by Noel Rowe)

response to the infant's distress calls. Upon the juvenile's approach the infant jumped onto her back, but the juvenile was too small to travel with the baby, and an adult eventually needed to come take the infant. Thus, juveniles appear to be too small to help with infant transport.

Food sharing was a commonly observed behavior, occurring as often as twelve times in one day. Adults shared food with infants as early as twenty-six days after their birth, allowing the infant to take parts of food items from their hand. Adults shared vertebrates, insects, fungi, and fruits with infants and juveniles.

The juvenile in her sixth month stole food from adult group members, chasing them and squealing until she received the desired food item. The juvenile was observed robbing food only once in May, five times in August, and fifteen times in October. This may be one strategy juveniles use after weaning and before they are experienced at foraging, in order to obtain sufficient food.

Mortality

The study group had a very high mortality rate. It is unclear if the adults that disappeared emigrated, died of disease, or were victims of predation (n = 4). It is very unlikely that the two infants and one juvenile that disappeared emigrated, however, and more likely they died of disease or predation.

DISCUSSION

Despite many similarities between callimicos and the other callitrichids, callimicos differ in several important aspects of reproduction and social organization. Examining these similarities and differences allows for a better understanding of the callitrichid radiation, particularly the evolution of variable reproductive systems, social organization, and twinning. The data collected in this study therefore provide a starting point for developing hypotheses concerning callimicos' rearing and reproductive strategies.

Male Reproductive Strategies

Results of this study suggest that callimico males may engage in mate guarding of breeding females as a means of increasing their reproductive success. This possibility needs to be confirmed with studies of marked animals and data on intragroup relations. In studies of pair formations among captive callimicos, males were observed to initiate affiliative behaviors and perform display behaviors more than females, suggesting that males are more concerned with maintaining bonds with the receptive females, than females are with males (Carroll 1985). Mate guarding has been reported in other tamarins and marmosets, and in moustached tamarins mate guarding occurred exclusively during times when the females could have been ovulating (Huck, Lottker, and Heymann 2004).

Besides mate guarding, other male strategies used by callitrichids may include aggression and competition among males. For example, physical competition for mates is considered to be a major source of weight loss among golden lion tamarins during the breeding season (Dietz, Baker, and Miglioretti 1994). In addition, Garber (1997) proposes that dominant callitrichid males, like dominant females, may be capable of hormonal suppression of subordinates (but see Barroso et al. 1997). Future studies are needed to test which of these strategies are employed by callimico males.

Female Reproductive Strategies

The study group in this project contained only one breeding female, but a neighboring group contained two. It appears from the limited evidence available from the field that groups containing two breeding females are found in roughly one third of callimico groups (Table 6–1), a proportion similar to common marmosets (Digby and Saltzman in prep.) but greater than lion tamarins or tamarins (Dietz and Baker 1993; Digby 1999; Garber et al. 1993). Future studies are needed to determine if groups with two breeders are mother and daughter pairs as suggested by Pryce and Colleagues (2002). Additionally, comparisons are needed of infant survival

Table 6–1 Maximum group sizes for wild callimico in which age classes were observed[1]

Reference	Group size
Focal group	6a, 1i
Group II	9a, 2i
Group III	2a, 1j
(Christen 1999)	6a, 2j, 2i
(Christen 1999)	4a, 1i
(Encarnación and Heymann 1998)	6a, 1i
(Encarnación and Heymann 1998)	9a, 1j, 2i
(Christen and Geissmann 1994)	4a
(Buchanan-Smith 1991a)	7a, 1j, 1i
(Pook and Pook 1981)	8a, 1i
(Masataka 1981)	6a, 2i*

a = adult and subadult

j = juvenile

i = infant

* excludes animals introduced into group

[1]From Porter 2001c, used with permission from Karger AG Publishers.

rates between groups containing one versus two breeders to determine if the number of helpers influences a mother's reproductive success.

Males and females are likely to have different strategies for achieving maximal reproductive success depending on the mating possibilities available to them. Goldizen and Terborgh (1989) propose that an individual may be forced to compromise between immediate reproductive success and long-term survival based on its age, body size, the composition of its natal group, and the composition of neighboring groups. Indeed, for callimicos, the large home range size (150 ha, Chapters 4 and 5) and infrequency of group encounters are likely to make dispersal more difficult for them than for individuals in species that are characterized by higher population densities. This in turn may increase the frequency of groups with two breeding females, as limited dispersal opportunities may increase a dominant female's tolerance of a related female breeding in her group. This hypothesis was proposed by Ferrari and Lopes Ferrari (1989) to explain differences between marmoset and tamarin group structure, but it has not consistently been supported by field data on these taxa (reviewed in Digby 1999; Garber 1994).

Once callimico females become breeders, they have the potential to reproduce biannually. The duration of callimicos' gestation in captivity (147–157 days: Table 6–2) is similar to all other callitrichids except golden lion tamarins, which have a shorter gestation period. As compared with other platyrrhines, gestation is relatively long for callitrichids considering their small body size (Table 6–2). Callimicos, like other callitrichids, undergo postpartum estrus, allowing rapid resumption of reproduction following parturition (Jurke et al. 1995; Ziegler, et al. 1989) resulting in an interbirth interval of 171 days in captivity (Buchanan-Smith et al. 1996). In this study the interbirth interval was approximately 165–180 days (Table 6–3).

Although postpartum estrus makes it possible for callitrichids to have two birth seasons per year, tamarin and lion tamarin females often have only one (Goldizen et al. 1988; Souza de Oliviera et al. 1999) and births are generally constrained to the rainy season (DiBitetti and Janson 2000). *Callithrix* and *Cebuella*, on the other hand, appear to have two birth seasons per year, perhaps as a result of their ability to exploit plant exudates, which provide a reliable food resource throughout the year (Ferrari and Lopes Ferrari 1989). Callimico births in this study were biannual, occurring at the end of the dry season and middle of the rainy season (Table 6–2). It is possible that fungus, the fallback resource for callimicos, like exudate resources for the marmosets, provides a stable resource that allows for two birth seasons per year.

Infant Care

Although callimicos have single rather than twin offspring, the burden of carrying an infant while simultaneously undergoing postpartum ovulation and conception is likely to be high for callimico females. In captivity,

Table 6-2 Summary of female reproduction and rearing strategies[1]

Genus	Adult body weight (g)	Neonatal body weight (g)*	Gestation length (days)*	Pattern of births	Mothers in group	Age at first infant transfer (days)	Age at weaning (months)
Wild							
Callimico	500^	—		Bimodal (this study)	1 or 2 (this study; Masataka 1981; Pook and Pook 1981)	4–10 (this study) 11–15 (Masataka 1981)	3.5 (this study)
Captive							
Callimico	463*	47	150	Bimodal (Buchanan-Smith et al. 1996)	1	16–27	2–3
Saguinus	419–534*	39–44	140–184	Birth peak, seasonal and bimodal†	See text Generally 1 (Garber et al. 1993; Goldizen and Terborgh 1989)	See Table 6–3 1 (Tardif et al. 1993)	See Table 6–3 2–3 (Yamamoto 1993)
Callithrix	352*	32	144	Bimodal or two peaks†	1 or 2 and (Digby 1999; Ferrari and Lopes Ferrari 1989)	1 (Tardif et al. 1993)	2–3 (Yamamoto 1993)
Leontopithecus	659*	57	128	Seasonal†	Generally 1 (Dietz and Baker 1993; Dietz et al. 1994)	9–17 (Kleiman 1978)	2–3 (Yamamoto 1993)
Cebuella	128*	16	131	Bimodal†	1 (Soini 1987)	1 (Tardif et al. 1993)	2–3 (Yamamoto 1993)
Aotus	1,000*	97	133	Seasonal†	1 (Wright 1984)	1 (Wright 1984)	8 (Wright 1984)
Saimiri	617–800*	102–114	153–155	Seasonal†	Multiple (Boinski 1987)	—	5–12 (Fragaszy et al. 1991)

*From Hartwig 1996
^From Porter and Garber 2003
†From DiBitetti and Janson 2000
[1] From Porter 2001c, used with permission from Karger AG Publishers.

115

Table 6-3 Summary of infant development in captive and wild callimicos

	Birth months	Interbirth interval (months)	Mothers in group	Age at first infant transfer (days)	Age infant first received food (days)	Age first observed off adult (days)	Age last seen nursing (months)
Captivity	Biannual- (Buchanan-Smith et al. 1996)	5.7 (Buchanan-Smith et al. 1996)	1 or 2 (Carroll 1988)	16–27 (Jurke and Pryce 1994; Schradin and Anzenberger 2001b)	28 (Carroll 1982)	43 (Jurke and Pryce 1994)	4 (Carroll 1982)
This study Infant 1	February	—	1	—	—	—	5
This study Infant 2	August	5.5	1	Between 4–20	26	26	3.5
This study Infant 3	March	6	1	Between 2–10	—	—	—
(Masataka 1981)	August–October	6	2	11–15	27	26	—
(Pook and Pook 1981)	December	—	—	—	—	—	—
(Christen 1998)	September–October	—	2	—	—	—	—

callimico neonates weigh 10% of the mother's body weight, more than the relative weight of a single callitrichid neonate, but less than the combined weight of callitrichid twins, which may reach 17–25% of their mother's body weight (see Table 6–2). Tardif (1994) suggests that infant transport exerts a higher cost on the foraging of cryptic animals than for noncryptic animals. Due to the highly cryptic nature of callimicos, group members may need to hold the infants on their backs in a concealed location in order to give the mother time to forage without exposing the infant to increased predation risk.

Unlike other callitrichid mothers who may transfer infants to a group member the day it is born, captive callimico mothers are usually the exclusive carriers of their infants for the first three weeks following birth (see Table 6–3). In captivity, the earliest reported transfer of a callimico infant to other group members (fathers and older siblings) occurred at sixteen days, and on average infants were first transferred during their third and fourth weeks. In this study, however, other individuals were helping transport infants at least by the fourth day after their birth.

Schradin and Anzenberger (2001b) showed that callimico mothers in captive, monogamous, family groups were able to reduce infant carrying when their mates and older offspring helped transport their infants. Infant transport has been shown to be energetically costly for tamarin and lion tamarin helpers who lose weight during months they help carry offspring (Dietz, Baker, and Migliotti 1994; Sanchez et al. 1999). In contrast, cotton-top tamarin mothers gain weight from the second week after parturition onward, with extramaternal infant transport appearing to allow the mother to recuperate from gestation, parturition, and lactation (Sanchez et al. 1999). Indeed, the number of successfully reared infants has been shown to be positively associated with the number of adult male helpers present in wild groups of tamarins (Garber 1997) and marmosets (Koenig 1995), but not for pygmy marmosets (Heymann and Soini 1999). The lack of correlation between infant survival and group size in pygmy marmosets may be due to its short day ranges that allow infants to be parked during feeding and foraging, rather than carried as in other longer-ranging callitrichids, thereby reducing infant rearing costs for pygmy marmosets (Heymann and Soini 1999).

Captive studies of callimicos indicate that mothers are able to reduce the time they spend carrying their infants as the number of helpers increase (Schradin and Anzenberger 2001b), suggesting that callimico mothers and infants may similarly benefit from allocare. The results of this study show that wild callimico mothers may transfer their infants between two and ten days, earlier than the time reported for captive mothers. It is possible that the higher costs of infant transport and foraging for wild callimicos necessitate the transfer of an infant at an earlier age than in captivity.

Although callimico infants' growth rates during the first three months are similar to those of other infant callitrichids (Garber and Leigh 1997), callimicos reach sexual maturity on average at fifty-seven weeks, faster than other callitrichids (see Table 6–2). In captivity, callimico infants first leave their parents on average at forty-three days, with the earliest reported age of independent movement at nineteen days (see Table 6–3). In this study the second infant was observed walking independently of an adult carrier at twenty-six days. Results from this study show infants are carried nearly 100% of the time during their first month, and 61–65% in the second month. In the third month there appears to be considerable variability between infants, with one baby carried during 46% of all scans, and another infant during only 7% of all scans. These results are similar to captive observations, where infants between five and six weeks of age begin to spend a considerable amount of time alone on a substrate (see Table 6–3). Tardif, Harrison, and Simek (1993) suggest that in callitrichids with long daily path lengths, infants are carried longer than in species that travel less. Indeed, callimicos follow the tamarin and lion tamarin pattern of more extensive infant transport, characteristic of long-ranging callitrichid species (Souza de Oliviera et al. 1999; Tardif, Harrison, and Simek 1993).

Nonmaternal care by callimico group members includes food provisioning as well as infant transport. In captive studies and during this study infants begin to be food provisioned at four weeks of age (Table 6–3). In the wild, adults provided food with both infants and juveniles actively (by sharing) and passively (by permitting food stealing). The month after the first infant was weaned, the frequency with which she stole food from adults peaked, probably as a means of acquiring sufficient food until she had improved her own foraging skills (Yamamoto 1993).

Based on the limited sample size from the wild, callimico infants appear to be permitted to nurse longer than other callitrichids, which are weaned between eight and fifteen weeks after parturition (Table 6–2). It is possible that a mother callimico, with one infant and extensive allocare available, is able to allow her single offspring to nurse more frequently and delay weaning more than are other callitrichid mothers that are raising twins. Continued studies of wild groups are necessary to determine if this pattern is consistent. Greater investment may lead to faster development rates, and may explain why callimicos reach sexual maturity faster than other callitrichids (Dettling and Pryce 1999).

Benefits of Allocare to Caregivers

Clearly mothers and infants benefit from allocare, but what benefits do these allocare givers gain from helping the mothers? Group members may receive several benefits that should compensate for the energetic loss associated with infant transport and food sharing. Fathers and siblings in a group may aid in rearing offspring to increase their inclusive fitness by increasing the chances that related infants survive (e.g., Rabenold 1985; Soltis and McElreath 2001). Long-term field data of tamarins and marmosets suggest that group members may spend several years in their natal group (Ferrari 1993; Garber, et al. 1993; Garber et al. 1984; Goldizen et al. 1996) . In this way, offspring are available to aid their parents in raising half or full siblings and in doing so can increase their inclusive fitness. Callimico males, both fathers and non fathers, show an increase in prolactin following the birth of infants, a change that likely promotes infant caretaking behavior (Schradin, et al. 2003).

Helpers may stay in a group due to limited extragroup breeding opportunities or due to the possibility of taking over a breeding position in the future. Due to the prevalence of polyandrous groups, many callitrichid females never breed (Goldizen et al. 1996); thus, it may be a worthwhile strategy to remain in a group as a helper if there is a chance to ascend to a breeding position (Goldizen et al. 1996; Dunbar 1995).

Alternatively, helpers may provide allocare for reasons of reciprocal altruism (Trivers 1971). Studies of food sharing among unrelated cotton-top tamarins show that individuals give more food to those that give back, indicating that callitrichids are capable of remembering their interactions with specific individuals, thereby providing the "psychological capacity for reciprocally mediated altruism" (Hauser et al. 2003, p. 2363). A dominant female may permit an individual to stay in her group if they help raise her offspring, a "work-to-stay" strategy. This strategy is beneficial if there are no vacant territories to move to and it is costly for an individual to leave its natal group due to predation and/or poor resource knowledge of areas outside the group's range. For example, although adult daughters may eventually be evicted from their natal groups, they can prolong the time before eviction and reduce aggression from their mothers by carrying their younger siblings (Sanchez, Pelaez, and Gil-Burmann 2002). As discussed earlier, given the difficulties that callimicos likely encounter when emigrating, staying as a helper in the natal group may be a reasonable strategy.

Some researchers have proposed that males may aid in allocare as a courtship strategy, whereby their help improves their chances of mating with the breeding female in the future (Ferrari 1992; Price 1992). Although this possibility exists for some species in the wild, Tardif and Bales (1997) have shown that among captive cotton-top tamarins infant carrying does not serve as a successful courtship strategy for males. It remains to be tested whether male callimicos that help with infant care have greater mating priority than males that do not help.

Allocare may provide subadults with the opportunity to gain experience rearing infants, so that they are more successful raising their own infants when they achieve reproductive status (Lancaster 1971). Among callitrichids, animals with experience in infant allocare are suggested to be better at raising their own offspring than animals that lack any training (Hoage 1978; Tardif, Richter, and Carson 1984). This hypothesis also needs to be tested for callimicos.

Why Don't Callimicos Twin?

Given the similarities between callimicos and other callitrichids in body size, allocare giving, and other life history traits, how can the lack of twinning be explained in this genus? Genetic evidence suggests that callimicos are not an ancestral callitrichid (Porter and Garber 2004). Therefore, there are two possibilities for litter-size evolution. First, callimicos and all other callitrichids may have evolved from an ancestor that twinned, and callimicos later lost this ability. Second, the ability to twin evolved separately among all callitrichid lineages except for callimicos (Porter and Garber 2004). Given the importance of litter size on reproductive success, it is unlikely that callimico litter size is the result of chance evolutionary events. It is most probable that ecological factors, such as food availability and quality, and/or reduced predation risk have led callimicos to lose the ability to twin and re-evolve single births (Porter and Garber 2004).

In addition, if callimico groups can support two breeding females, then callimico females may have greater reproductive opportunity than in species in which two breeding females are rarely found. If this is the case, callimico females may actually achieve greater reproductive success in their lifetimes than other callitrichids whose breeding positions are more scarce. Clearly, a better understanding of how often different social structures occur in callimico populations is necessary to understand their reproductive strategies.

A better understanding of callimico reproductive strategies and potential reproductive output are necessary in order to plan for the species' management and conservation in the wild. For example, are the low densities of callimicos due to high mortality rates, low reproductive output, or high habitat selectivity? These questions will be further addressed in the next chapter.

7

Conservation

"These monkeys [callimicos] seem everywhere rare, with thinly scattered patchy populations, and they are often unknown to local people. Apparent rarity puts this species at potential risk, but its true status and even its exact geographic range are unknown." (Emmons and Feer 1997, p. 120)

CONSERVATION STATUS OF CALLIMICOS

Callimicos are considered an endangered species by some classification systems (United States Endangered Species Act: Littel 1992) while other systems have determined the species to be near threatened but not endangered (IUCN 2006 Red list: www.redlist.org, May 4, 2006). Determining a species' conservation status can be difficult and may vary depending on the criteria used (Arita, Robinson, and Redford 1990; Dobson and Yu 1993; Gaston 1994; Rabinowitz, Cairns, and Dillon 1981) and the spatial scale being considered (Quinn, Gaston, and Arnold 1996). The problem with assessing the status of callimicos is that few data are available on its population density, habitat requirements, and geographic distribution. Until these data are available the conservation strategies we adopt for this species will be provisional.

Many studies have suggested that rare species are more likely to become extinct than common species (Gaston 1994). Rare species are more severely affected by demographic, genetic, and environmental stochastic events (Cowlishaw and Dunbar 2000), as small populations can be quickly exterminated by events such as a year of high infant mortality, the appearance of harmful mutations in a gene pool, or a year of food shortage due to drought. Unfortunately, the relationship between rarity and extinction among primates is not well understood, and Harcourt, Copperto, and Parks (2002) suggest that more detailed studies of primate population dynamics are needed. Despite our limitations in understanding the exact links between rarity and extinction, it is useful to examine rare species closely in order to obtain information that is likely to help in conservation management plans.

Cody (1986) divided rare species into three different categories: alpha rarity describes species with low population densities; beta rarity describes species with narrow habitat tolerance; and gamma rarity describes species with small geographic ranges. Among primates, species can be found exhibiting all combinations of these forms of rarity (Jones 1997). In this chapter, I will review the evidence for speciation among callimico populations, callimico population density, habitat specificity, and distribution in order to assess the reasons for its apparent rarity. Then, I will discuss the role of callimicos in their ecosystems, and the pressures that callimicos face in their habitats of northern Bolivia.

SPECIATION

It is unclear if there is only one type of callimico throughout its range. Although only one species of callimico, *Callimico goeldii,* is currently recognized in South America, genetic evidence from captive callimicos suggests that more than one subspecies or species may exist. Genetic studies of captive callimicos indicate that animals show the results of both outbreeding and inbreeding effects (Vasarhelyi 1999, 2000). Inbreeding depression occurs when closely related individuals breed with one another, causing their offspring to become more genetically homogeneous than offspring born to unrelated parents. This reduction in genetic diversity is often detrimental as it can result in an increase in the frequency of rare genetic diseases that are present in inbred offspring. Inbreeding depression is common in captive populations that were founded by just a few individuals, and to which no new breeding individuals were added. Outbreeding, on the other hand, occurs when distantly related individuals (belonging to populations that would not regularly interbreed) breed with one another. In this case, matings between distantly related individuals can create combinations of genes that do not normally appear together, and may result in health problems for the outbred individuals. Both outbreeding and inbreeding can result in higher infant mortality rates than would occur in a "normal" breeding population (Cowlishaw and Dunbar 2000). Vasarhelyi (1999, 2000) suggests that evidence of outbreeding in captive populations of callimicos in Europe and North America indicate that the founders of these populations were captured from genetically isolated subspecies of callimicos in different regions of the Amazon.

Although callimicos are reported to be the same coloration (black) throughout their range, coloration indicates little about the genetic diversity that may exist across populations. Other primates with little variation in pelage coloration have been shown to represent different subspecies throughout their ranges (e.g., sportive lemurs, *Lepilemur*) (Tattersall 1982). Rivers often form physical barriers for gene flow between populations in the Amazon basin, and river barriers form the boundaries of many primate species and subspecies distributions (Eeley and Lawes 1999). The owl monkeys, genus *Aotus*, for example, were once considered a single species, but are now recognized to have five to seven different species, with many species appearing to have arisen, through isolation, on different banks of South American rivers (Ford 1994).

Pygmy marmosets, which have a similar distribution range to callimicos (from Colombia south to Bolivia) have just one recognized species, *Cebuella pygmaea*, and individuals across all its populations are similar in appearance. In contrast, other callitrichid genera are represented by several different species that look different, and the species additionally have populations that are distinct looking, and are therefore divided into subspecies. For example, the tamarin genus (*Saguinus*) has fifteen recognized species (Rylands et al. 2000), and one species within this genus—the saddle-back tamarin (studied in this project)—has twelve recognized subspecies within the range of callimicos (see Figures 1-4 and 2-2).

The reasons some taxa of callitrichids are more speciose and subspeciose than others are uncertain. If tamarins dispersed across the Amazon before callimicos and pygmy marmosets, they would have had more time to accumulate genetic differences, some of which could manifest themselves as facial and body markings and colorations. Alternatively, the same rivers that divide saddle-back tamarin subspecies may also define different subspecies of callimicos, but they may not be recognized. If there is selection for callimicos to remain black for crypsis, callimicos, unlike tamarins, may appear the same, even if populations are genetically distinct. Comparisons of the genes of callimicos from different populations across their range are necessary to determine if speciation as or has not occurred. Work with other primates has shown that although populations may look the same across wide geographic areas, genetically the populations may actually represent different species (e.g., owl monkeys [*Aotus*]: reviewed in Ford, 1994).

There is debate among biologists as to how subspecies should be defined and whether they are valid taxonomic and conservation units. Species are commonly defined using the Biological Species Concept, which states that species are organisms that can successfully interbreed with one another to produce fertile offspring (reviewed in Isaac, Mallet, and Mace 2004). There is no common definition for subspecies. They are variably defined on the basis of genetic, ecological, and/or behavioral differences that are found to exist among populations of a species that are geographically separated from one another (Stanford 2001). As there is no consensus as to how many differences must exist between two populations for them to be considered distinct, subspecies are often divided on the basis of one or more arbitrarily chosen characters (Grubb et al. 2003; Isaac, Mallet, and Mace 2004; Zink 2004).

Despite the lack of standard criteria for defining a subspecies, they can be useful conservation units. If a species has a broad geographic distribution, it may be comprised of populations (subspecies) that are uniquely adapted to different ecological conditions that exist across the species' range. In this situation, any one population represents a unique group of organisms' specifically adapted to a local environment that could not be replaced with individuals from other areas (Mayr 1982). These locally adapted subspecies would be important conservation units, as no other population could replace them in the event of their extinction.

If, however, different subspecies are not uniquely adapted to local environments, and one population could be replaced by another, then each subspecies may be of less importance as conservation units. If conservation funds are limited, efforts may be better focused on managing a species in its entirety, as a metapopulation, rather than focusing on each subspecies (Isaac, Mallet, and Mace 2004). Certainly more data on callimico populations from different parts of their distribution range are needed to determine if they differ genetically, morphologically, ecologically, and/or behaviorally. Only with this data is it possible to determine if callimicos should be treated as one large metapopulation, or as several smaller micropopulations.

POPULATION DENSITY

Populations of species at low densities decline more rapidly than populations of species at high densities in the same-sized area, putting low-density populations at greater risk of extinction (Davies, Margules, and Lawerence 2000; Terborgh and Winter 1980). In this study, there were six groups of saddle-back and red-bellied tamarins in the area occupied by one group of callimicos (with six individuals) that had a home range of 150 ha (see Chapter 5). I have also followed two additional groups of callimicos with five and four individuals at my study site in Bolivia, whose home ranges were 80 ha and 114 ha respectively (Porter 2003; Porter, Sterr, and Garber in prep.). If I use these three home ranges to calculate an average callimico group's home range size (115 ha), and the three group sizes to calculate an average group size (five individuals), I can calculate a density of callimicos at the study site of 4.4 individuals/km^2. This estimate is clearly limited in its accuracy by the small sample size. Although home range data are very limited, additional group counts of callimicos are available from the literature and can be used to increase the accuracy of the density estimate. If I use all group counts of callimicos published in the literature (Table 7–1), I calculate a mean group size of 6.4 individuals, and the density estimate increases slightly to 5.6 individuals/km^2.

As densities of callimicos may vary across sites, it is important to compare the estimate of density from my field site to those at other locations. During a survey of northwestern Bolivia, I counted the number of callimico groups I encountered along line transects at five different sites (Porter 2006). Using 6.4 individuals as an average-sized group, I then calculated densities across

Table 7–1 Summary of callimico observations in the Pando, Bolivia Acre, Brazil and Madre de Dios, Peru

Reference	Map number or location	Callimico observed? Y/N	Group count	Estimated density per km²
Azvedo Lopes 2004	NW Acre	Y	3, 5*	
Alverson et al. 2000	1–3	N		
	4	Y		
Alverson et al. 2003a	5–7	N		
Alverson et al. 2003b	8–13	N		
Buchanan-Smith 1991b	14	N		
Buchanan-Smith 1991a	15	Y	9*	
Buchanan-Smith et al. 2000	14, 16–20	N	7*	
	4	Y		
	21	Y		
Cameron et al. 1989	15, 22–24	Y	1–8	9.6 individuals
	25	N		
Christen 1999	26–31	N		
	32	Y	6*	
Christen and Geissmann 1994	33–37	Y	2.5, 3, 3.3, 4.5*	
Encarnación and Heymann 1998	38	Y	7, 12*	
Ferrari et al. 1998	39	Y		
Hardie 1998	33, 40	Y		
	41	N		
Izawa and Bejarano 1981	23, 42	Y	7*	
Izawa and Yoneda 1981	43	Y	9*	
Kohlhaas 1988	44	N		
Masataka 1981	43	Y	8^	
Pook and Pook 1981	23	Y	8*	0.25 groups
Porter (this study)	4	Y	9, 4*	6.1 individuals
Porter (in press)	45	Y		37 individuals
	46	Y		
	47–49	N		
Rehg 2003	50	Y	8*	1.2 groups

* indicates the group counts were used to calculate an average group size

^ group size was changed by the release of pets into the group

From Porter 2006 used with permission from Wiley-Liss Publishers

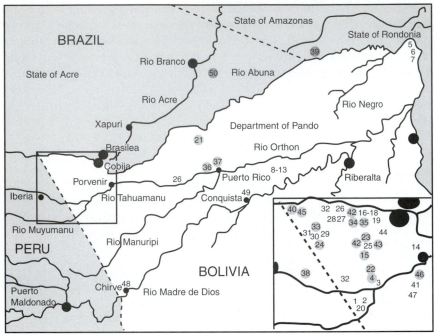

Figure 7–1 Observations of callimicos throughout the Pando and neighboring areas From Porter 2006 used with permission from Wiley-Liss Publishers

these sites. I found callimico groups to be at high densities (37 individuals/km^2) only at one of the five survey sites (#45 in Figure 7–1). The density at this site, the forest just south of the Yaminahua village in the Territorio Communal de Origin Yaminahua—Machineri, was 37 individuals/km^2. This estimate is far greater than at my study site (6.1 individuals/km^2, see above), or at any other site surveyed in the northwestern region of Bolivia, where estimates range from 2–9.6 individuals km^2 (see Table 7–1).

Unfortunately there are limited quantifiable data with which I can compare these different sites to determine what factors may influence callimico densities. In my own survey I estimated habitat abundance, and found that the Yaminahua site has a larger quantity of bamboo (49% of the forest), than I found at other survey sites, and at the study site described in this volume (where bamboo is just 1% of the forest).

Accurate estimates of callimico densities outside Bolivia are available only from Acre, Brazil. Rehg (2003) estimated callimico densities at 1.2 groups/km^2 and tamarins (saddle-back and red-bellied) at 2 groups/km^2. Anecdotal evidence from other parts of the callimico's range such as the Manu National Park suggests it is rare in many parts of its range. In the Manu National Park, callimicos were observed only twice in four years during an intense investigation of five primate species at the site (Terborgh

1983). Similarly, although Izawa (1979) surveyed sites in Colombia, Peru, and Bolivia looking for callimicos and was told that it inhabited these regions, he only observed callimicos in northwestern Bolivia, suggesting that callimicos are at higher densities in this region.

Further studies of callimicos at different sites (outside of Pando) are necessary to determine if callimicos are consistently found at higher densities in areas with abundant bamboo than in areas with little bamboo. As more groups are studied, and home range data are collected, a more accurate calculation of population densities will be possible, as estimates based on a few study groups can vary widely due to small sample sizes (Fashing and Cords 2000).

Although callimicos may achieve high densities in a few isolated habitats, such as in the northwestern corner of the Pando, tamarins can reach densities of around 50 individuals/km² across wide geographic areas (Cameron et al. 1989; Porter 2006). Thus, callimicos are likely to be more vulnerable to extinction than other callitrichids that can maintain higher densities throughout their range. In this regard, callimicos would fit in the alpha rarity category; they are apparently at low density throughout most of their range.

GEOGRAPHIC RANGE

Density is only one factor that should be considered in assessing a species' risk of extinction. Geographic range is also important for assessing the area a species covers, and its degree of protection from anthropogenic disturbance within that area (Happel, Noss, and Marsh 1987). Unfortunately, as a result of its low density, callimicos may be missed during primate surveys (e.g., Freese et al. 1982; Kohlhaas 1988), even in areas where it actually exists (Christen and Geissmann 1994; Ferrari et al. 1998). Thus, the geographic range of callimicos is not well defined, particularly their eastern limits.

Izawa (1979) surveyed the western Amazon basin to assess the distribution limits of callimicos and concluded that the northern limit of the species is the Río Caqueta in Colombia, and the southern limit is the Río Manuripi in Bolivia (further north than the limit proposed by Hershkovitz [1977] at the Río Madre de Dios) (Figure 7–1). During my own census of northwestern Bolivia (Porter 2006) I found callimicos south of the Tahuamanu River, but not south of the Manuripi River. Many sites in northwestern Bolivia have been surveyed and the total results indicate that callimicos are found throughout the region between the Tahuamanu and Acre Rivers, but are rare between the Tahuamanu and Manuripi Rivers, and are absent to the south of the Manuripi River (see Table 7–1), thereby supporting Izawa's proposed range (Izawa 1979).

Hershkovitz (1977) proposed that the Andean foothills limit the species' distribution to the west, but factors limiting the species' eastern limit are less certain. Although the Rio Acre was thought to be callimico's eastern range limit in Brazil (Ferrari et al. 1998; Hershkovitz 1977; Izawa 1979), Rehg's studies east of the Acre River at the Fazenda Experimental Catuaba (2003), and documentation of callimicos north of the Rio Abuná in Brazil, in the state of Rondonia proved this to be incorrect (Ferrari et al. 1998) (Figure 7–1). Thus, the eastern distribution limits of callimicos remain unknown.

Geologists working in the Amazon basin suggest that in the early–mid Miocene the Andes were slowly rising due to continental uplifting, resulting in the formation of a large inland body of water (it is unclear if it was a lake or sea) in the Amazon basin (Hoorn et al. 1995; Rasanen et al. 1995). This large body of water may have acted as a geographic barrier, trapping some callitrichid populations to the west (Ford in prep). The shores of this lake or sea may have acted as the callimicos' eastern boundary and therefore may partially explain its present-day distribution pattern. Although some species of callitrichids— such as the saddle-back tamarins—successfully invaded the forests that formed in the central Amazon once the water subsided, callimicos did not.

HABITAT REQUIREMENTS

Food availability affects animals' distribution patterns. Emmons (1999) suggests that the callitrichids (including callimicos), and several other small-bodied monkeys such as the titi monkeys (*Callicebus*), and squirrel monkeys (*Saimiri*) show a patchy distribution in the Neotropics as a result of their high sensitivity to seasonal resource variability and/or their competitive disadvantage with other larger-bodied animals. Although sensitivity and competition may explain the limited distribution of small-bodied primates in general as compared to other platyrrhines, it does not explain why callimicos have an even patchier and more restricted distribution than other small-bodied monkeys.

As shown in Chapter 3, the callimicos' diet is distinctly different from other callitrichids in their extensive reliance on fungi as a food resource. Hanson (2000) found that the production of jelly fungi (*Auricularia*) and bamboo fungi (*Ascopolyporous*) was substantially less than the production of fruit per unit forest area. She proposed, therefore, that the reliance on fungi would increase the home range size of callimicos in comparison to sympatric tamarin species. Thus the abundance of fungi within a forest may affect the density of callimicos, with home-range size and population densities tightly linked with fungi availability. Clearly, estimates of diet and home-range size at other sites are necessary to test this hypothesis.

Diet and habitat are clearly linked, as the location of food resources partially determines where an animal can live. Diamond (1980) proposed that a species may show a patchy distribution pattern if it is confined to a narrow range of habitats. Callimicos were considered by some scientists to be bamboo and disturbed forest specialists (Buchanan-Smith 1991a; Ferrari et al. 1998; Izawa 1979), but others reported their presence in mature forests in some parts of its range (Christen 1999; Christen and Geissmann 1994). As demonstrated in Chapter 4, callimicos during this study used primary forest with dense understory during 76% of observations, while bamboo forest was used during 10%, and secondary forest during only 3% of all observations. Although callimicos only used bamboo occasionally, they used bamboo forest more than either sympatric tamarin species, and at slightly higher frequency than expected based on availability. Thus, callimicos may require a forest with a mosaic of habitats on which to forage for fruits, arthropods, and fungi.

Bamboo, stream-edge, and tree falls are all habitats that would promote the production of the jelly fungi and bamboo fungi eaten by callimicos. Hanson (2000) determined that fungi eaten by callimicos are more abundant in stream-edge forest than other habitat types, and Pook and Pook (1981) had earlier noted that callimicos appear to have an affinity for stream-edge habitats, a preference that may be due to the presence of fungi in these areas. Although bamboo fungi are difficult to locate—making abundance estimates difficult—they should be more abundant in bamboo forests than other habitats, which may explain why callimicos can be found in areas with extensive bamboo.

As mentioned previously, I found that the Yaminahua site had the highest densities of callimicos in the Pando and was also the site with the highest abundance of bamboo and stream-edge habitats (see Figure 7–2). As I surveyed only five sites, additional studies need to be conducted to compare densities of callimicos and densities of different habitats. In addition, many other factors must be controlled for in order to establish a correlation between the abundance of callimicos and bamboo, including food availability, predator abundance, and forest patch size. Aerial surveys of the northwestern Pando show that the forests of the western Pando that form the frontier with Peru are the southeastern edge of the "greatest bamboo patch in South America" (Alverson, Moskovitz, and Shopland 2000, p. 19). They indicate that this bamboo patch continues 500 km to the north and west into Peru and Brazil. This area may be ideal for callimicos.

In addition to bamboo, dead wood is also an important source of fungi (genus *Auricularia*), and callimicos may select forests containing a high density of tree falls. The forest used for the present study has been documented to have a high occurrence of *Tachigali* (locally known as Palo santo), a monocarpic species that flowers only once and then dies (Alverson, Moskovitz, and Shopland 2000). These trees die at a younger age than other large emergent trees, and likely lead to a higher number of tree falls per hectare and a more discontinuous canopy than in forests where the tree is less abundant (Alverson, Moskovitz, and Shopland 2000). These high tree fall rates may enable callimicos to exploit fungi growing on rotting wood.

Wright and Jernvall (1999) found that primate species that used one type of primary habitat (tropical rain forest, deciduous forest, swamp

Figure 7–2 Bamboo habitat in the forests just south of the Acre River and the indigenous community of the Yaminahua (photo by the author)

forest, scrub forest, savanna) are at higher risk of extinction due to their
narrow habitat ranges. Although callimicos can be considered to be a habitat specialist in that it requires tropical rain forest, it has a distinct advantage over other habitat specialists that require undisturbed forest. As
bamboo often reforests areas that have been cleared for agriculture or pasture, callimicos may be able to use regenerating forests, whereas other
monkey species cannot. Additional studies are therefore needed to determine the degree of tolerance that callimicos have for different habitats
ranging from exclusively bamboo to exclusively primary forest. With this
knowledge it will be possible to assess how well callimicos will be able to
cope with increasing anthropogenic disturbance of Amazonian forests.

REPRODUCTION

Although callimicos do not produce twin offspring like other marmosets
and tamarins, they are capable of producing two infants a year with a biannual birth season. One wild callimico female was observed to produce an

infant every six to seven months (Chapter 6), giving it an equivalent annual reproductive output to a tamarin producing twins once a year, but less than a marmoset producing twins twice a year (Ferrari and Lopes Ferrari 1989; Goldizen et al. 1988; Kleiman 1978; Souza de Oliviera et al. 1999). Although more rapidly reproducing species are generally found at higher densities than species with longer interbirth intervals (Happel, Noss, and Marsh 1987), callimicos show low density despite high reproductive output. This suggests that resource availability or high mortality rates, not reproductive output, limits callimicos' population densities.

Understanding a species' reproductive potential is important for assessments of a population's ability to recover from natural and human-induced disasters. Although I have provided preliminary data on interbirth interval, many aspects of the callimicos' life history are still unclear. For example, it is unknown how many females in a population breed at any one time. If callimico groups regularly contain two breeding females, then there should be less competition for breeding positions than in other callitrichids in which groups generally contain only one breeding female. Polygynous groups may permit callimico females to acquire breeding positions at earlier ages and to have longer reproductive tenures than females in polyandrous groups. However, in this study the group contained only a single breeding female, thus this hypothesis requires further testing. In addition, the mortality rates of infants, juveniles, and adults are needed to assess how quickly a population will grow. High mortality rates obviously will prevent population growth. Long-term data on a population of callimicos would allow the collection of these life history data.

INTERSPECIFIC COMPETITION

Izawa (1979) proposed that callimicos might be limited in their distribution through competitive interactions with saddle-back tamarins. Indeed, saddle-back tamarins and callimicos were found to travel and forage extensively in the understory (Chapter 4) and to consume many of the same fruit species (Chapter 3). As it difficult to assess the effects of competitive interactions in wild populations (Schoener 1982), no direct test of this hypothesis is possible; however, my data do not support this suggestion.

First, despite their similarities in overall foraging, callimicos and saddle-back tamarins relied on different food resources during periods of fruit scarcity in the dry season: callimicos consumed fungi while saddle-back tamarins consumed nectar and exudates (Chapter 3). Second, the two species were also found to differ in the manner in which they foraged for arthropods (Chapter 3). Different arthropod foraging techniques have been shown to reduce dietary overlap for arthropod prey between other species of sympatric tamarins in Peru (Nickle and Heymann 1996). Thus, the differences in arthropod foraging techniques between callimicos and tamarins are also likely to reduce dietary overlap and competition between these species. Third, although both species were found to associate frequently, there were few incidents of interspecific aggression between them (Chapter 5).

These data therefore suggest that interspecific competition between saddle-back tamarins and callimicos does not limit their distributions. Although it is possible that in forests with severely limited food, tamarins can out-compete the callimicos, it is more likely that resource availability (particularly of fungi) has prevented callimicos from expanding into the eastern Amazon. This possibility needs to be tested by comparing fungi ability at sites in the Amazon basin where callimicos are present to areas where they are absent.

ROLE OF CALLIMICOS IN THEIR ECOSYSTEM

Although some primate species are seed predators, many have been shown to be important seed dispersers (Dew and Wright 1998; Gathua 2000). Tamarins (genus *Saguinus*) are reported to serve as seed dispersers for a wide variety of plants, including several of the same plants eaten by callimicos in this study (Garber 1996; Knogge and Heymann 2002). Passage of seeds through primate guts can be neutral, helpful, or harmful for a seed, depending if the seeds pass unharmed through the gut, are slightly modified by stomach acids thereby accelerating germination, or are destroyed (Schupp 1993). Seeds pass unharmed through tamarin guts, suggesting that tamarins act as effective seed dispersers (Knogge, Tirado Herrera, and Heymann 2003). In addition, tamarins defecate seeds up to 500 m away from the parent plant (Garber 1996), and in areas with both primary and secondary forest they can serve as important dispersers of seeds from one habitat to another (Oliveira and Ferrari 2000). Oliveira and Ferrari (2000) believe that tamarins play an important role in regeneration of secondary forest habitats.

It is possible that callimicos also serve as a seed disperser, given their similarities with tamarins in swallowing seeds whole (personal observation). Studies of germination rates of seeds that have passed through callimicos' digestive system are necessary, however, to assess their effect on seeds. In addition, given that callimicos have larger home ranges than tamarins, it is possible that they carry seeds even greater distances from their parent plants. Finally, as callimicos spend more time in bamboo forests than tamarins, callimicos may also serve as important agents in bringing plant seeds into bamboo habitats, a practice that may help to start the succession of bamboo forests back into primary forest. Studies that measure dispersal distances, seed survivorship, and dispersal across habitats are needed to determine callimicos' role as seed dispersers.

Although callimicos are fungi predators, they may also act as dispersers for fungi, as they eat the fruiting bodies of fungi (where the fungi make and store spores). If the spores pass unharmed through the callimicos digestive system, they would be deposited in the callimicos' feces far from the parent, allowing their dispersal through the forest. Other mammals that consume fungi are considered to be an important component of forest ecosystems, as they disperse the spores of fungi to new habitats (Mangan and Adler 2000; Maser, Trappe, and Nussbaum 1978; Reddel, Spain, and Hopkins 1997). Although the fungi callimicos consume are epigeous fungi (sporocarps grow aboveground) which are generally wind dispersed, examination of callimicos' feces and ranging patterns are necessary to determine if it aid in fungi dispersal.

PEOPLE AND FORESTS IN THE DEPARTMENT OF THE PANDO

Callimicos appear to be more abundant in the Department of the Pando, Bolivia than any other area in its distribution range. In order to consider the future of the callimico, it is necessary to examine the history of the Pando, and the current state of the Pando's forests. The Pando has a long history of both human occupation and high primate diversity, but rapid changes in the last several decades threaten the potential for their continued coexistence.

Botanical surveys of the Pando suggest that indigenous peoples have been present in the region for more than 500 years. Archaeological evidence from Brazil indicates that large-scale settlements were present in at least some regions of the Amazon between 1250 and 1600 AD (Heckenberger et al. 2003). In addition, other archaeological sites in Brazil demonstrate that humans inhabited the Amazon basin as early as 10,000 years ago (Roosevelt et al. 1996). No archaeological work has been conducted in the Pando, but given long-term human presence in what is now the Brazilian Amazon, it is likely they also inhabited what is now the Pando. The forests provide evidence that these indigenous peoples historically made patchy but widespread clearings in the region and cultivated hardwoods, rubber, and fig trees throughout the forest to increase their abundance (Alverson, Moskovitz, and Shopland 2000). For example, the density of fig trees (of the genus *Ficus*), in the inland forests of northwestern Pando are higher than any other area surveyed in the Neotropics (Alverson, Moskovitz, and Shopland 2000).

Indigenous peoples inhabited Northern Bolivia and southwestern Brazil nearly exclusively until 1880 when an American explorer found a navigable route from Bolivia into Brazil, an area which was also rich in wild rubber trees (*Hevea brasiliensis* and *Hevea lutea*). Within twenty years after this exploration, the population in the northern sector region of Bolivia (which now includes the Brazilian state of Acre and the Bolivian Department, Pando) had gone from a few hundred colonists to 60,000 colonists in response to the booming rubber trade (Fifer 1972) (Figure 7–3).

The development of Asian rubber plantations reduced the price of rubber, and caused the crash of Bolivian rubber trade by 1915 (Fifer 1972). Thus,

Figure 7–3 A rubber tapper (seringuero) cutting a rubber tree to collect its sap (photo by the author)

only a few rubber tappers remained in the Pando, subsisting on small-scale rubber trade, and agriculture. In 1930, Bolivia began exporting Brazil nuts (*Bertholletia excelsa*) from the Pando, creating a new but seasonal product for the colonists (Figure 7–4).

The low density of Brazil nut trees and rubber trees in the forest of Pando requires that each family use a large tract of forest in order to harvest sufficient

Figure 7–4 The outer shells of Brazil nuts that were harvested in the forest (photo by the author)

quantities of these products to make a living. As a result, the population densities of the Pando remained low throughout most of the twentieth century (0.4–0.9 people/km^2) (Cameron and Buchanan-Smith 1991–1992; Christen and Geissmann 1994). Families living in the forest (campesinos) create small-scale subsistence agricultural plots to grow bananas, papayas, yucca, beans, and rice. Due to the small size of these clearings they are not considered to be a significant threat to the forest (Alverson, Moskovitz, and Shopland 2000; Cameron and Buchanan-Smith 1991–1992). Campesinos also hunt for wild game, with preference for large animals such as peccary, deer, large monkeys (such as howler monkeys), and large birds. The largest primates of the Pando have suffered from this hunting pressure. Woolly monkeys (*Lagothrix lagotricha*) historically lived in the Pando but they are now extinct throughout the region, and spider monkeys are locally extinct from many areas (Alverson, Moskovitz, and Shopland 2000). In contrast, hunting pressure on smaller-bodied primates appears to have been sustainable throughout the twentieth century, as several species have maintained high densities in the Pando to the present day (Buchanan-Smith et al. 2000; Cameron and Buchanan-Smith 1991–1992; Porter 2006).

In the 1970s, commercial trapping of primates began, targeting red-bellied and emperor tamarins. Thousands of these primates left the Pando from 1974–1981 (Cameron and Buchanan-Smith 1991–1992) even though Bolivia joined CITES and theoretically prohibited the sale of wild primates from Bolivia in 1979 (www.cites.org/eng/disc/parties/chronolo. html, April 25, 2005). In addition, saddle-back tamarins were exported from the Pando from 1977–1987 (Cameron and Buchanan-Smith 1991–1992). Callimicos that were trapped during this phase were also exported and some were given to zoological gardens, forming the founders of some captive colonies (Vincent Sodaro, Brookfield Zoo, personal communication). Despite these large-scale exportation efforts, callitrichids are present throughout the Pando, and often at high density (Buchanan-Smith et al. 2000; Cameron and Buchanan-Smith 1991–1992; Porter 2006), although it is impossible to know if the callitrichids have recuperated from the population numbers that existed prior to the 1970s.

More recently other industries have been started in the Pando, and these new activities threaten to decrease biodiversity of all plant and animal species. A large portion of the Pando has been divided into forestry concessions and many areas have been logged for hardwoods such as mahogany (*Swietenia macrophylla*), cedro (*Cedrela* sp.) and roble (*Amburana cearensis*) (Alverson, Moskovitz, and Shopland 2000; Pacheco 1998) (Figure 7–5). The timber trade has resulted in a dramatic increase in the number of roads built through the forest. These roads have facilitated human settlement of forests across all of northwestern Pando (Alverson, Moskovitz, and Shopland 2000). Although large lumber companies controlled much of the lumber trade in the past decades, the national land reform has shifted management of forests to local communities; now the lumber trade is conducted by families and communities (Pacheco 1998).

Although logging has created wide-scale forest disturbance across the Pando, and changed human settlement patterns, selective logging leaves most of the forest standing. Although logging companies create temporary roads to haul out the most valuable hardwoods, thereby increasing secondary growth, much of the forest remains intact. In contrast, ranchers cut and burn forests completely to create open fertile land for growing grass for cattle (Figure 7–6). It is unclear how long or even if reforestation of large pastures will occur (Faminow 1998). Ranches have expanded

Figure 7–5 The author with Edilio Nacimento, Rafael Suarez, and Orlando Pereira, in front of a large mahogany tree (photo by the author)

Figure 7–6 A small cattle ranch in the Pando. Notice the forest that still remains in the background (photo by the author)

along all the roads leading out of the city of Cobija, and have resulted in the destruction of thousands of hectares of forest. Although campesinos generally have only a few cattle and therefore need limited pastureland, a few wealthy individuals own hundreds, if not thousands, of heads of cattle and have cleared extensive plots of forest for pastureland.

In addition to the pressures of logging and ranching, human population in the Pando is increasing rapidly through immigration from other regions of Bolivia and Brazil, and through improved health care. For example, in 1976 the population of the capital city of the Pando, Cobija, was 3,636 people, whereas in 1992 the population was 10,001; in 2001 the population was 20,820 (www.citypopulation.de/Bolivia, May 6, 2005). It is unclear what employment options are available to these new immigrants, but one project currently underway is the creation of a large meat-packing plant outside of Cobija. This plant will certainly encourage more ranching, as it will create more demand for cattle for sale to local and international markets. Clearly the growth of the cattle industry in the Pando will be devastating for the forests, just as it was for the forests in many regions of Brazil (Faminow 1998).

FUTURE CONSERVATION IN THE DEPARTMENT OF THE PANDO

In order to ensure the survival of callimicos and the other plants and animals in its ecosystem, it is necessary to start conservation programs for its protection. There is considerable scientific interest in the flora and fauna of the northwestern Pando due to the high biodiversity found in the region. In 1996, a scientific assessment of aquatic ecosystems in northwestern Bolivia found the area to be potentially the richest area of aquatic biodiversity within Bolivia, and possibly within the entire Amazon River Basin (Chernoff and Willink 1999). In 1999, an assessment of terrestrial flora and fauna in the same region also found the area to be high in biodiversity, with thirteen species of primates and numerous species of other large mammals, as well as numerous first records of reptiles, amphibians, and plants for Bolivia (Alverson, Moskovitz, and Shopland 2000).

Despite more than one hundred years of human colonization by rubber tappers and their descendants, and a longer but unknown period of inhabitation by indigenous groups, the forest has retained a high diversity of flora and fauna. Thus the area has the potential to be an extractive reserve in which humans collect products such as Brazil nuts to sell to a national and international market. Some biologists argue that sustainable harvest of forest products inevitably leads to degradation of the forest, and that there is no substitute for totally protected areas (e.g. Struhsaker 1998; Terborgh 1999) while others argue that sustainable harvest programs—when implemented correctly—are a necessary means for effective conservation of wildlife ecosystems (McLarney 1999; Medellin 1999). Several factors suggest that with proper regulation and management the Pando could be used both as an extractive reserve and a conservation area. The relatively high density of extractive products in the Pando (principally rubber and Brazil nuts) make the forest of potentially greater value than logged forest or land cleared for pasture, if programs to raise the market value of the products are initiated.

The biggest challenge for the Pando, therefore, will be to decide how to help and employ the large numbers of immigrants that have arrived, and will continue to arrive in the city of Cobija. Although people have lived in the area for long periods of time, biodiversity remains high; however, this pattern will only continue if human population densities remain low in rural areas. If new immigrants to Cobija are encouraged to establish their own agricultural plots or ranches outside of the city, the forests of Pando will disappear rapidly, along with the biodiversity that currently makes the region unique. Even if people stay close to the city, the growing population will need more food supplies. Improved agricultural methods that prevent erosion of soils and improved crop production are needed to reduce the continual burning of forests for new agricultural land (Anderson 1990a). In addition, alternatives to beef as a source of protein for the residents of Cobija are needed, as well as improved management of grazing land and reforestation projects for pasture that has been abandoned.

Education programs are also essential. Although long-term residents of the Pando are aware of the diversity of their forests, they are unaware of its value to the world as a potential source of pharmaceutical drugs; as a carbon sink for greenhouse gasses; as a key player in the movement of fresh water in clouds, rain, and rivers; and as a natural and irreplaceable wonder (Cracraft and Grifo 1999). Recent immigrants to the Pando generally have no knowledge of the tropical forests surrounding the city of Cobija, and should be given the opportunity to learn about their new environment. Only in this way will the forests be viewed as valuable resources in themselves, rather than areas whose value lies in their destruction for pasture and agricultural land.

8

Summary

While planning th is study from my graduate school on Long Island in New York, far from the tropical forests of Bolivia, I tried to picture how callimicos would behave in the wild. My images were basically that of a very shy, very black tamarin. Although callimicos do behave like tamarins in many respects, they diverge from the tamarin behavioral and ecological repertoire in ways I had never imagined. The most surprising finding of this study is that callimicos eat fungi almost every day, from dead trees rotting on the ground and from bamboo stalks and branches. This reliance on fungi as a food resource influences many other behaviors including locomotion, ranging, and habitat choice. In addition, it is clear that mycophagy influences reproductive strategies, social structure, and social organization. In this chapter I will synthesize the results of this project from ecological, evolutionary, and conservation perspectives. The goal of this synthesis is to make recommendations for future studies that will improve our understanding not just of callimicos but of primates in general.

DIET

Since the completion of this study, two additional research projects have investigated the diet of callimicos: my own study of a second group in Bolivia (with observations taken in 2002 and 2003), and a study by Rehg at a site in the state of Acre, Brazil, completed in 2003. Callimicos consumed large quantities of fungi in both of these studies. My work shows that 38% of this second Bolivian groups' diet is fungi (Porter, Sterr, and Garber in prep.) and

Rehg's work shows 19% of her Brazilian groups' diet is fungi (Rehg 2003). Thus, mycophagy appears to be part of the normal callimico diet in different years and study sites. Additional studies of callimicos in the north of their range in Colombia are needed to confirm whether mycophagy is a consistent feeding strategy across its entire distribution range.

Given that mycophagy is common among callimicos at least in the southern part of its range, it remains to be determined how they are able to digest this low-quality resource. Other mycophagous mammals have specialized digestive tracts to house microbes that aid in the digestion of the protein and structural carbohydrates found in fungi. Anatomical studies are needed to determine if the callimico's gut has similar adaptations for mycophagy. In addition, given the close genetic relationship between callimicos and marmosets, it is important to consider whether a gut designed for gummivory is also useful for digesting fungi. This may be an example of an exaptation, whereby traits that evolved for one particular purpose (gummivory), are by chance useful for another purpose entirely (mycophagy). In a study of marmosets in Brazil, Mestre Correa (1995) found that the buffy tufted-ear marmoset (*Callithrix aurita*) diet was 12% fungi, making it the only other primate for which high amounts of mycophagy have been reported in South America. The observations of mycophagy in a marmoset, known to be a specialized gummivore, suggest that a gut designed for digesting exudates may also serve for digesting fungi. This possibility needs to be tested through comparative anatomy studies and digestive trials of gum and fungi in different callitrichids.

HABITAT USE

Callimicos do not inhabit bamboo forests exclusively but can be found in areas with a mixed set of habitats including primary, secondary, bamboo, and stream-edge forests. Census data of many sites in the Pando (reviewed in Chapter 7), indicate that callimico densities increase where bamboo availability increases. The correlation between the abundance of callimico and the abundance of bamboo needs to be confirmed with further study across sites where habitat abundance and other factors, such as forest disturbance due to logging, pasture, hunting, and agriculture, are also taken into consideration. In addition, it is important to assess whether callimico home-range sizes change according to habitat availability. If home-range sizes decrease in a given habitat, then population densities have the potential to increase in areas containing an abundance of that habitat.

Only when data from several sites and several groups are collected will it be possible to assess the breadth of habitat tolerance of this species. Even at one study site, habitat use and availability may vary considerably among neighboring groups. The data presented in Chapter 4 demonstrate that callimicos use primary forest with dense understory during 76% of observations and bamboo (10%), stream-edge (8%), and secondary forest (2%) during the remainder of observations. In contrast, a neighboring group of callimico I have studied recently (Porter, Sterr, and Garber in prep.) used secondary forests most frequently (50% of observations), and primary forest with dense understory (30%), bamboo forest (17%), primary forest with open understory (2%), and stream-edge forest (1%) less often. Rehg's work (2003) shows her callimico study group used bamboo forests (secondary bamboo, taboca, and disturbed bamboo) during 58% of observations, and primary forest with dense understory (disturbed primary, tree falls, and primary thick understory) during 37% of observations. Although studies of three groups at two sites do not provide sufficient data to accurately assess the species' habitat needs across its entire distribution range, these data suggest that forests containing dense understory habitats with wet areas, frequent tree falls, and bamboo can be used with various levels of intensity by callimicos.

REPRODUCTIVE STRATEGIES

Callimico reproductive strategies are like the other callitrichids in several respects: groups may contain just one breeding female; all group members help with the transport and sharing of food with infants; and females have the potential for biannual births. These similarities exist despite their fundamental difference in litter size—callimicos, unlike all other callitrichids, almost never twin (Warneke 1992). Communal care strategies among callitrichids are thought to have evolved in order to permit high reproductive output in response to high mortality, and as a strategy for rapidly colonizing new habitats when they become available (Garber 1997). Communal care provides one mechanism whereby females can produce twins (rather than the normal single births of all other anthropoids) and have short interbirth intervals by becoming pregnant while lactating, due to their ability to leave infant transport up to other group members. This system provides females with the potential for biannual births. Caretakers are considered necessary in this strategy as a breeding female alone would not have enough energy to lactate, transport rapidly growing twin infants, and be pregnant simultaneously. The observation of communal care in callimicos indicates that twinning is not necessary to explain this behavior, and that communal care occurs even within a single-birth strategy.

In this study, one breeding female had a single offspring every six months, giving her a reproductive output of two infants per year. Tamarins, although they have the potential for biannual births, generally have twins just once a year, giving them a reproductive output of two infants per year, similar to callimicos (Dietz, Baker, and Miglioretti 1994; Goldizen et al. 1996; Savage et al. 1996). It is only the marmosets, which have both twins and biannual births, that regularly surpass the callimicos' reproductive output, as marmosets can produce four infants per year (Digby 1995). It is thought that the greater occurrence of biannual births among marmosets is due to their ability to create exudate feeding sites, giving them a steady, year-round source of food. In contrast, tamarins experience periods of food shortage, and at least in one study were shown to lose substantial amounts of weight during the dry season, a pattern that limits biannual births only to years of exceptional food availability (Goldizen et al. 1988).

Callimicos, like marmosets, have a reliable year-long food source in fungi, and this may explain their ability to reproduce twice per year. It is unclear, however, if biannual births occur regularly. During my postdoctoral research, I followed one group of callimicos for an entire year and biannual births did not occur. Following the birth of an infant in August, the group's sole adult female was not observed with an infant for the next year (Porter and Garber in prep.). Thus, additional long-term data are needed to determine how often biannual and annual births occur in callimico populations.

Regardless of whether callimicos are regularly capable of biannual births, why would they have single infants rather than twins? It may be that having single infants allows parents and other group members to invest more heavily in an offspring, giving it a greater chance of surviving to maturity. Callimico infants have higher rates of infant development and reach sexual maturity faster than other callitrichids (Garber and Leigh 1997), a pattern that may be possible due to greater access to milk and solid foods shared by group members. Greater investment in single offspring in turn may be possible if predation rates are lower for callimicos than for other callitrichids. Given their extremely cryptic nature, their use of dense vegetation, and high scanning rates, infants might have greater chances of survival than infants in other callitrichid species. The results of this study do not support this hypothesis, however, as one infant and one juvenile disappeared during the course of the study period, and an additional infant disappeared two months later (see Chapter 6). It is likely that these disappearances were a result of predation or disease. With long-term data it will be possible to compare survival rates among populations of callimicos and other callitrichids. Further investigation into the factors that influence litter size, growth, and parental investment in callimicos will provide important clues toward explaining the evolution of life history among all primates. Currently, the reasons callimicos have single births are still unclear.

SOCIAL ORGANIZATION

Callimicos, like all other callitrichids, appear to have a flexible social organization, with monogamy, polyandry, and polygynandry all possible. Groups of callimicos of all sizes have been observed in the wild, including groups with as few as two adults to as many as nine adults (see Table 7–1). In addition, in groups with two adult females, some groups have just one breeding female, whereas others have two (see Chapter 6). In a recent study of callimicos, we were able to identify individual group members, and found that the group was polyandrous. One adult female mated with two adult males, and both males helped transport and share food with the female's infant (Porter and Garber in prep.), indicating that callimicos, like other callitrichids, benefits from communal care.

Detailed studies of social behaviors are needed to understand the relationships among group members, and the circumstances that lead callimicos to form polyandrous, monogamous, or promiscuous social groups. For example, it is unclear if groups with several adult males have one male that consistently can impregnate the female. In groups with two breeding females, it is uncertain if the females are mother-daughter pairs or unrelated individuals. In addition, it is unknown if group members invest differentially in infant care, and if so whether the differences are due to their degree of relatedness to the infants, or their relationship with the dominant female. Studies of genetic relatedness among group members can help answer these questions and address the evolution of social behaviors in the context of kin selection and/or sexual selection. Data on emigration and immigration between callimico groups is also necessary to understand their social behavior. If dispersal opportunities are limited, adults may choose to cooperate with the group's dominant individuals while waiting for breeding opportunities to arise, or they may choose to compete with dominant individuals to obtain breeding rights in the same group.

CALLIMICOS AND THE ADAPTIVE RADIATION OF CALLITRICHIDS

The members of the family Callitrichidae are a highly successful radiation that are distributed from Panama throughout the Amazon basin and the Atlantic coastal forests of Brazil. The success of the callitrichid lineage is likely due to their flexibility in social and reproductive strategies and their ability to consume a wide variety of foods in a diverse set of habitats. All callitrichids are capable of using secondary and disturbed forest, a characteristic that likely provided them with a means of avoiding competition with other larger-bodied platyrrhines that rely more heavily on undisturbed forest. Within this radiation, callimicos evolved their own distinctive specializations that provided them with their own ecological niche, that of the understory specialist (Table 8–1).

Although the small body size, inconspicuous coloration, and timid nature of callimicos have led some people to regard them as an insignificant twig on the primate evolutionary tree, the results of my research and other recent studies have revealed that callimicos provide an interesting model for addressing questions concerning the evolution of life history variables and niche specialization. Chaves and colleagues (1999) suggest

Table 8–1 Comparison of ecological specializations among callitrichids[1]

Genus	Habitat preference	Height preference[†]	Dietary niche
Callimico	Mixed—Bamboo, Stream, 1°	Understory–lower canopy	Fungi
Saguinus	Edge, 2° (Rylands 1996)	Lower-middle canopy	Omnivory
Mico	Edge, 2°*	Middle canopy (Heymann and Buchanan-Smith 1997)	Exudates*
Callithrix	Dry, Seasonal (Rylands 1996)	Understory-middle canopy (Rylands 1982; Ferrari, 1988)	Exudates*
Cebuella	Inundated, Riverine (Rylands 1996)	Understory-lower canopy (Youlatos 1999)	Exudates*
Leontopithecus	1°*	Lower-middle canopy (Kierulff et al. 2002)	Omnivory*

[†] Understory 0–5 m; lower canopy 5–10 m; middle canopy 10–15 m

* From Rylands et al. 2000

[1]Modified from Porter, L.M. and P. A. Garber. 2004.

that the earliest callitrichids date to around 14 Mya, and that the ancestor of callimicos diverged from the marmoset lineage around 11 Mya. Thus, the specializations we see among callimicos—principally: reduced litter size, specialized limbs for trunk-to-trunk leaping in the understory, and mycophagy—likely represent adaptations established over several million years. The study of callimico ecology, anatomy, and reproductive biology will help determine the evolutionary mechanisms by which callimicos were able to diverge from an ancestral callitrichid population into an understory, mycophagous animal.

CONSERVATION

The northwestern region of Pando, Bolivia, the southeastern region of Acre, Brazil, and the eastern portion of the Madre de Dios, Peru, are the only areas where callimicos are well documented. Without more information on species distribution and density in other areas, it is impossible to know how well-protected it is across its range, and what other sites might effectively help to protect substantial numbers of the species. As Defler (2003) writes of callimicos in Colombia, "A first step for the conservation and management of Goeldi's monkey [callimico] is a detailed knowledge of the precise locus of all known populations, so that each can be protected" (p. 15). Currently we have detailed data of only two populations—those between the Acre and Tahuamanu Rivers in Bolivia, and those further to the northeast in the state of Acre, Brazil. This represents an extremely small portion of the species' entire geographic range; more

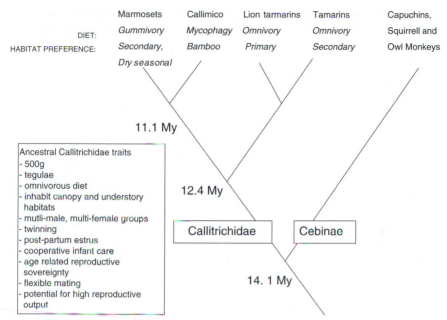

Figure 8–1 Phyologenetic tree for the callitrichids, including the divergence of dietary and forest niches among taxa. From Porter and Garber 2004, used with permission from Wiley-Liss Publishers

studies are needed across the northern and western edge of the Amazon basin.

Taped playbacks of callimico contact calls (Christen 1999; Christen and Geissmann 1994) or an experienced guide's imitations of callimico and tamarin long calls (Porter 2006) are particularly useful for locating wild callimico groups, as they often responded to these vocalizations, and are easier to hear than to observe. Using these techniques it may be possible to more accurately determine the geographic range limits and densities of callimicos. In addition, although surveys in the wet season are logistically difficult due to frequent rains, observations of callimicos are likely to be easier at this time than in the dry season as they use open habitats more, associate more frequently with tamarins, and forage more frequently for fruits higher in the canopy.

In addition to determining the geographic limits of its range, two other factors need to be established in order to adequately plan for the conservation of callimicos. First, do callimicos represent a single species across the Amazon, or are different species or subspecies present in different regions? Using genetic data from animals in different regions of the Amazon, it should be possible to determine if callimicos represent a single, continuous population. Second, the reasons for the species' patchy distribution across its range should be established. Does the abundance of bamboo, streams, and tree falls create its patchy distribution pattern across its distribution range as my data indicates?

The forests of the Amazon are under increasing pressure from anthropogenic disturbance. Ranching, in particular, is taking an increasingly high toll on Amazon forests, and threatens to reduce the biodiversity and abundance of monkeys. Callimicos can tolerate—and indeed may benefit from—small-scale disturbance of the forest; however, they will go extinct if the Amazon forests are permanently converted into pasture and agricultural land. In addition, rising population growth and immigration into the Amazon basin will necessitate greater food production and the creation of employment opportunities. Balancing the needs of humans with that of the flora and fauna in the Amazon will not be easy but the establishment of programs that promote conservation and sustainable development are essential if callimicos and the ecosystems they are found in are to survive into the twenty-second century.

References Cited

Abbott, D. H., J. Barrett, and L. M. George. 1993. Comparative aspects of the social suppression of reproduction in female marmosets and tamarins. In *Marmosets and tamarins: Systematics, behavior and ecology*, ed. A. B. Rylands, 152–163. New York: Oxford University Press.

Alverson, W., D. Moskovitz, and J. Shopland (eds.). 2000. *Rapid Biological Inventory: Northwestern Pando, Bolivia*. Report 01. Chicago: Chicago Field Museum.

Alverson, W., D. Moskovits, and I. Halm (eds.). 2003a. *Rapid Biological Inventory: Bolivia Pando, Madre de Dios*. Report 05. Chicago: Chicago Field Museum.

Alverson, W., D. Moskovits, and I. Halm (eds.). 2003b. *Rapid Biological Inventory: Bolivia Pando, Frederico Roman*. Report 06. Chicago: Chicago Field Museum.

Anderson, A. (Ed.). 1990a. *Alternatives to deforestation: Steps toward sustainable use of the Amazon rain forest*. New York: Columbia University Press.

Anderson, A. 1990b. Deforestation in Amazonia: Dynamics, causes and alternatives. In *Alternatives to deforestation: Steps towards sustainable use of the Amazon rain forest*, ed. A. Anderson, 3–24. New York: Columbia University Press.

Arita, H., J. Robinson, and K. Redford. 1990. Rarity in Neotropical forest mammals and its ecological correlates. *Conservation Biology* 4:181–192.

Azvedo Lopes, M., and J. Rehg. 2004. Observations of *Callimico goeldii* with *Saguinus imperator* in the Serra do Divisor National Park, Acre, Brazil. *Neotropical Primates* 11:181–183.

Bales, K., J. Dietz, A. Baker, K. Miller, and S. Tardif. 2000. Effects of allocare-givers on fitness of infants and parents in callitrichid primates. *Folia Primatologica* 71:27–38.

Barroso, C., H. Schneider, M. Schneider, S. I. M. Harada, J. Czelusniak, and M. Goodman. 1997. Update on the systematics of New World monkeys: Further DNA evidence for placing the pygmy marmoset (*Cebuella*) within the genus *Callithrix*. *International Journal of Primatology* 18:651–674.

Barton, R., A. Whiten, S. C. Strum, R. W. Byrne, and A. J. Simpson. 1992. Habitat use and resource availability in baboons. *Animal Behaviour* 43:831–844.

Beck, B., D. Anderson, J. Ogden, B. Rettberg, C. Brejla, R. Scola, and M. Warneke. 1982. Breeding the Goeldi's monkey at Brookfield Zoo, Chicago. *International Zoo Yearbook* 22:106–114.

Begon, M., J. L. Harper, and C. R. Townsend. 1986. *Ecology: Individuals, populations and communities*. Oxford: Blackwell.

Bergallo, H., and C. Rocha. 1994. Spatial and trophic niche differentiation in two sympatric lizards (*Tropidurus torquatus* and *Cnedmidophorus ocellifer*) with different foraging tactics. *Australian Journal of Ecology* 19:72–75.

Bermejo, M., G. Illera, and J. Sabater Pi. 1994. Animals and mushrooms consumed by bonobos (*Pan paniscus*): New records from Lilungu (Ikela), Zaire. *International Journal of Primatology* 15:879–898.

Bicca-Marcques, J. C., and P. A. Garber. 2003. Experimental field study of the relative costs and benefits of wild tamarins (*Saguinus imperator* and *S. fuscicollis*) of exploiting contestable food patches as single- and mixed-species troops. *American Journal of Primatology* 60:139–153.

Bicca-Marques, J. C. 1999. Hand specialization, sympatry, and mixed-species associations in callitrichines. *Journal of Human Evolution* 36:349–378.

Bicca-Marques, J. C. 2003. Sexual selection and foraging behavior in male and female tamarins and marmosets. In *Sexual selection and reproductive competition in primates: New perspectives and directions*, ed. C. Jones, 455–475. Norman, Oklahoma: American Society of Primatologists.

Boinski, S. 1987. Birth synchrony in squirrel monkeys (*Saimiri oerstedii*). *Behavioral Ecology and Sociobiology* 21:393–400.

Brown, A., and D. Rumiz. 1985. Distribución y conservación de los primates en Bolivia—estado actual de su conocimiento. *A Primatologia no Brasil*, 1:335–363. Belo Horizonte: Fundação Biodiversitas and Socieda de Brasilera de Primatologia.

Buchanan-Smith, H. 1990. Polyspecific association of two tamarin species, *Saguinus labiatus* and *Saguinus fuscicollis*, in Bolivia. *American Journal of Primatology* 22:205–214.

Buchanan-Smith, H. M. 1991a. Field observations of Goeldi's monkey, *Callimico goeldii*, in northern Bolivia. *Folia Primatologica* 57:102–105.

Buchanan-Smith, H. M. 1991b. A field study on the red-bellied tamarin, *Saguinus labiatus*, in Bolivia. *International Journal of Primatology* 12:259–276.

Buchanan-Smith, H. M. 1999. Tamarin polyspecific associations: Forest utilization and stability of mixed-species groups. *Primates* 40:233–247.

Buchanan-Smith, H. M., S. M. Hardie, C. Caceres, and M. J. Prescott. 2000. Distribution and forest utilization of *Saguinus* and other primates of the Pando Department, northern Bolivia. *International Journal of Primatology* 21(3):353–379.

Buchanan-Smith, H. M., S. M. Hardie, M. Prescott, J. Stronge, and M. Challis. 1996. Callitrichids at the Belfast Zoo, North Ireland. *Neotropical Primates* 4:143–146.

Burt, W. 1943. Territoriality and home range concepts as applied to mammals. *Journal of Mammalogy* 24:346–352.

Caine, N. G. 1993. Flexibility and co-operation as unifying themes in *Saguinus* social organization and behaviour: The role of predation pressure. In *Marmosets and tamarins: Systematics, behavior and ecology*, ed. A. B. Rylands, 200–219. New York: Oxford University Press.

Caine, N. G. 1984. Visual scanning by tamarins. *Folia Primatologica* 43:59–67.

Cameron, R., and H. M. Buchanan-Smith. 1991–1992. Primates of the Pando, Bolivia. *Primate conservation* 12–13:11–14.

Cameron, R., C. Wiltshire, C. Foley, N. Dougherty, X. Aramayo, and L. Rea. 1989. Goeldi's monkey and other primates in northern Bolivia. *Primate Conservation* 10:62–70.

Cannon, C., and M. Leighton. 1994. Comparative locomotor ecology of gibbons and macaques: Selection of canopy elements for crossing gaps. *American Journal of Physical Anthropology* 93:505–524.

Carroll, J. B. 1982. Maintenance of the Goeldi's monkey at Jersey Wildlife Preservation Trust. *International Zoo Yearbook* 22:101–105.

Carroll, J. B. 1985. Pair bonding in the Goeldi's Monkey. *Dodo: Jersey Wildlife Preservation Trust* 22:57–71.

Carroll, J. B. 1988. The stability of multifemale groups of Goeldi's monkey, *Callimico goeldii* in captivity. *Dodo* 25:37–43.

Carroll, J. B., D. Abbott, L. M. George, J. E. Hindle, and R. D. Martin. 1990. Urinary endocrine monitoring of the ovarian cycle and pregnancy in Goeldi's monkey (*Callimico goeldii*). *Journal of Reproduction and Fertility* 89:149–161.

Cartmill, M. 1974. Pads and claws in arboreal locomotion. In *Primate locomotion*, ed. F. Jenkins, 45–83. New York: Academic Press.

Chapman, C. A. 1987. Flexibility in the diets of three species of Costa Rican primates. *Folia Primatologica* 49(2):90–105.

Chapman, C. A., and L. J. Chapman. 1991. The foraging itinerary of spider monkeys: When to eat leaves? *Folia Primatologica* 56:162–166.

Chapman, C. A., and L. J. Chapman. 1996. Mixed-species primate groups in the Kibale Forest: Ecological constraints on association. *International Journal of Primatology* 17:31–50.

Chapman, C. A., and L. J. Chapman. 2000. Interdemic variation in mixed-species association patterns: Common diurnal primates of Kibale National Park, Uganda. *Behavioral Ecology and Sociobiology* 47:129–139.

Chapman, C. A., and L. M. Fedigan. 1990. Dietary differences between neighboring *Cebus capucinus* groups: Local traditions, food availability or response to food profitability. *Folia Primatologica* 54:177–186.

Chaves, R., I. Sampaio, M. Schneider, H. Schneider, S. Page, and M. Goodman. 1999. The place of *Callimico goeldii* in the Callitrichinae phylogenetic tree: Evidence from the von Willebrand Factor gene intron II sequences. *Molecular Phylogenetics and Evolution* 13(2):392–404.

Chernoff, B., and P. Willink. 1999. *A Biological assessment of the aquatic ecosystems of the Upper Rio Orthon Basin, Pando, Bolivia* (Bulletin of Biological Assessment 15). Washington, DC: Conservation International.

Christen, A. 1998. The most enigmatic monkey in the Bolivian rain-forest—*Callimico goeldii*. *Neotropical Primates* 6(2):35–37.

Christen, A. 1999. Survey of Goeldi's monkeys (*Callimico goeldii*) in northern Bolivia. *Folia Primatologica* 70:107–111.

Christen, A., and T. Geissmann. 1994. A primate survey in northern Bolivia, with special reference to Goeldi's monkey, *Callimico goeldii*. *International Journal of Primatology* 15:239–273.

Churchfield, S., V. Nesterenko, and E. Shvarts. 1999. Food niche overlap and ecological separation amongst six species of coexisting forest shrews (Insectivora: Soricidae) in the Russian Far East. *Journal of Zoology London* 248:349–359.

Claridge, A., and T. May. 1994. Mycophagy among Australian mammals. *Australian Journal of Ecology* 19:251–275.

Claridge, A., J. Trappe, S. Cork, and D. Claridge. 1999. Mycophagy by small mammals in the coniferous forests of North America: Nutritional value of sporocarps of *Rhizopogon vinicolor*, a common hypogeous fungus. *Journal of Comparative Physiology B* 169:172–178.

Clutton-Brock, T. H. 1977a. A comparative study of the feeding strategies of two sympatric species of leaf monkeys: *Presbytis senex* and *Presbytis entellus*. In *Primate ecology: Studies of feeding and ranging behaviour in lemurs, monkeys and apes*, ed. T. Clutton-Brock, 323–353. New York: Academic Press.

Clutton-Brock, T. H. 1977b. Some aspects of intraspecific variation in feeding and ranging behaviour in primates. In *Primate ecology*, ed. T. Clutton-Brock, 504–538. London: Academic Press.

Clutton-Brock, T. H., and P. H. Harvey. 1977. Species differences in feeding and ranging behaviour in primates. In *Primate ecology: Studies of feeding and ranging behavior in lemurs, monkeys and apes*, ed. T. Clutton-Brock, 557–584. New York: Academic Press.

Cody, M. 1986. Diversity, rarity, and conservation in Mediterranean-climate regions. In *Conservation Biology: The Science of Scarcity and Diversity*, edited by M. Soulé. Sunderland, MA: Sinauer Associates, Inc.,

Coimbra-Filho, A. 1977. Natural shelters of *Leontopithecus rosalia* and some ecological implications (Callitrichidae: Primates). In *The biology and conservation of the Callitrichidae*, ed. D. Kleiman, 79–89. Washington, DC: Smithsonian Institution Press.

Conklin-Brittain, N., R. Wrangham, and K. Hunt. 1998. Dietary response of chimpanzees and cercopithecines to seasonal variation in fruit abundance. II. Macronutrients. *International Journal of Primatology* 19:971–997.

Cords, M. 1987. *Mixed-species association of* Cercopithecus *monkeys in the Kakamega Forest, Kenya*, Vol. 117. Berkeley: University of California Publications in Zoology.

Cords, M. 1990a. Mixed-species association of East African guenons: General patterns or specific examples? *American Journal of Primatology* 21:101–114.

Cords, M. 1990b. Vigilance and mixed-species association of some East African forest monkeys. *Behavioral Ecology and Sociobiology* 26:297–300.

Cowlishaw, G., and R. Dunbar. 2000. *Primate conservation biology*. Chicago: Chicago University Press.

Cracraft, J., and F. Grifo. 1999. *The living planet in crisis*. New York: Columbia University Press.

Crandlemire-Sacco, J. 1986. *The ecology of the saddle-backed tamarin* (Saguinus fuscicollis), *of southeastern Peru*. Pittsburgh: University of Pittsburgh.

Davies, K., C. Margules, and J. Lawerence. 2000. Which traits of species predict population declines in experimental forest fragments? *Ecology* 81:1450–1461.

Davis, L. M. 1996. Functional and phylogenetic implications of ankle morphology in Goeldi's Monkey (*Callimico goeldii*). In *Adaptive radiations of Neotropical primates*, ed. M. Norconk, A. Rosenberger, and P. Garber, 134–156. New York: Plenum Press.

Davis, L. M. 2002. *Functional morphology of the forelimb and long bones in the Callitrichidae (Platyrrhini: Primates)*. Ph.D. thesis, Southern Illinois University at Carbondale.

Dawson, G. 1979. The use of time and space by the Panamanian tamarin, *Saguinus oedipus*. *Folia Primatologica* 31:253–284.

Day, R., and R. Elwood. 1999. Sleeping site selection by the golden-handed tamarin *Saguinus midas midas*: The role of predation risk, proximity to feeding sites, and territorial defense. *Ethology* 105(12):1035–1051.

De Vleeschouwer, K., K. Leus, and L. Van Elsacker. 2003. Characteristics of reproductive biology and proximate factors regulating seasonal breeding in captive golden-headed lion tamarins (*Leontopithecus chrysomelas*). *American Journal of Primatology* 60:123–137.

Defler, T. R. 2003. Conservation priorities for Colombian primates. *Primate Conservation* 19:10–18.

Demes, B., W. L. Jungers, T. S. Gross, and J. G. Fleagle. 1995. Kinetics of leaping primates: Influences of substrate orientation and compliance. *American Journal of Physical Anthropology* 96:419–429.

Dettling, A., and C. R. Pryce. 1999. Hormonal monitoring of age at sexual maturation in female Goeldi's Monkeys (*Callimico goeldii*) in their family groups. *American Journal of Primatology* 48:77–83.

Dew, J. L., and P. C. Wright. 1998. Frugivory and seed dispersal by four species of primates in Madagascar's eastern rain forest. *Biotropica* 30:425–437.

Diamond, J. 1980. Patchy distributions of tropical birds. In *Conservation biology*, ed. M. Soulé and B. Wilcox, 57–74. Sunderland, MA: Sinauer Associates.

DiBitetti, M. S., and C. H. Janson. 2000. When will the stork arrive? Patterns of birth seasonality in Neotropical primates. *American Journal of Primatology* 50:109–130.

DiBitteti, M. S., E. M. L. Vidal, M. C. Baldovino, and V. Benesovsky. 2000. Sleeping site preferences in tufted capuchin monkeys (*Cebus apella nigritus*). *American Journal of Primatology* 50:257–274.

Dietz, J., and A. Baker. 1993. Polygyny and female reproductive success in golden lion tamarins, *Leontopithecus rosalia*. *Animal Behavior* 46:1067–1078.

Dietz, J. M., A. J. Baker, and D. Miglioretti. 1994. Seasonal variation in reproduction, juvenile growth, and adult body mass in golden lion tamarins (*Leontopithecus rosalia*). *American Journal of Primatology* 34:115–132.

Digby, L. J. 1995. Infant care, infanticide, and female reproductive strategies in polygynous groups of common marmosets (*Callithrix jacchus*). *Behavioral Ecology and Sociobiology* 37:51–61.

Digby, L. J. 1999. Sexual behavior and extragroup copulations in a wild population of common marmosets (*Callithrix jacchus*). *Folia Primatologica* 70:136–145.

Digby, L. J., and S. F. Ferrari. 1994. Multiple breeding females in free-ranging groups of *Callithrix jacchus*. *International Journal of Primatology* 15:389–397.

Digby, L., and W. Saltzman. In prep. Balancing cooperation and competition in callitrichine primates: Examining the relative risk of infanticide across species. In *The smallest anthropoids: The marmoset/callimico radiation*, ed. L. C. Davis, S. M. Ford, and L. M. Porter. New York: Springer.

Dobson, F., and J. Yu. 1993. Rarity in Neotropical forest mammals revisited. *Conservation Biology* 7:586–591.

Dunbar, R. I. M. 1992. A model of the gelada socio-ecological system. *Primates* 33: 69–83.

Dunbar, R. I. M. 1995. The mating system of callitrichid primates: II. The impact of helpers. *Animal Behaviour* 50:1071–1089.

Dunbar, R. I. M., and Dunbar, P. 1988. Maternal time budgets of gelada baboons. *Animal Behavior* 36:970–980.

Eeley, H., and M. Lawes. 1999. Large-scale patterns of species richness and species range size in anthropoid primates. In *Primate communities*, ed. J. Fleagle, C. Janson, and K. Reed, 191–219. Cambridge: Cambridge University Press.

Emmons, L. 1999. Of mice and monkeys: Primates as predictors of mammal community richness. In *Primate communities*, ed. J. Fleagle, C. Janson, and K. Reed, 171–188. Cambridge: Cambridge University Press.

Emmons, L., and F. Feer. 1997. *Neotropical rainforest mammals*. Chicago: The University of Chicago Press.

Encarnación, F., and E. W. Heymann. 1998. Body mass of wild *Callimico goeldii*. *Folia Primatologica* 69:368–371.

Estrada, A., S. Juan-Solano, T. Ortiz Martinez, and R. Coates- Estrada. 1999. Feeding and general activity patterns of a howler monkey (*Alouatta palliata*) troop living in a forest fragment at Los Tuxtlas, Mexico. *American Journal of Primatology* 48(3):167–183.

Faminow, M. D. 1998. Cattle, deforestation, and development in the Amazon: An economic, agronomic, and environmental perspective. New York: CAB International.

Fashing, P., and M. Cords. 2000. Diurnal primate densities and biomass in the Kakamega Forest: An evaluation of census methods and a comparison with other forests. *American Journal of Primatology* 50:139–152.

Ferrari, S. 1988. *The behaviour and ecology of the buffy-headed marmoset,* Callithrix flaviceps (O. Thomas, 1903). Ph.D. thesis, University College London.

Ferrari, S. 1992. The care of infants in a wild marmoset (*Callithrix flaviceps*) group. *American Journal of Primatology* 26:109–118.

Ferrari, S. F. 1993. Ecological differentiation in the Callitrichidae. In *Marmosets and tamarins, sytstematics, behaviour, and ecology*, ed. A. B. Rylands, 314–328. Oxford: Oxford University Press.

Ferrari, S. F., M. Aparecida Lopes and A. Krause. 1993. Gut morphology of *Callithrix nigriceps* and *Saguinus labiatus* from western Brazilian Amazonia. *American Journal of Physical Anthropology* 90:487–493.

Ferrari, S. F., F. S. Iwanaga, E. M. Ramos, M. R. Messias, P. C. Ramos, and E. da Cruz Neto. 1998. Expansion of the known distribution of Goeldi's monkey (*Callimico goeldii*) in Southwestern Brazilian Amazon. *Folia Primatologica* 70:112–116.

Ferrari, S. F., and M. Lopes Ferrari. 1989. A re-evaluation of the social organization of the Callitrichidae, with reference to the ecological differences between genera. *Folia Primatologica* 52:132–147.

Ferrari, S. F., and M. Lopes Ferrari. 1990. Predator avoidance behavior in the buffy-headed marmoset, *Callithrix flaviceps*. *Primates* 31(3):323–338.

Ferrari, S. F. and E. Martins. 1992. Gummivory and gut morphology in two sympatric callitrichids (*Callithrix emiliae* and *Saguinus fuscicollis weddelli*) from western Brazilian Amazonia. *American Journal of Physical Anthropology* 88:97–103.

Fifer, J. 1972. *Bolivia: Land, location and politics since 1825*. Cambridge: Cambridge University Press.

Fitzgibbon, C. D. 1990. Mixed-species grouping in Thomson's and Grant's gazelles: The antipredator benefits. *Animal Behavior* 31:1116–112.

Fleagle, J. G. 1999. *Primate adaptation and evolution*, 2nd ed. San Diego: Academic Press.

Fleagle, J. G., R. F. Kay, and M. R. L. Anthony. 1997. Fossil New World monkeys. In *Vertebrate paleontology in the Neotropics: The Miocene fauna of La Venta, Colombia*, ed. R. Kay, R. Madden, R. Cifelli, and J. Flynn, 473–495. Washington, DC: Smithsonian Institution Press.

Fleagle, J. G., and R. A. Mittermeier. 1980. Locomotor, behavior, body size, and comparative ecology of seven Surinam monkeys. *American Journal of Physical Anthropology* 52:301–314.

Ford, S. M. 1986. Systematics of the New World monkeys. In *Comparative primate biology*, ed. D. Swindler and J. Erwin, 73–135. Vol. 1, *Systematics, evolution and anatomy*. New York: Alan R. Liss.

Ford, S. M. 1994. Taxonomy and distribution of the owl monkey. In *Aotus: The owl monkey*, ed. J. Baer, R. Weller, and I. Kakoma, 1–57. San Diego: Academic Press.

Ford, S. M. In prep. Biogeographic patterns of the Atelinae across the northern tier of South America.

Ford, S., and L. Davis. 1992. Systematics and body size: Implications for feeding adaptations in New World monkeys. *American Journal of Physical Anthropology* 88:415–468.

Fragaszy, D. M., J. Baer, and L. Adams-Curtis. 1991. Behavioral development and maternal care in tufted capuchins (*Cebus apella*) and squirrel monkeys (*Saimiri sciureus*) from birth through seven months. *Developmental Psychobiology* 24:375–393.

Freese, C., P. Heltne, N. Castro, and G. Whitesides. 1982. Patterns and determinants of monkey densities in Peru and Bolivia, with notes on distributions. *International Journal of Primatology* 3(1):53–90.

French, J. A., and B. J. Inglett. 1989. Female-female aggression and male indifferences in response to unfamiliar intruders in lion tamarins. *Animal Behaviour* 37:487–497.

Ganzhorn, J. U. 1988. Food partitioning among Malagasy primates. *Oecologica* 75:436–450.

Ganzhorn, J. U., and P. C. Wright. 1994. Temporal patterns in primate leaf eating: The possible role of leaf chemistry. *Folia Primatologica* 63:203–208.

Garber, P. A. 1980. Locomotor behavior and feeding ecology of the Panamanian tamarin (*Saguinus oedipus geoffroyi*, Callitrichidae, Primates). *International Journal of Primatology* 1:185–201.

Garber, P. A. 1984. Proposed nutritional importance of plant exudates in the diet of the Panamanian tamarin, *Saguinus oedipus geoffroyi. International Journal of Primatology* 5:1–15.

Garber, P. A. 1988a. Diet, foraging patterns, and resource defense in a mixed species troop of *Saguinus mystax* and *Saguinus fuscicollis* in Amazonian Peru. *Behavior* 105:18–34.

Garber, P. A. 1988b. Foraging decisions during nectar feeding by tamarin monkeys (*Saguinus mystax* and *Saguinus fuscicollis,* Callitirichidae, Primates) in Amazonian Peru. *Biotropica* 20:100–106.

Garber, P. A. 1992. Vertical clinging, small body size, and the evolution of feeding adaptations in the Callitrichinae. *American Journal of Physical Anthropology* 88:469–482.

Garber, P. A. 1993. Feeding ecology and behavior of the genus *Saguinus.* In *Marmosets and tamarins: Systematics, behavior and ecology* ed. A. B. Rylands, 273–295. New York: Oxford University Press.

Garber, P. A. 1994. Phylogenetic approach to the study of tamarin and marmoset social systems. *American Journal of Primatology* 34:199–219.

Garber, P. A. 1996. The ecology of seed dispersal in two species of callitrichid primates (*Saguinus mystax* and *Saguinus fuscicollis*). *American Journal of Primatology* 10:155–170.

Garber, P. A. 1997. One for all and breeding for one: Cooperation and competition as a tamarin reproductive strategy. *Evolutionary Anthropology* 5:187–199.

Garber, P. A., and J. Bicca-Marques. 2002. Evidence of predator sensitive foraging in small and large-scale space in free-ranging tamarins (*Saguinus fuscicollis, Saguinus imperator* and *Saguinus mystax*). In *Eat or be eaten: Predator sensitive foraging in primates,* ed. L. Miller, 138–153. Cambridge: Cambridge University Press.

Garber, P. A., G. E. Blomquist, and G. Anzenberger. 2005. Kinematic analysis of trunk-to-trunk leaping in *Callimico goeldii. International Journal of Primatology* 26:223–240.

Garber, P. A., F. Encarnación, L. Moya, and J. Pruetz. 1993. Demographic and reproductive patterns in moustached tamarin monkeys (*Saguinus mystax*): Implications of reconstructing platyrrhine mating systems. *Amercian Journal of Primatology* 29:235–254.

Garber, P. A., and S. Leigh. 1997. Ontogenetic variation in small- bodied New World primates: Implications for patterns of reproduction and infant care. *Folia Primatologica* 68:1–22.

Garber, P. A., and S. Leigh. 2001. Patterns of positional behavior in mixed-species troops of *Callimico goeldii, Saguinus labiatus,* and *Saguinus fuscicollis* in northwestern Brazil. *American Journal of Primatology* 54:17–31.

Gaston, K. 1994. *Rarity.* London: Chapman & Hall.

Gathua, M. 2000. The effects of primates and squirrels on seed survival of a canopy tree, *Afselia quanzensis,* in Arabuko-Sukoke Forest, Kenya. *Biotropica* 32:127–132.

Gause, G. 1934. *The struggle for existence.* Baltimore: Williams and Witkins.

Gautier-Hion, A., J. M. Duplantier, R. Quris, F. Feer, C. Sourd, J. P. Decoux, G. Dubost, L. Emmons, C. Erard, P. Hecketsweiler, A. Moungazi, C. Roussilhon, and J. M. Thiollay. 1985. Fruit characters as a basis of fruit choice and seed dispersal in a tropical forest vertebrate community. *Oecologica* 65:324–337.

Gentry, A., and L. Emmons. 1987. Geographical variation in fertility, phenology, and composition of the understory of Neotropical forests. *Biotropica* 19(3):216–227.

Goldizen, A. W., J. Mendelson, M. van Vlaardingen, and J. Terborgh. 1996. Saddle-back tamarin (*Saguinus fuscicollis*) reproductive strategies: Evidence from a 13-year study of a marked population. *American Journal of Primatology* 38:57–83.

Goldizen, A. W., and J. Terborgh. 1989. Demography and dispersal patterns of a tamarin population: Possible causes of delayed breeding. *American Naturalist* 134(2):208–224.

Goldizen, A. W., J. Terborgh, F. Cornejo, D. Porras, and R. Evans. 1988. Seasonal food shortage, weight loss, and the timing of births in saddle-back tamarins (*Saguinus fuscicollis*). *Journal of Animal Ecology* 57:893–901.

Goldizen, A. W. 1990. A comparative perspective on the evolution of tamarin and marmoset social systems. *International Journal of Primatology* 11:63–83.

Goldsmith, F. 1998. Tropical rain forests—what are they really like? In *Tropical rain forest: A wider perspective*, ed. F. Goldsmith, 1–17. London: Chapman and Hall.

Goodman, S. M., S. O'Conner, and O. Langrand. 1993. A review of predation on lemurs: Implications for the evolution of social behavior in small, nocturnal primates. In *Lemur social systems and their ecological basis*. Ed. P. M. Kappeler, and J. U. Ganzhorn, 51–66. New York: Plenum Press.

Grubb, P., T. Butynski, J. Oates, S. Bearder, T. Disotell, C. Groves, and T. Struhsaker. 2003. Assessment of the diversity of African primates. *International Journal of Primatology* 24(6):1301–1357.

Hamrick, M. 1998. Functional and adaptive significance of primate pads and claws: Evidence from New World anthropoids. *American Journal of Physical Anthropology* 106:113–127.

Hanson, A. M. 2000. *Habitat use in relation to diet, with particular emphasis on mycophagy, by Callimico goeldii in Pando, Bolivia*. Master's thesis, State University of New York at Stony Brook.

Hanson, A. M., M. Hall, L. M. Porter, and B. Lintzenich. 2006. Composition and nutritional characteristics of fungi consumed by *Callimico goeldii* in Pando, Bolivia. *International Journal of Primatology* 27:323–349.

Hanson, A. M., and L. M. Porter. 2000. Nutrient composition and distribution of fungal sporocarps consumed by Goeldi's monkeys in northern Bolivia. *American Journal of Primatology* 51:60.

Hanya, G. 2004a. Diet of a Japanese macaque troop in the coniferous forest of Yakushima. *International Journal of Primatology* 25(1):55–71.

Hanya, G. 2004b Seasonal variations in the activity budget of Japanese macaques in the coniferous forest of Yakushma: effects of food and temperature. *American Journal of Primatology* 63:165–177.

Happel, R., J. Noss, and C. Marsh. 1987. Distribution, abundance, and endangerment of primates. In *Primate conservation in the tropical rain forest*, ed. C. Marsh and R. Mittermeier, 63–82. New York: Alan Liss.

Harcourt, A. H., S. A. Copperto, and S. A. Parks. 2002. Rarity, specialization and extinction in primates. *Journal of Biogeography* 29:445–456.

Hardie, S. M. 1995. Do subordinate female *Callimico* disperse from their social groups? *Folia Primatologica* 64:192–195.

Hardie, S. M. 1998. Mixed-species tamarin groups *Saguinus fuscicollis* and *Saguinus labiatus* in northern Bolivia. *Primate Report* 50:39–62.

Hardie, S., and H. Buchanan-Smith. 1997. Vigilance in single- and mixed-species groups of tamarins (*Saguinus labiatus* and *Saguinus fuscicollis*). *International Journal of Primatology* 18:217–234.

Hartwig, W. C. 1996. Perinatal life history traits in New World monkeys. *American Journal of Primatology* 40:99–130.

Hauser, M. D., M. K. Chen, F. Chen, and E. Chuang. 2003. Give unto others: Genetically unrelated cotton-top tamarin monkeys preferentially give food to those who altruistically give food back. *Proceedings of the Royal Society of London, B* 270:2363–2370.

Heckenberger, M. J., A. Kuikuro, U. T. Kuikoro, J. C. Russell, M. Schmidt, C. Fausto, and B. Franchetto. 2003. Amazonia 1492: Pristine forest or cultural parkland? *Science* 301:1710–1713.

Heltne, P. G., J. F. Wojcik, and A. G. Pook. 1981. Goeldi's monkey, genus *Callimico*. In *Ecology and behavior of neotropical primates*, ed. A. Coimbra-Filho and R. Mittermeier, Vol. 1, 169–209. Rio de Janeiro: Academia Brasileira de Ciencias.

Hershkovitz, P. 1977. *Living New World monkeys (platyrrhini)*, Vol. 1. Chicago: University of Chicago Press.

Heymann, E. W. 1995. Sleeping habits of tamarins, *Saguinus mystax* and *Saguinus fuscicollis* (Mammalia: Primates: Callitrichidae), in north-eastern Peru. *Journal of Zoology* 237(2):211–226.

Heymann, E. W. 1997. The relationship between body size and mixed-species troops of tamarins (*Saguinus spp.*). *Folia Primatoligica* 68:287–295.

Heymann, E. W., and H. M. Buchanan-Smith. 2000. The behavioural ecology of mixed-species troops of callitrichine primates. *Biological Review* 75:169–190.

Heymann, E. W., and A. C. Smith. 1999. When to feed on gums: Temporal patterns of gummivory in wild tamarins, *Saguinus mystax* and *Saguinus fuscicollis* (Callitrichinae). *Zoo Biology* 18(6):459–471.

Heymann, E. W., and P. Soini. 1999. Offspring number in pygmy marmosets, *Cebuella pygmaea*, in relation to group size and the number of adult males. *Behavioral Ecology and Sociobiology* 46:400–404.

Heymann, E. W. 1990. Interspecific relations in a mixed-species troop of moustached tamarins, *Saguinus mystax*, and saddle-back tamarins, *Saguinus fuscicollis* (Platyrrhini: Callitrichidae), at the Rio Blanco, Peruvian Amazonia. *American Journal of Primatology* 21:115–127.

Hill, W. 1966. The anatomy of *Callimico goeldii* (Thomas). *Transactions of the American Philosophical Society* 49:1–116.

Hinton, P. 1995. *Statistics explained: a guide to the social science student*. Philadelphia: Routledge.

Hoage, R. 1978. Parental care in *Leontopithecus rosalia rosalia*: Sex and age differences in carrying behavior and the role of prior experience. In *The biology and conservation of the Callitrichidae*, ed. D. Kleiman, 293–305. Washington, DC: Smithsonian Institution Press.

Hodge, M. A., and G. W. Uets. 1996. Foraging advantages of mixed-species association between solitary and colonial orb-weaving spiders. *Oecologia* 107:578–587.

Holenweg, A.-K., R. Nöe, and M. Schabel. 1995. Waser's Gas Model applied to associations between red colobus and diana monkeys in the Tai National Park, Ivory Coast. *Folia Primatologica* 67:125–136.

Hoorn, C., J. Guerrero, G. Sarmiento, and M. Lorente. 1995. Andean tectonics as a cause for changing drainage patterns in Miocene northern South America. *Geology* 23:237–240.

Horovitz, I., and A. Meyer. 1997. Evolutionary trends in the ecology of New World monkeys inferred from a combined phylogenetic analysis of nuclear, mitochondrial, and morphological data. In *Molecular evolution and adaptive radiation*, ed. T. Givnish and K. Sytsma, 189–224. Cambridge: Cambridge University Press.

Huck, M., P. Lottker, and E. Heymann. 2004. Proximate mechanisms of reproductive monopolization in male moustached tamarins (*Saguinus mystax*). *American Journal of Primatology* 64:39–56.

Hutchinson, G. 1959. Homage to Santa Rosalia: Why are there so many species? *Amercian Naturalist* 93:145–159.

Hutchinson, G. 1978. *An introduction to population ecology.* New Haven: Yale University Press.

Ilse, L., and E. Hellgren. 1995. Resource partitioning in sympatric populations of collared peccaries and feral hogs in southern Texas. *Journal of Mammology* 76(3):784–799.

Isaac, N., J. Mallet, and G. Mace. 2004. Taxonomic inflation: Its influence on macroecology and conservation. *Trends in Ecology and Evolution* 19(9):464–469.

Isbell, L. A. 1990. Sudden short-term increase in mortality of vervet monkeys (*Cercopithecus aethiops*) due to predation in Amboseli National Park, Kenya. *American Journal of Primatology* 21:41–52.

Izawa, K. 1979. *Studies on peculiar distribution pattern of callimico: Kyoto University overseas research reports,* 1–19. Kyoto: Kyoto University.

Izawa, K., and G. Bejarano. 1981. Distribution ranges and patterns of nonhuman primates in western Pando, Bolivia: *Kyoto University overseas research reports.* Kyoto: Kyoto University, 1–11.

Izawa, K., and M. Yoneda. 1981. Habitat utilization of nonhuman primates in a forest of the Wetern Pando, Bolivia: *Kyoto University overseas research reports.* Kyoto: Kyoto University, 13–22.

Janson, C. H. 1983. Adaptation of fruit morphology to dispersal agents in a Neotropical forest. *Science* 219:187–189.

Janson, C. H. 1988. Intra-specific food competition and primate social structure: A synthesis. *Behaviour* 105:1–17.

Janson, C. H. 1992. Evolutionary ecology of primate social structure. In *Evolutionary ecology of human behavior,* ed. E. Smith and B. Winterhalder, 95–130. New York: Aldine.

Janson, C. H., and C. Chapman. 1999. Resources and primate community structure. In *Primate communities,* ed. J. Fleagle, C. Janson, and K. Reed, 237–267. Cambridge: Cambridge University Press.

Janson, C. H., and M. L. Goldsmith. 1995. Predicting group size in primates: Foraging costs and predation risks. *Behavioral Ecology* 6:326–336.

Janson, C. H., J. Terborgh, and L. H. Emmons. 1981. Non-flying mammals as pollinating agents in the Amazonian forest. *Biotropica* 13:1–6.

Jones, C. B. 1997. Rarity in primates: Implications for conservation. *Mastozoologia Neotropical* 4(1):35–47.

Jordan, C. 1985. Soils of the Amazon rainforest. In *Key environments amazonia,* ed. G. Pfance and T. Lovejoy, 83–94. Oxford: Pergamon Press.

Jouffroy, F., M. Godinot, and Y. Nakano. 1993. Biometrical characteristics of primate hands. In *Hands of primates,* ed. H. Preuschoft and D. Chivers, 133–171. New York: Springer-Verlag.

Jurke, M. H., and C. R. Pryce. 1994. Parental and infant behavior during early periods of infant care in Goeldi's monkey, *Callimico goeldii. Animal Behavior* 48:1095–1112.

Jurke, M. H., C. R. Pryce, A. Hug-Hodel, and M. Dobeli. 1995. An investigation into the socioendocrinology of infant care and postpartum fertility in Goeldi's monkey (*Callimico goeldii*). *International Journal of Primatology* 16:453–474.

Karasov, W. H. 1992. Daily energy expenditure and the cost of activity in mammals. *American Zoology* 32:238–248.

Kay, R. F. 1975. The functional adaptations of primate molar teeth. *American Journal of Physical Anthropology* 43:195–215.

Kay, R. F. 1984. On the use of anatomical features to infer foraging behavior in extinct primates. In *Adaptations for foraging in nonhuman primates: Contributions to an organismal biology of prosimians, monkeys and apes,* ed. P. Rodman and J. Cant, 21–53. New York: Columbia University Press.

Kierulff, M. C. M., B. E. Raboy, P. Procopio de Oliveira, K. Miller, F. Passos, and F. Prado. 2002. Behavioral ecology of lion tamarins. In *Lion tamarins: biology and conservation,* eds. D. Kleiman and A. Rylands. Washington, D.C: Smithsonian Institution Press, 157–187.

Kinzey, W. G., A. L. Rosenberger, P. S. Heisler, D. L. Prowse, and J. S. Trilling. 1977. A preliminary field investigation of the yellow handed titi monkey (*Callicebus torquatus torquatus*) in northern Peru. *Primates* 18:159–181.

Kirkpatrick, R. C., Y. C. Long, and L. Xiao. 1998. Social organization and range use in the Yunnan snub-nosed monkey *Rhinopithecus bieti. International Journal of Primatology* 19:13–51.

Kleiman, D. G. 1978. Characteristics of reproduction and sociosexual interactions in pairs of Lion tamarins (*Leontopithecus rosalia*) during the reproductive cycle. In *Biology and conservation of the Callitrichidae,* ed. D. Kleiman, 181–190. Washington, DC: Smithsonian Institution Press.

Knogge, C. E., and E. W. Heymann. 2002. Seed dispersal by sympatric tamarins, *Saguinus mystax* and *Saguinus fuscicollis*: Diversity and characteristics of plant species. *Folia Primatologica* 74(33–47).

Knogge, C., E. Tirado Herrera, and E. W. Heymann. 2003. Effects of passage through tamarin guts on the germination of potential dispersed seeds. *International Journal of Primatology* 24:1121–1128.

Koenig, A. 1995. Group size, composition, and reproductive success in wild common marmosets (*Callithrix jacchus*). *American Journal of Primatology* 35:311–317.

Koenig, A. 1998. Visual scanning by common marmosets (*Callithrix jacchus*): Functional aspects and the special role of adult males. *Primates* 39:85–90.

Kohlhaas, A. 1988. Primate populations in northern Bolivia. *Primate Conservation* 9:93–97.

Kurland, J. A., and S. J. C. Gaulin. 1987. Comparability among measures of primate diets. *Primates* 28:71–77.

Lambert, J. E. 1998. Primate digestion: Interactions among anatomy, physiology, and feeding ecology. *Evolutionary Anthropology* 7(1):8–20.

Lancaster, J. B. 1971. Play mothering: The relationships between juvenile females and young infants among free-ranging vervet monkeys (*Cercopithecus aethiops*). *Folia Primatologica* 15:161–182.

Landeau, L., and J. Terborgh. 1986. Oddity and the "confusion effect" in predation. *Animal Behavior* 34:1372–1380.

Littel, R. 1992. *Endangered and other protected species: Federal law and regulation.* Washington, DC: The Bureau of National Affairs, Inc.

Lopes, M. A., and S. F. Ferrari. 1994. Foraging behavior of a tamarin group (*Saguinus fuscicollis weddelli*) and interactions with marmosets (*Callithrix emiliae*). *International Journal of Primatology* 15(3):373–387.

Loettker, P., M. Huck, E. W. Heymann, and M. Heistermann. 2004. Endocrine correlates of reproductive status in breeding and nonbreeding wild female moustached tamarins. *International Journal of Primatology* 25:919–937.

Luiselli, L., G. Akani, and D. Capizzi. 1998. Food resource partitioning of a community of snakes in a swamp rainforest of south-eastern Nigeria. *Journal of Zoology London* 246:125–133.

MacKinnon, J. R., and K. S. MacKinnon. 1980. Niche differentiation in a primate community. In *Malayan forest primates,* ed. D. Chivers, 167–190. New York: Plenum.

Mangan, S., and G. Adler. 2000. Consumption of arbuscular mycorrhizal fungi by terrestrial and arboreal small mammals in a Panamanian cloud forest. *Journal of Mammology* 81(2):563–570.

Martin, P., and P. Bateson. 1993. *Measuring behaviour: An introductory guide.* Cambridge: Cambridge University Press.

Martin, R. D. 1990. *Primate origins and evolution: A phylogenetic reconstruction.* Princeton: Princeton University Press.

Martin, R. D. 1992. Goeldii and the dwarfs: The evolutionary biology of the small New World monkeys. *Journal of Human Evolution* 22:367–393.

Masataka, N. 1981. A field study of the social behavior of Goeldi's monkeys (*Callimico goeldii*) in north Bolivia: I group composition, breeding cycle, and infant development. *Kyoto University overseas research reports*, 23–32. Kyoto: Kyoto University.

Masataka, N. 1982. A field study on the vocalizations of Goeldi's Monkeys (*Callimico goeldii*). *Primates* 23(2):206–219.

Masataka, N. 1983. Categorical responses to natural and synthesized alarm calls in Goeldi's monkeys (*Callimico goeldii*). *Primates* 24(1):40–51.

Maser, C., J. Trappe, and R. Nussbaum. 1978. Fungal-small mammal interrelationships with emphasis on Oregon coniferous forests. *Ecology* 59:799–809.

Mayr, E. 1982. Of what use are subspecies? *Auk* 99:593–595.

McGraw, W. S. and R. Bshary. 2002. Association of terrestrial mangabeys (*Cercocebus atys*) with arboreal monkeys: Experimental evidence for the effects of reduced ground predator pressure on habitat use. *International Journal of Primatology* 23:311–325.

McIlwee, A., and C. Johnson. 1998. The contribution of fungus to the diets of three mycophagous marsupials in Eucalyptus forests, revealed by stable isotope analysis. *Functional Ecology* 12:223–231.

McLarney, W. 1999. Sustainable development: A necessary means for effective biological conservation. *Conservation Biology* 13:4.

Medellin, R. 1999. Sustainable harvest for conservation. *Conservation Biology* 13:225.

Mestre Correa, H. K. M. 1995. *Ecologia e comportamento alimentar de um grupo de Saguis-da-Serra-Escuros* (Callithrix aurita E.Geoffroy 1812) *no Parque Estadual da Serra do Mar, Nucleo Cunha, Sao Paulo, Brasil* (Masters thesis, zoology). Minas Gerais: Universidade Federal de Minas Gerais.

Miller, L. E. 1997. Methods of assessing dietary intake: A case study from wedge-capped capuchins in Venezuela. *Neotropical Primates* 5(4):104–108.

Milton, K. 1980. *The foraging strategy of howler monkeys: A study in primate economics.* New York: Columbia University Press.

Milton, K. 2000. Quo vadis? Tactics of food search and group movement in primates and other animals. In *On the move: How and why animals travel in groups,* ed. S. Boinski and P. A. Garber, 375–417. Chicago: The University of Chicago Press.

Mitani, J. C., and P. S. Rodman. 1979. Territoriality: The relation of ranging pattern and home range size to defensibility, with an analysis of territoriality among primate species. *Behavioral Ecology and Sociobiology* 18:87–100.

Mitani, J. C., W. J. Sanders, J. S. Lwanga, and T. L. Windfelder. 2001. Predatory behavior of crowned hawk-eagles (*Stephanoaetus coronatus*) in Kibale National Park, Uganda. *Behavioral Ecology and Sociobiology* 49:187–195.

Mitani, J., and D. Watts. 1997. The evolution of non-maternal caretaking among anthropoid primates: Do helpers help? *Behavioral Ecology and Sociobiology* 40:213–220.

Munn, C. A., and J. W. Terborgh. 1979. Multi-species territoriality in Neotropical foraging flocks. *Condor* 81:338–347.

Nash, L. T. 1986. Dietary, behavioral and morphological aspects of gummivory in Primates. *Yearbook of Physical Anthropology* 29:113–137.

Nickle, D. A., and E. W. Heymann. 1996. Predation on Orthoptera and other orders of insects by tamarin monkeys, *Saguinus mystax mystax* and *Saguinus fuscicollis nigrifrons* (Primates: Callitrichidae), in north-eastern Peru. *Journal of Zoology London* 239:799–819.

Nievergelt, C. M., L. J. Digby, U. Ramakrishnan, and D. S. Woodruff. 2000. Genetic analysis of group composition and breeding system in a wild common marmoset (*Callithrix jacchus*) population. *International Journal of Primatology* 21:1–20.

Nöe, R., and R. Bshary. 1997. The formation of red colobus–diana monkey associations under predation from chimpanzees. *Proceedings of the Royal Society of London, B* 264:253–259.

Norconk, M. A. 1986. *Interactions between primate species in a Neotropical forest: Mixed-species troops of* Saguinus mystax and S. fuscicollis *(Callitrichinae).* Ph.D. thesis, Southern Illinois University at Carbondale.

Norconk, M. A. 1990. Mechanisms promoting stability in mixed Saguinus mystax and S. fuscicollis troops. *American Journal of Primatology* 21:159–170.

Oates, J. F. 1986. Food distribution and foraging behavior. In *Primate societies*, ed. B. Smuts, D. Cheney, R. Seyfarth, R. Wrangham, and T. Struhsaker, 197–209. Chicago: University of Chicago Press.

Oates, J. F., and G. H. Whitesides. 1990. Association between Olive Colobus (*Procolobus verus*), Diana Guenons (*Cercopithecus diana*), and other forest monkeys in Sierra Leone. *American Journal of Primatology* 21:129–146.

Oliveira, A. C. M., and S. F. Ferrari. 2000. Seed dispersal by black-handed tamarins, *Saguinus midas niger* (Callitrichinae, Primates): Implications for the regeneration of degraded forest habitats in eastern Amazonia. *Journal of Tropical Ecology* 16:709–716.

Overdorff, D. J. 1993. Similarities, differences, and seasonal patterns in the diets of *Eulemur fulvus rufus* in the Ranomafana National Park, Madagascar. *International Journal of Primatology* 14(5):721–753.

Oversluijs Vasquez, M. R., and E. W. Heymann. 2001. Crested eagle (*Mophnus guanensis*) predation on infant tamarins (*Saguinus mystax* and *Saguinus fuscicollis,* Callitrichinae). *Folia Primatologica* 72:301–303.

Pacheco, P. 1998. Magnitud y causas de la deforestación y degradación de los bosques en Bolivia. World Rainforest Movement. www.wrm.org.uy/deforestation/America/Bolivia.html., May 1, 2006.

Pastorini, J., M. R. J. Forstner, R. D. Martin, and D. J. Melnick. 1998. A reexamination of the phylogenetic position of *Callimico* (Primates): Incorporation of new mitochondrial DNA sequence data. *Journal of Molecular Evolution* 47:32–41.

Penny, N., and J. Arias. 1982. *Insects of an Amazon forest.* New York: Columbia University Press.

Peres, C. A. 1989. Costs and benefits of territorial defense in wild golden tamarins, *Leontopithecus rosalia. Behavioral Ecology and Sociobiology* 25:227–233.

Peres, C. A. 1992a. Consequences of joint-territoriality in a mixed-species group of tamarin monkeys. *Behavior* 123:220–246.

Peres, C. A. 1992b. Prey-capture benefits in a mixed-species group of Amazonian tamarins, *Saguinus fuscicollis* and *S. mystax. Behavioral Ecology and Sociobiology* 31:339–347.

Peres, C. A. 1993. Anti-predation benefits in a mixed-species group of Amazonian tamarins. *Folia Primatologica* 61:61–76.

Peres, C. A. 1996. Food patch structure and plant resource partitioning in interspecific associations of Amazonian tamarins. *International Journal of Primatology* 17:695–724.

Peres, C. A. 1997. Primate community structure at twenty western Amazonian flooded and unflooded forest. *J. Trop. Ecol.* 13(3):381–405.

Peres, C. A. 2000. Territorial defense and the ecology of group movements in small-bodied Neotropical primates. In *On the move: How and why animals travel in groups*, ed. S. Boinski and P. Garber, 100–124. Chicago: Chicago University Press.

Pianka, E. 1981. Competition and niche theory. In *Theoretical ecology: Principles and applications*, 2nd ed., R. May, 167–196. Oxford: Blackwell Scientific Publications.

Podolsky, R. D. 1990. Effects of mixed-species association on resource use by *Saimiri sciureus* and *Cebus apella*. *American Journal of Primatology* 21:147–158.

Pook, A. G., and G. Pook. 1982. Polyspecific association between *Saguinus fuscicollis, Saguinus labiatus, Callimico goeldii* and other primates in north-western Bolivia. *Folia Primatologica* 38:196–216.

Pook, A. G., and G. Pook. 1981. A field study of the socio-ecology of the Goeldi's monkey (*Callimico goeldii*) in northern Bolivia. *Folia Primatologica* 35:288–312.

Popp, J. W. 1988. Scanning behavior of finches in mixed-species groups. *The Condor* 90:510–511.

Porter, L.M. 2001a. *Callimico goeldii* and *Saguinus*: Dietary differences between sympatric callitrichines in northern Bolivia. *International Journal of Primatology* 22:961–992.

Porter, L.M. 2001b. Benefits of polyspecific associations for the Goeldi's monkey (*Callimico goeldii*). *American Journal of Primatology* 54:143–158.

Porter, L.M. 2001c. Social organization, reproduction and rearing strategies of Callimico goeldii: New clues from the wild. *Folia Primatologica* 72:62–79.

Porter, L. M. 2003. Goeldi's monkeys (*Callimico goeldii*) population densities and use of home range in northwestern Bolivia.

Porter, L.M. 2004. Differences in forest utilization and activity patterns among three sympatric callitrichines: Callimico goeldii, *Saguinus fuscicollis* and *S. labiatus*. *American Journal of Physical Anthropology* 124:139–153.

Porter, L. M. 2006. Distribution and density of *Callimico goeldii* in northwestern Bolivia. *American Journal of Primatology* 68:235–243.

Porter, L. M., and P. A. Garber. 2004. Goeldi's monkeys: A primate paradox? *Evolutionary Anthropology* 13:104–115.

Porter, L. M., and P. A. Garber. In prep. Social relations among wild Goeldi's monkeys.

Porter, L. M., A. M. Hanson and E. Nacimento. 2001. Group demographics and dispersal in a wild group of Goeldi's monkeys (*Callimico goeldii*). *Folia Primatologica* 72(2):100–110.

Porter, L. M., S. M. Sterr, and P. A. Garber. In prep. Habitat use, diet, and ranging patterns of *Callimico goeldii*.

Power, M. L. and O. T. Oftedal. 1996. Differences among captive callitrichids in the digestive responses to dietary gum. *American Journal of Primatology* 40:131–144.

Prescott, M. J., and H. M. Buchanan-Smith. 1999. Foraging efficiency in single- and mixed-species troops of tamarins. *Folia Primatologica* 70:221–231.

Price, E. C. 1992. The benefits of helpers: Effects of group and litter size on infant care in tamarins (*Saguinus oedipus*). *American Journal of Primatology* 26:179–190.

Pryce, C. R., J. Pastorini, K. Vasarhelyi, and A. Christen. 2002. Bio-behavioral description of social and reproductive relationships in captive Goeldi's monkeys. *Evolutionary Anthropology* 11(S1):190–194.

Puertas, P., F. Encarnación, and R. Aquino. 1995. Analisis poblacional del Pichico Pecho Anaranjado, *Saguinus labiatus*, en el sur oriente Peruano. *Neotropical Primates* 3:4–7.

Pulliam, H. 1973. On the advantages of flocking. *Journal of Theoretical Biology* 38:419–422.

Quinn, R., K. Gaston, and H. Arnold. 1996. Relative measures of geographical range size: Empirical comparisons. *Oecologica* 107:179–188.

Rabenold, K. N. 1985. Cooperation in breeding by nonreproductive wrens: Kinship, reciprocity, and demography. *Behavioral Ecology and Sociobiology* 17:1–7.

Rabinowitz, D., S. Cairns, and T. Dillon. 1981. Seven forms of rarity and their frequency in the flora of the British Isles. In *Conservation biology: The science of scarcity and diversity*, ed. M. Soulé, 182–304. Sunderland, MA: Sinauer Associates.

Raboy, B. E., and J. M. Dietz. 2004. Diet, foraging, and use of space in wild golden-headed lion tamarins. *American Journal of Primatology* 63:1–15.

Rasa, O. 1994. Altruistic infant care or infanticide: The dwarf mongooses' dilemma. In *Infanticide and parental care*, ed. S. Parmigiani and F. vom Saal, 301–320. Chur, Switzerland: Harwood Academic Publishers.

Rasanen, M., A. Linna, J. Santos, and F. Negri. 1995. Late Miocene tidal deposits in the Amazonian foreland basin. *Science* 273:124–125.

Reddel, P., A. Spain, and M. Hopkins. 1997. Dispersal of spores of mycorrhizal fungi in scats of native mammals in tropical forests of northeastern Australia. *Biotropica* 29(2):184–192.

Rehg, J. A. 2003. *Polyspecific associations of* Callimico goeldii, Saguinus labiatus, and Saguinus fuscicollis *in Acre, Brazil*. Ph.D. thesis. University of Illinois at Urbana-Champaign.

Roberts, G. 1996. Why individual vigilance declines as groups size increases. *Animal Behavior* 51:1077–1086.

Roosevelt, A. C., M. Lima da Costa, C. Lopes Machado, M. Michab, N. Mercier, H. Valladas, J. Feathers, W. Barnett, M. Imazio da Silveira, A. Henderson, J. Silva, B. Chernoff, D. S. Reese, J. A. Holman, N. Toth, and K. Schick. 1996. Paleoindian cave dwellers in the Amazon: The peopling of the Americas. *Science* 272(5260):373–383.

Rose, L. M. and L. M. Fedigan. 1995. Vigilance in white-faced capuchins, *Cebus capucinus*, in Costa Rica. *Animal Behavior* 49:63–70.

Rosenberger, A. L. 1981. Systematics: the higher taxa. In *Ecology and behavior of neotropical primates*, ed. A. Coimbra-Filho and R. Mittermeier, Vol. 1, 9–27. Rio de Janeiro: Acadamia Brasileira da Ciencias.

Ross, C. 1988. The intrinsic rate of natural increase and reproductive effort in primates. *Journal of Zoology, London* 214:199–219.

Ross, C. 1991. Life history patterns of New World monkeys. *International Journal of Primatology* 12:481–502.

Ruhiyat, Y. 1983. Socio-ecological study of *Presbytis aygula* in west Java. *Primates* 24:344–359.

Rylands, A. B. 1982. *The behaviour and ecology of three species of marmosets and tamarins (Callitrichidae, Primates) in Brazil*. Ph.D. thesis, University of Cambridge.

Rylands, A. B., ed. 1993. *Marmosets and tamarins: Systematics, behavior, and Ecology*. New York: Oxford University Press.

Rylands, A. B. 1996. Habitat and the evolution of social and reproductive behavior in Callitrichidae. *American Journal of Primatology* 38:5–18.

Rylands, A. B., A. Coimbra-Filho, and R. Mittermeier. 1993. Systematics, geographic distribution, and some notes on the conservation status of the Callitrichidae. In *Marmosets and tamarins: Systematics, behavior, and ecology*, ed. A. B. Rylands. New York: Oxford University Press.

Rylands, A. B., H. Schneider, A. Langguth, R. A. Mittermeier, C. P. Groves, E. Rodriguez-Luna. 2000. An assessment of diversity of New World primates. *Neotropical Primates* 8(2): 61–93.

Saltzman, W. 2003. Reproductive competition among female common marmosets (*Callithrix jacchus*): Proximate and ultimate causes. In *Sexual selection and reproductive competition in primates: New perspectives and directions*, ed. C. Jones, 197–229. Norman, Oklahoma: American Society of Primatologists.

Sanchez, S., F. Pelaez, C. Gil-Burmann, and W. Kaumanns. 1999. Costs of infant-carrying in the cotton-top tamarin. *American Journal of Primatology* 48:99–111.

Sanchez, S., F. Pelaez, and C. Gil-Burmann, and W. Kaumanns. 2002. Why do cotton-top tamarin female helpers carry infants? A preliminary study. *American Journal of Primatology* 57:43–49.

Savage, A., C. T. Snowdon, L. H. Giraldo, and L. H. Soto. 1996. Parental care patterns and vigilance in wild cotton-top tamarins (*Saguinus oedipus*). In *Adaptive radiations of Neotropical primates*, ed. M. Norconk, A. Rosenberger, and P. A. Garber. 187–200. New York: Plenum Press.

Schneider, H., I. Sampaio, M. L. Harada, C. M. L. Barroso, M. P. C. Schneider, J. Czelusniak, and M. Goodman. 1996. Molecular phylogeny of the New World monkeys (Platyrrhini, Primates) based on two unlinked nucelear genes: IRBP Intron 1 and epsilon-globin sequences. *American Journal of Physical Anthropology* 100:153–179.

Schoener, T. 1968. The *Anolis* lizards of Bimini: Resource partitioning in a complex fauna. *Ecology* 49:704–726.

Schoener, T. 1974. Resource partitioning in ecological communities. *Science* 185:27–39.

Schoener, T. 1982. The controversy over interspecific competition. *American Scientist* 70:586–595.

Schradin, C., and G. Anzenberger. 2001a. Costs of infant carrying in common marmosets, *Callithrix jacchus*: An experimental analysis. *Animal Behaviour* 62:289–295.

Schradin, C., and G. Anzenberger. 2001b. Infant carrying in family groups of Goeldi's monkeys (*Callimico goeldii*). *American Journal of Primatology* 53:57–67.

Schradin, C., D. Reeder, S. Mendoza, and G. Anzenberger. 2003. Prolactin and paternal care: Comparison of three species of monogamous New World monkeys (*Callicebus cupreus*, *Callithrix jacchus*, and *Callimico goeldii*). *Journal of Comparative Psychology* 117:166–175.

Schupp, E. 1993. Quantity, quality and the effectiveness of seed dispersal by animals. *Vegetatio* 107/108:15–29.

Slater, P. 1994. Niche overlap between three sympatric, short-billed honeyeaters in Tasmania. *Emu* 94:186–192.

Sodaro, V. 2004. Housing of callimico in zoological parks. In *Callimico species survival plan husbandry manual*, ed. V. Sodaro. Brookfield, IL: Chicago Zoological Park.

Soini, P. 1987. Ecology of the saddle-backed tamarin *Saguinus fuscicollis illegri* on the Rio Pacaya, Northeastern Peru. *Folia Primatologica* 49:11–32.

Soini, P. 1993. The ecology of the pygmy marmoset, *Cebuella pygmaea*: Some comparisons with two sympatric tamarins. In *Marmosets and tamarins: Systematics, behavior and ecology*, ed. A. B. Rylands, 257–261. New York: Oxford University Press.

Sokal, R., and F. Rohlf. 1995. *Biometry*, 3rd ed. New York: W. H. Freeman and Company.

Soltis, J., and R. McElreath. 2001. Can females gain extra paternal investment by mating with multiple males? A game theoretical approach. *American Naturalist* 158(5):519–529.

Souza de Oliviera, M., F. A. Lopes, C. Alonso, and M. E. Yamamoto. 1999. The mother's participation in infant carrying in captive groups of *Leontopithecus chrysomelas* and *Callithrix jacchus*. *Folia Primatologica* 70:146–153.

Stanford, C. B. 2001. The subspecies concept in primatology: The case of the mountain gorillas. *Primates* 42(4):309–318.

Strier, K. B. 1987. Activity budgets of woolly spider monkeys, or muriquis (*Brachyteles arachnoides*). *American Journal of Primatology* 13:385–395.

Struhsaker, T. T. 1998. A biologist's perspective on the role of sustainable harvest in conservation. *Conservation Biology* 12:930–932.

Sussman, R. W., and P. A. Garber. 2004. Rethinking sociality: Cooperation and aggression among primates. In *Origins and nature of sociality*. Ed. R. W. Sussman, and A. R. Chapman, 161–190. Hawthorne, NY: Aldine de Grutyer.

Sussman, R. W., and W. Kinzey. 1984. The ecological role of the Callitrichidae: A review. *American Journal of Physical Anthropology* 64:419–449.

Tan, C. L. 1999. Group composition, home range size, and diet of three sympatric bamboo lemur species (Genus *Hapalemur*) in Ranomafana National Park, Madagascar. *International Journal of Primatology* 20(4):547–566.

Tardif, S. D. 1994. Relative energetic costs of infant care in small-bodied Neotropical primates and its relation to infant-care patterns. *American Journal of Primatology* 34:133–143.

Tardif, S. D., and K. Bales. 1997. Is infant-carrying a courtship strategy in callitrichid primates. *Animal Behaviour* 53:1001–1007.

Tardif, S. D., M. L. Harrison, and M. A. Simek. 1993. Communal infant care in marmosets and tamarins: Relation to energetics, ecology, and social organization. In *Marmosets and tamarins: Systematics, behavior and ecology*, ed. A. B. Rylands, 220–234. New York: Oxford University Press.

Tardif, S. D., M. Power, O. T. Oftedal, R. A. Power, and D. G. Layne. 2002. Lactation, maternal behavior and infant growth in common marmoset monkeys (*Callithrix jacchus*): Effects of maternal size and litter size. *Behavioral Ecology and Sociobiology* 51:17–25.

Tardif, S. D., C. B. Richter, and R. L. Carson. 1984. Effects of sibling rearing experience on future reproductive success in two species of Callitrichidae. *American Journal of Primatology* 11:103–110.

Tattersall, I. 1982. *The primates of Madagascar*. New York: Columbia University Press.

Terborgh, J. 1983. *Five New World primates*. Princeton: Princeton University Press.

Terborgh, J. 1990. Mixed flocks and polyspecific associations: Costs and benefits of mixed groups to birds and monkeys. *American Journal of Primatology* 21:87–100.

Terborgh, J. 1999. *Requiem for nature*. Washington, DC: Island Press.

Terborgh, J., and B. Winter. 1980. Some causes of extinction. In *Conservation biology*, ed. M. Soulé and B. Wilcox. Sunderland, MA: Sinauer Associates, Inc.

Thompson, S. D., M. L. Power, C. E. Rutledge, and D. G. Kleiman. 1994. Energy metabolism and thermoregulation in the golden lion tamarin (*Leontopithecus rosalia*). *Folia Primatologica* 63:131–143.

Treves, A. 1998. The influence of group size and neighbors on vigilance in two species of arboreal monkeys. *Behaviour* 135:453–481.

Trivers, R. L. 1971. The evolution of reciprocal altruism. *Quarterly Review of Biology* 46:35–57.

Ungar, P. S. 1995. Fruit preferences of four sympatric primate species at Ketambe, northern Sumatra, Indonesia. *International Journal of Primatology* 16:221–246.

van Schaik, C. P. 1983. Why are diurnal primates living in groups? *Behavior* 87:120–144.

Vasarhelyi, K. 1999. The nature of relationships among founders in the captive population of Goeldi's monkey (*Callimico goeldii*). *Evolutionary Anthropology* 11 (Supplement 1):155–158.

Vasarhelyi, K. 2000. Is *Callimico* monotypic? A reassessment in the light of new data. *Dodo* 36:20–29.

Vasey, N. 2000. Niche separation in *Varecia variegata rubra* and *Eulemur fulvus albifrons*: Interespecific patterns. *American Journal of Primatology* 112(3):411–431.

Von Dornum, M., and M. Ruvolo. 1999. Phylogenetic relationships of the New World monkeys (Primates, Platyrrhini) based on nuclear G6PD DNA sequences. *Molecular Phylogenetics and Evolution* 11:459–476.

Vrcibradic, D., and C. Rocha. 1996. Ecological differences in tropical sympatric skinks (*Mabuya macrorhyncha* and *Mabuya agilis*) in southeastern Brazil. *Journal of Herpetology* 30(1):60–67.

Wachter, B., M. Schabel, and R. Nöe. 1997. Diet overlap and poly-specific associations of red colobus and diana monkeys in the Tai National Park, Ivory Coast. *Ethology* 103:514–526.

Walter, G. 1991. What is resource partitioning? *Journal of Theoretical Biology* 150:137–143.

Warneke, M. 1992. *Callimico goeldii II: 1992 international studbook*. Chicago: Chicago Zoological Society.

Waser, P. M. 1982. Primate polyspecific associations: Do they occur by chance? *Animal Behavior* 30:1–8.

Waser, P. M. 1984. "Chance" and mixed-species associations. *Behavioral Ecology and Sociobiology* 15:197–202.

Whitesides, G. H. 1989. Interspecific associations of Diana monkeys, *Cercopithecus diana*, in Sierra Leone, West Africa: Biological significance or chance? *Animal Behavior* 37:760–776.

Wolda, H. 1981. Similarity indices, sample sizes and diversity. *Oecologia* 50:296–302.

Wolters, S., and K. Zuberbuhler. 2003. Mixed-species associations of Diana and Campbell's monkeys: The costs and benefits of forest phenomenon. *Behaviour* 140:371–385.

Wrangham, R. N. 1977. Feeding behavior of chimpanzees in Gombe National Park, Tanzania. In *Primate ecology*, ed. T. Clutton-Brock, 504–538. London: Academic Press.

Wrangham, R., N. Conklin Brittain, and K. Hunt. 1998. Dietary response of chimpanzees and cercopithecines to seasonal variation in fruit abundance. I. Antefeedants. *International Journal of Primatology* 1998:949–969.

Wright, P. C. 1984. Biparental care in *Aotus trivirgatus* and *Callicebus moloch*. In *Female primates: studies by women primatologists*, ed. M. Small. New York: Alan R. Liss, Inc., 59–75.

Wright, P. C. 1989. The nocturnal primate niche in the New World. *Journal of Human Evolution* 18:635–658.

Wright, P. C. 1998. Impact of predation risk on the behavior of *Propithecus diadema edwardsi* in the rain forest of Madagascar. *Behaviour* 135:483–512.

Wright, P. C., and J. Jernvall. 1999. The future of primate communities: A reflection of the present? In *Primate communities*, ed. J. Fleagle, C. Janson, and K. Reed, 295–309. Cambridge: Cambridge University Press.

Yamamoto, M. E. 1993. From dependence to sexual maturity: The behavioral ontogeny of Callitrichidae. In *Marmosets and tamarins: Systematics, behaviour and ecology*, ed. A. B. Rylands, 235–254. New York: Oxford University Press.

Yoneda, M. 1981. *Ecological studies of Saguinus fuscicollis and Saguinus labiatus with reference to habitat segregation and height preference. Kyoto Universtiy overseas research reports*. Kyoto: Kyoto University, 43–50.

Yoneda, M. 1984. Comparative studies on vertical separation, foraging behavior and traveling mode of saddle-backed tamarins (*Saguinus fuscicollis*) and red-chested moustached tamarins (*Saguinus labiatus*) in northern Bolivia. *Primates* 25:414–422.

Youlatos, D. 1999. Positional behavior of *Cebuella pygmaea* in Yasuni National Park, Ecuador. *Primates* 40:543–550.

Ziegler, T. E., C. T. Snowdon, and M. Warneke. 1989. Postpartum ovulation and conception in Goeldi's monkey, *Callimico goeldii*. *Folia Primatologica* 52:206–210.

Zink, R. 2004. The role of subspecies in obscuring avian biological diversity and misleading conservation policy. *Proceedings of the Royal Society of London B* 271:561–564.

INDEX

A

Activity budgets
    factors affecting, 63–64
    findings, 70–72
Activity periods, 68–70, 77–78
Aggressive interactions, 56
Allocare, 103, 105, 110–112, 117–118,
    144–145. see also Communal care
    benefits to caregivers, 118–120
Alpha rarity, 122
Antipredation benefits of polyspecific
    associations, 84–85, 101
Arthropods
    feeding behavior study data collection, 35
    feeding behavior study findings, 47–51,
      56, 78
    polyspecific associations and feeding on,
      96–97, 101–102
Ascopolyporous
    see bamboo fungi
Associations
    see Polyspecific associations
Auricularia
    see jelly fungi

B

Bamboo fungi, 35, 36–38, 128–129
    nutritional composition of, 58–59
Basal callitrichids, 4
Behavior
    activity budgets, 63–64, 70–72
    of callitrichidae, 8–10
    categories of, 65

feeding, see Feeding behavior study
habitat use study, see Habitat use study
implementation of Chi-squared test for
    independence in comparisons of, 67,
    70, 71
polyspecific associations, see Polyspecific
    associations
social, see Social organization
Behavioral reproductive suppression,
    104–105
Beta rarity, 122
Biannual birth season, 108–109, 130–131,
    143, 144
Biological Species Concept, 123
Bolivia, 18–22
    see also Department of the pando
Breeding
    combinations, 103
    females, 104–105, 107, 108–109
    males, 107–108

C

Caecums, 58
Callimico goeldii, see Callimicos
Callimicos (*Callimico goeldii*)
    anatomy of, 1
    appearance of, 1, 30, 78
    associations with tamarins, 70–71, 81,
      89–93, 99
    conservation, see Conservation
    discovery of, 1
    distinguishing characteristics, 1
    geographic range of, 2, 6, 127–128,
      146–147

Callimicos (*Continued*)
limb proportions, 62
offspring, 1, 4, 11, 102, 105
polyspecific associations, see Polyspecific
associations
polyspecific associations with tamarins,
89–93, 99
protections for, 2
studies of, 17–18
study groups, 23–27
taxonomy, 2–6
traits, 4
Callithrix, see Marmosets
Callitrichidae, 3–6
distribution, behavior and ecology of, 6–11
Campesinos, 135, 138
Cebuella, see Pygmy marmosets
Christen studies, 18
Claws, 3, 4, 63, 80
Climate, 20
Color variations, regional, 6
Communal care, 10, 103, 110–112, 117–118,
143, 144. see also Allocare
Competition
among callitrichids, 9
feeding behavior study findings,
55–56, 60
for food, 29–30, 51–52, 54, 55–56, 60,
83–84, 99, 131–132
for fruit, 54, 131
interspecific, 131–132
niche partitioning, 9
for vertebrate prey, 51–52, 57
Conservation
efforts, 138–139
knowledge base, 146–148
status, 2, 121–122

D

Department of the Pando study site, 18–22
challenges facing, 136–139
forests of, 20–22, 133–138
peoples of, 133–138
Diet
habitat and, 128–130
studies of, 128–130, 141–142. see also
Feeding behavior study
Dietary niches, 29–30, 60
feeding behavior study, see Feeding
behavior study
Diet overlap
feeding behavior study findings,
55, 56–57

feeding behavior study methodology,
33–34
Distribution of callitrichidae, 2, 6, 16–17
Dominant females, 10, 104, 119

E

Ecological niches, 9
Ecology of callitrichidae, 10–11
Ecosystem, role of callimico in, 132–133
Energy expenditure, 63–64, 70–72
Estrus, postpartum, 114
Extinction
geographic range as factor in, 127
population density as factor in, 124, 127
relationship of rare species to, 121–122
Exudate feeding sites, 8, 30
feeding behavior study findings, 44–47,
57, 80

F

Fallback foods, 30, 57
Feeding
comparisons of feeding records, 66–67
frequencies, 95–96
polyspecific associations effect on, 95–96,
99, 101–102
Feeding behavior study
arthropod consumption findings, 47–51,
56, 78
arthropod data, 35
behavioral observations, 32–33
competition, 55–56, 60
diet overlap data collection, 33–34
diet overlap findings, 55, 56–57
distinctions found, 56
exudate consumption, 44–47, 57, 80
food categories, 34
foraging, 53–54, 60, 131
fruit consumption, 42–44, 53–54,
56–57, 78
fungi consumption findings, 35–38,
57–60, 77
fungi data, 34–35
group scans, 32–33
methodology, 32–35
nectar consumption findings, 38–41, 57
plant data, 34
results, 35–56
vertebrates consumption findings,
51–53, 57
vertical stratification: height class use,
53–54, 56

Females
    breeding, 104–105, 107, 108–109
    dominant, 10, 104, 119
    interbirth intervals, 106, 108–109, 114,
        130–131, 143
    postpartum estrus, 114
    reproductive strategies, 113–114
Food
    categories, 34
    competition for, 29–30, 51–52, 54, 55–56,
        60, 83–84, 99, 131–132
    fallback foods, 30, 57
Foraging
    feeding behavior study findings, 53–54,
        60, 131
    habitat use study findings, 68–70, 78,
        131–132
    height comparisons, 53–54, 60
    polyspecific associations effect on, 96–97,
        101–102
Fruit
    competition for, 54, 131
    feeding behavior study findings, 42–44,
        53–54, 56–57, 60, 78
    morning consumption of, 68, 70
    percentage of diet, 42–44, 56–57
Fungi, 32, 68, 99–100, 128, 141–142
    bamboo fungi, 35, 36–38, 58–59,
        128–129
    digestion of, 77, 142
    dispersal of, 132–133
    evening consumption of, 68, 77
    feeding behavior study data collection,
        34–35
    feeding behavior study findings, 35–38,
        57–60, 77
    jelly fungi, 35, 36–38, 58–59, 128–129
    nutritional composition of, 58–59

G

Gamma rarity, 122
Geographic range, 127–128, 146–147. see
    also Home range
Geographic range of, 2, 6
Goeldi, Emilio Augusto, 1
Group-size effect, 85
Gummivory, 57, 142

H

Habitat requirements, 128–130
Habitat use, 142–143
    polyspecific associations effect on, 93

Habitat use study
    activity periods, 68–70, 77–78
    analyses, 66–67
    comparisons, 66–67
    criteria used in defining habitats, 66
    feeding activity, 68–70, 77–78
    foraging, 68–70, 78, 131–132
    habitat specialization, 61–63
    height class use data collection, 67
    height class use findings, 73, 79
    home range, 63, 64–65
    home range size and density findings,
        67–68
    locomotor behavior data collection, 66
    locomotor behavior findings, 72, 79–80
    methodology, 64–67
    microhabitat use data collection, 65
    microhabitat use findings, 73–76, 80–81
    results, 67–76
    seasonal effects on activity, 72, 78
    seasonal effects on microhabitat use,
        75–76, 80–81
    sleeping site findings, 68, 77
    sleeping sites, 63, 64, 70
    substrate use data collection, 72–73
    substrate use findings, 72–73
    tests used in comparisons, 67
Hand morphology, 31
Height class use
    feeding behavior study findings, 53–54, 56
    habitat use study data collection, 67
    habitat use study findings, 73, 79
    polyspecific associations effect on, 93, 100
Hindgut fermentation, 58
Home range, 63, 127–128
    calculation of, 64–65
    effect of polyspecific associations on,
        97–99
Hormonal reproductive suppression, 104

I

Inbreeding depression, 122
Index of Niche Overlap, 33–34
Infant care, 103, 105, 110–112, 114–118. see
    also Allocare; Communal care
Infant-care behavior, 107
Infant development, 110, 118
Infanticide, 104
Insect foraging benefits of polyspecific
    associations, 86
Insectivory, 47, 50
Interbirth intervals, 106, 108–109, 114,
    130–131, 143

Intergroup interactions, see Polyspecific associations
Intermembral index, 62
Interspecific competition, 131–132

J

Jelly fungi, 35, 36–38, 128–129
  nutritional composition of, 58–59

K

Keystone resources, 30

L

Lion tamarins *(Leontopithecus)*, 3
Locomotor behavior
  see also Trunk-to-trunk leaping
  data collection, 66
  factors affecting, 61–63
  findings on, 62
  habitat use study findings, 72, 79–80
  intermembral index as predictor of, 62
Logging, 20, 22, 136–138

M

Males
  breeding, 104, 107–108
  infant care, 110, 117, 119
  prolactin increase, 119
  reproductive strategies, 112–113
Marmosets *(Callithrix* and *Mico)*, 1, 3
  exudate feeding sites, 8, 30
  procumbent incisors, 7–8
Mate guarding, 112
Mating strategies, 10. see also Reproductive strategies
Mico, see Marmosets
Microhabitats, 61
  defining, 65
  effect of seasonal changes on, 75–76, 80–81
  habitat use study data collection, 65
  habitat use study findings, 73–76, 80–81
Molars, 1, 4, 31
Molecular data, 4, 6
Mortality rate, 112, 131
Mycophagy, 32, 35, 77–78, 141–142, 146
  polyspecific associations effect on, 97

N

Nectar consumption, 38–41, 57
Niche partitioning, 9, 29

O

Offspring, 1, 4
  communal care, 10, 103, 110–112, 117–118, 143, 144
  twinning, 10–11, 102, 105, 120, 130–131, 143
One:zero sampling, 86–87
Orthopterans, 48
Outbreeding, 122

P

Pando, Department of the, see Department of the Pando study site
Patchiness, 2, 6, 128
Physical association, 86
Pook studies, 17–18
Polyspecific associations, 9–10, 15, 16
  analyses, 87–89
  antipredation benefits, 84–85, 101
  arthropod feeding, 96–97, 101–102
  callimicos associations with tamarins, 89–93, 99
  effects on behavior of callimicos, 93–97
  foraging, 96–97, 101–102
  habitat use, 93
  height class use, 93, 100
  home range, 97–99
  insect foraging benefits, 86
  leadership data collection, 87
  location data, 87
  one:zero sampling, 86–87
  patterns of associations, 89–93
  potential costs and benefits of, 83–86, 99
  resource knowledge benefits, 85–86
  saddle-back tamarins associations with red-bellied tamarins, 91
  scanning of environment, 93–95, 100–101
  study methodology, 86–89
  study results, 89–97
  use of Waser's Gas Model, 87–88
Population density, 2, 6
  calculating, 124–127
Postpartum estrus, 114
Predators, 10–11, 84–85
  antipredation benefits of polyspecific associations, 84–85, 101
  effect on social organization, 108

Primate community, Department of the Pando, 22
Prolactin, 119
Pygmy marmosets *(Cebuella)*, 3, 6

R

Rainfall, 18
Ranching, 138, 148
Rare species
  categories of, 122
  relationship of extinction to, 121–122
Red-bellied tamarin *(Saguinus labiatus)*, 2, 13
  appearance of, 78
  geographic range of, 6, 16–17
  polyspecific associations, 9–10, 14, 89–93, 99
  studies of, 16
  study groups, 25–27
Reproductive biology, 1, 4, 102. see also Offspring
Reproductive strategies, 102, 143–144. see also Offspring
  biannual birth season, 108–109, 130–131, 143
  birth season, 108–109
  breeding females, 104–105, 107
  breeding males, 107–108
  female, 113–114
  interbirth intervals, 106, 108–109, 114, 130–131, 143
  male, 112–113
  results of study, 107–110
  social organization, see Social organization
Research plan, 13–15
  study area, 18–22
  study groups, 23–27
  study species, 15–18
  trail/grid system, 22–23, 24
Resource knowledge benefits of polyspecific associations, 85–86
Resting behaviors, 65, 70–71
Rubber trees, 133–134

S

Saddle-back tamarin *(Saguinus fusciollis)*, 2, 13
  appearance of, 78
  geographic range of, 6, 16–17
  polyspecific associations, 9–10, 14, 15–16, 89–93, 99
  studies of, 15–16
  study groups, 24–27
Saguinus, see Tamarins
Saguinus fusciollis, see Saddle-back tamarin
Saguinus labiatus, see Red-bellied tamarin
San Sebastian research camp, 20
Scanning of environment, 65, 85
  polyspecific associations effect on, 93–95, 100–101
Schoener's Index of Niche Overlap, 33–34
Seasonal changes
  effects on activity, 72
  effects on microhabitat use, 75–76, 80–81
Seed dispersers, 132–133
Short-term field studies of 1970s and 1990s, 1–2
Sleeping sites, 63, 64, 70
  habitat use study findings, 68, 77
Social organization
  allocare, 103, 105, 110–112, 117–118, 144–145
  among females, 104–105
  birth season, 108
  breeding combinations, 103
  communal care, 103, 110–112, 117–118, 143, 144
  dispersal of group members, 108
  infant care, 103, 105, 110–112, 114–118
  infant development, 110
  methodology of study, 107
  mortality, 112
  predation, 108
  study results, 107–112
Speciation, 122–124
Species
  defined, 123
  rare species, 122
Stomachs, 58
Study area, 18–22
Study groups, 23–27
Study species, 15–18
Subspecies, 15–16, 122–124
Substrate use, 72–73

T

Tamarins *(Saguinus)*, 1, 3
  appearance of, 78
  associations between, 70–71, 81, 89–93, 99
  exudate feeding sites, 44, 57
  polyspecific associations, 89–93, 99
Taxonomy, callimicos, 2–6

Tegulae, 3, 4, 63, 80
Territoriality, 63
Thermoregulation, 64
Trail/grid system, 22–23, 24
Travel, 95
Tropical rainforest, 61–63
Trunk-to-trunk leaping, 62, 63, 72, 79, 146
Twinning, 10–11, 102, 105, 120,
      130–131, 143

U

Understory, 53–54, 73, 79

V

Vertebrates, consumption of, 51–53, 57
Vertical stratification
      feeding behavior study findings, 53–54, 56
      height class use, see Height class use
      locomotor styles, 79
Vocal association, 86–87

W

Waser's Gas Model, 87–88
"Work-to-stay" strategy, 119